Redesigning
Liberal Education

Redesigning Liberal Education

Innovative Design for a Twenty-First-Century Undergraduate Education

Edited by William Moner, Phillip Motley, and Rebecca Pope-Ruark

Foreword by Michael S. Roth

Johns Hopkins University Press | Baltimore

© 2020 Johns Hopkins University Press
All rights reserved. Published 2020
Printed in the United States of America on acid-free paper
9 8 7 6 5 4 3 2 1

Johns Hopkins University Press
2715 North Charles Street
Baltimore, Maryland 21218-4363
www.press.jhu.edu

Library of Congress Cataloging-in-Publication Data

Names: Moner, William, 1975- editor. | Motley, Phillip, 1969- editor. | Pope-Ruark, Rebecca, editor.
Title: Redesigning liberal education : innovative design for a twenty-first-century undergraduate education / edited by William Moner, Phillip Motley, and Rebecca Pope-Ruark. Foreword by Michael S. Roth.
Description: Baltimore : Johns Hopkins University Press, 2020. | Includes bibliographical references and index.
Identifiers: LCCN 2019040506 | ISBN 9781421438214 (hardcover) | ISBN 9781421438221 (ebook)
Subjects: LCSH: Education, Higher—Aims and objectives—United States. | Education, Higher—Curricula—United States. | Education, Humanistic—United States. | Education, Higher—Aims and objectives—United States—Case studies. | Education, Higher—Curricula—United States—Case studies. | Education, Humanistic—United States—Case studies.
Classification: LCC LA227.4 .R43 2020 | DDC 370.11/2—dc23
LC record available at https://lccn.loc.gov/2019040506

A catalog record for this book is available from the British Library.

Special discounts are available for bulk purchases of this book. For more information, please contact Special Sales at specialsales@press.jhu.edu.

Johns Hopkins University Press uses environmentally friendly book materials, including recycled text paper that is composed of at least 30 percent post-consumer waste, whenever possible.

Contents

Foreword, by Michael S. Roth ix
Acknowledgments xvii

Introduction. A Radical Vision for Redesigning Liberal Education 1
William Moner, Phillip Motley, and Rebecca Pope-Ruark

Part One. Case Studies 17

1 Problem-Focused Liberal Education in a First-Year Learning Community at the University of Wisconsin–Green Bay 19
Denise S. Bartell, Alison K. Staudinger, and David J. Voelker

2 Attending to Local Context, Culture, and Language at Florida International University 32
Isis Artze-Vega, Phillip M. Carter, and Heather Russell

3 The Experiential Liberal Arts: An Integrative Model for Twenty-First-Century Education at Northeastern University 44
Chris W. Gallagher and Uta G. Poiger

4 Creating Connections: An Intentional, Integrated Liberal Education at Connecticut College 58
Michael Reder and Ann Schenk

5 Building a Developmental, Interdisciplinary General Education Curriculum for the Future: Foundations in the Liberal Arts at Rollins College 72
Emily Russell, Susan Rundell Singer, and Toni Strollo Holbrook

6 Exploring the Borderlands: Using Interdisciplinarity to Build Civic Literacy at the College of the Holy Cross 85
Laurie Ann Britt-Smith

7 Redesigning Learning through Multidisciplinary Teaching: Voices from a Sophomore Core Experience at Lasell University 98
Michael J. Daley, Dennis A. Frey Jr., and Catherine Zeek

8 Intergenerational Partnerships to Support Liberal Learning Goals at Brown University 111
Mary C. Wright, Maud S. Mandel, Jessica Metzler, and Christina Smith

9 The Design Thinking Initiative at Smith College 124
Borjana Mikic

10 Immersive Learning in the Studio for Social Innovation at Elon University 138
Rebecca Pope-Ruark, William Moner, and Phillip Motley

11 Failing Forward: Writing, Design, and Organic Curricular Change at Georgetown University 151
Maggie Debelius, Sherry Lee Linkon, and Matthew Pavesich

12 Educating Business Leaders for a Better World at George Mason University 163
Lisa Gring-Pemble, Anne M. Magro, and Jacquelyn Dively Brown

13 Educating for Global Civic Participation and a Career: German Studies in the Twenty-First Century at Elon University 177
Scott Windham, Andrea A. Sinn, Kristin Lange, Derek Lackaff, Anthony Hatcher, Evan A. Gatti, and Janelle Papay Decato

14 Pursuing Major Passions: Innovative Minors That Blend Professional Skills and Liberal Education Values for Civic Pursuits at Susquehanna University 190
John Bodinger de Uriarte and Betsy Verhoeven

Part Two. Visions for the Future of Liberal Education 203

15 The Future Has Gone Soft on Skills: Why Campuses Should Be Working Harder to Cement Personal and Social Development with Learning 205
    Ashley Finley

16 Can We Liberate Liberal Education? 221
    Randy Bass

17 Aligning Liberal Education for an Age of Inequality 239
    William M. Sullivan

18 Slow: Liberal Learning for and in a Fast-Paced World 254
    Nancy L. Chick and Peter Felten

19 Shifting Paradigms: College Admissions as a Lever for Systemic Change in Liberal Education 266
    Kristína Moss Gudrún Gunnarsdóttir and Meredith Twombly

20 Scholartistry: Creativity and the Future of the Liberal Arts 282
    Michael Shanks and Connie Svabo

Afterword. The Age of Connectedness 299
Leo Lambert

Appendix 1 307
Appendix 2 310
Contributors 311
Index 323

Foreword

Michael S. Roth
President, Wesleyan University

Commentators on higher education like saying that colleges today are much as they were in the Middle Ages, with the sage on the stage facing a docile group of young people writing down what they hope to memorize. However, almost from the start, education has given rise to self-criticism and to efforts at "continuous improvement." Sure, there are still scholars lecturing, but the content and the form have evolved as schools dominated by religion have changed into centers of scientific inquiry and as the aspirations of students have transformed from desires to enter the church to desires for invention and entrepreneurship. Whenever there are significant changes in the economy and culture, there are significant pressures on the educational system of the day to adapt to those changes—either to better prepare students to participate in the new ventures or to protect the status quo from the upstarts creating innovation. Today, higher education is buffeted by demands from a variety of perspectives, and this book examines how liberal education is adapting to those demands, their challenges, and their opportunities. Whether through general studies, interdisciplinary programs, or project-based learning, the case studies here show the vitality of liberal education and how it remains pragmatic in the contemporary American context, while the vision chapters outline the possibilities for liberal education's continued relevance.

What Is a Liberal Education?

Of course, liberal education is not just an American idea; its roots extend to the ancient world. In Western traditions going back to the Greeks, a liberal education was to be liberating, requiring freedom to study and aiming at freedom through understanding. The medieval emphasis on the seven liberal arts—grammar, logic, rhetoric, arithmetic, geometry, music, and astronomy—pictured all of them within a framework set either by philosophy/theology or by rhetoric/oratory.

Although today in education we tend to emphasize inquiry as the fruit of these traditions (as if the seeds of modern research were planted with the sympathetic skepticism of the Socratic method), for centuries a liberal arts education was thought to consist in the deepening appreciation of great cultural achievements. A good student would be a person who knew the canons in those fields deemed to contain the finest achievements of civilization (which almost always meant Western civilization). This was a rhetorical tradition into which one was initiated so as to learn the virtues associated with the monumental works; it was not a philosophical commitment to discover truths. Several commentators on liberal education have emphasized how the philosophical and rhetorical traditions have uneasily coexisted in the American context, especially with respect to the humanities.[1]

In contrast with the initiation offered by the rhetorical current, the philosophical stream is skeptical and focused on inquiry and critical thinking—not an initiation into civilized rites, but rather practice at taking them down a peg. The rhetorical stream is reverential, focused on bringing new members into the common culture. The two approaches have been rechanneled in a variety of ways, giving rise to educational models that serve the "whole person"—to use a phrase popular in contemporary Chinese discussions of liberal learning.[2]

At least since the eighteenth-century Enlightenment, these models have been significantly reconfigured in the West, not least because of the challenges that the sciences have posed to either a theologically or a classically oriented education. Inquiry and critique have replaced religion and knowledge of ancient languages as hallmarks of the modern research university, which spread from Germany to the United States in the late nineteenth century. This model of the research university has shaped higher education practices until very recently, though the reverential rhetorical tradition lingers on, especially in core curricula at the undergraduate level. Liberal education often refers to the combination of the philosophical and rhetorical traditions of how we learn as a whole person: we learn how to learn so that we can continue both inquiry and cultural participation throughout our lives. Learning becomes part of who we are.[3]

The Association of American Colleges and Universities puts it this way:

> Liberal education is an approach to learning that empowers individuals and prepares them to deal with complexity, diversity, and change. It provides students with broad knowledge of the wider world (e.g., science, culture, and society) as well as in-depth study in a specific area of interest. A liberal education helps students develop a sense of social responsibility, as well as strong and transferable intellectual and practical skills such as communication, analytical and problem-solving skills, and a demonstrated ability to apply knowledge and skills in real-world settings.[4]

What Are the Challenges to Liberal Education Today?

Many of the educators in this volume share the ambition to create institutions that protect experimental, wide-ranging learning while also opening up to "real-world settings" that might squash it. On one hand, ours is a commercial republic, but few champions of liberal education want to subject all lessons to the pressures of the marketplace. On the other hand, those who want an education of the whole person are not content with isolating the university, protecting inquiry but dooming it to irrelevancy in the real world. The innovations described in this book balance the need for university protection with the objective of having an impact beyond the borders of the campus.

The beginning of the twenty-first century does seem to be another age of great agitation in higher education. At the beginning of the twentieth century, Harvard president Charles Eliot helped reshape America's idea of a modern research university. To serve the needs of the industrializing economy, Eliot led higher education away from memorization and a fixed curriculum and toward specialization and electives. In the digital twenty-first century our economy is vastly different, and many inside and outside of academia are trying to reconceptualize our universities in relation to how we get information, disseminate it, and learn from it.

Many of the authors in this book are following the lead of Cathy Davidson in calling for a more student-centered university.[5] Most of the students in the United States attend public institutions, and it is important to recognize the damage done by policies that have defunded community colleges and public universities since the economic dislocations of 2008. Forty-five states spent less per student in 2016 than they did before the Great Recession. The privatization of state universities and the rise of for-profit schools promising quick training for the newest jobs have had disastrous consequences for millions of students. As completion rates at these institutions have declined, student debt has soared. As student debt has increased, the range of choices that students have after graduation has decreased.

The challenges facing a more student-centered university today are great: rising tuition and onerous student debt, drastic cuts to state support of public institutions, poor measures of real student learning, the debilitating effects of inequality, groupthink, sexual violence, poorly paid adjunct professors, and the disconnect at many institutions between the impetus for new research and the core mission of teaching undergraduates. But none of these problems should frighten us into abandoning the model of pragmatic liberal learning that has made America's best colleges and universities the envy of the world.

How Can the Past Inform the Future of Liberal Education?

We've seen this many times before in US history. Booker T. Washington wanted to help formerly enslaved people acquire practical skills so they could become self-sufficient after the Civil War. And around the time of World War I, chambers of commerce and labor federations united to back legislation for a dual-track secondary educational system. According to that plan, some young people would be trained for specific jobs, while others would get a broad education, allowing them to continue their studies in college. The movement led to the Smith-Hughes Act of 1917, which financed vocational instruction.

Those who opposed this vocational turn certainly realized that people needed skills to get jobs. But they also realized that this kind of tracking would only exacerbate social and economic inequality. W. E. B. Du Bois argued that a broad education was a form of empowerment that must be accessible to those disenfranchised by the economy or by legacies of discrimination. He criticized the call for education to be more vocational, writing that "there is an insistence on the practical in a manner and tone that would make Socrates an idiot and Jesus Christ a crank."[6] Jane Addams rejected narrow vocationalism and sought out opportunities to connect education to the pressing problems of the most vulnerable around us.[7] Her notion of engaged learning, a tradition taken up by some of the authors in this volume, ensured that people would learn from one another through exercising reciprocal sympathetic understanding.

As John Dewey wrote, some of us "are managers and others are subordinates. But the great thing for one as for the other is that each shall have had the education which enables him to see within his daily work all there is in it of large and human significance."[8] Education should aim to enhance our capacities, Dewey argued, so that we are not reduced to being somebody else's tool.

What Does Reform in Liberal Education Look Like?

This is what some of today's reformers are missing in their willingness to tailor programs to the existing industrial regime's immediate needs. Some of the case studies in this volume connect to practical concerns off campus, and some of them use technological innovations, but at the heart of these changes is something else: recognizing the benefits students receive in developing a lifelong learning capacity in addition to acquiring immediately marketable skills. The reforms that get results at community colleges, at large public universities, or at small private liberal arts colleges are changes that put student learning—broad and measurable—as the highest priority. This means schools have to treat teachers fairly, too, attending to their work conditions and opportunities for continued learning, which means providing opportunities to do research. Although these reforms might not immediately lead to enrollment increases or upticks in the rankings, they will lead to sustainable educational progress.

Educational reform goes back a long way. Nineteenth-century reformers also argued for active learning, and in this regard they were building on ancient Socratic traditions. In the early twentieth century, as college enrollments increased, many innovators called for more vocational paths through higher education, paths more attuned to the economy of that era. Others, such as Addams, Du Bois, and Dewey, resisted the effort to turn a broad liberal education into narrow training. Du Bois argued that education should lead to the empowerment of the whole person and not just to a sharpening of skills with short-term value. Dewey, while acknowledging that education must be relevant to its time, rejected the specialization called for by educational reformers with the memorable line: "The kind of vocational education in which I am interested is not one which will 'adapt' workers to the existing industrial regime; I am not sufficiently in love with the regime for that."[9]

Victor Butterfield was one of my predecessors as president of Wesleyan University, and he certainly saw himself in the pragmatist tradition that was reinvigorating American liberal education after World War II and through the 1960s. But he also knew something about the limited relevance of pronouncements on this subject from on high: "Whatever the President might say about liberal education in community discussion, or in the college catalog, or in his speeches, he could not really define that education or affect it where it counts; that is, in hearts and minds of students. It is defined and takes effect from what and how a teacher teaches, how both he and his students think, how they both listen and read, what they both ask, and by how vitally and imaginatively they respond to each other."[10] Butterfield led Wesleyan from being a liberal arts college steeped in rhetorical traditions to being a small university eager to break down curricular silos and social barriers through inquiry and critical thinking. Along with faculty and students, he led the charge for interdisciplinary colleges as engines of pedagogical innovation, for small research-based graduate programs in the sciences and ethnomusicology that would shape new fields, and for creating a much more diverse and engaged student body than a New England liberal arts school had ever had before.

Butterfield was a philosophical pragmatist, and he saw the need for institutional changes that would revitalize liberal education in a time of increasing political turbulence and polarization. When he retired from the presidency in 1967, many were skeptical about the continued relevance of a broad contextual education that would prepare students not for the most immediate job opportunity but for a lifetime of learning and meaningful work. Once again today we face renewed skepticism about liberal education, but we also have deep resources for reimagining integrated, broadly pragmatic, and holistic forms of learning.

The authors in this book respond to that skepticism with concrete examples. They are in the tradition of Addams, Du Bois, Dewey, and Butterfield, a pragmatist tradition that puts impactful inquiry first and sees learning through the potential of the full, complex human beings students can become. If liberal education is to remain successful, whatever its use of technology, it will build on this tradition as teachers and students "vitally and imaginatively . . . respond to each other" and to the changing times in which they live.

Notes

1. See, for example, Bruce Kimball, *Orators and Philosophers: A History of the Idea of Higher Education* (New York: Teachers College Press, 1986); Robert Orrill, ed., *The Condition of American Liberal Education: Pragmatism and a Changing Tradition* (New York: College Board, 1995); Francis Oakley, *Community of Learning: The American College and the Liberal Arts Tradition* (New York: Oxford University Press, 1992); W. B. Carnochan, *The Battleground of the Curriculum: Liberal Education and the American Experience* (Stanford, CA: Stanford University

Press, 1993); and Geoffrey Galt Harpham, *The Humanities and the Dream of America* (Chicago, IL: University of Chicago Press, 2011).

2. The increasing interest in liberal education in China, Singapore, and Korea has been seen as a reaction against policies of rote learning that emphasize standardized testing and as tapping into Confucian notions of whole-person education. See, for example, the work of Tu Wei-Ming and Vera Schwartz on ideas about the Enlightenment in China. See also Daniel Bell's *China's New Confucianism: Politics and Everyday Life* (Princeton, NJ: Princeton University Press, 2010), chap. 7; Stephen Angle, *Sagehood: The Contemporary Significance of Neo-Confucian Philosophy* (Oxford: Oxford University Press, 2012), part 3. I have written on this topic in the following: Michael S. Roth, "American Liberal Education Is Happening in Singapore," *Atlantic*, October 16, 2015, https://www.theatlantic.com/education/archive/2015/10/american-liberal-education-happens-better-in-singapore/410869; Roth, "Why Pragmatic Liberal Education Matters Now More than Ever," *Washington Post*, January 13, 2017, https://www.washingtonpost.com/news/answer-sheet/wp/2017/01/13/why-pragmatic-liberal-education-matters-now-more-than-ever; Roth, "Isn't It Pragmatic?" *Inside Higher Ed*, April 5, 2017, https://www.insidehighered.com/views/2017/04/05/indian-students-are-embracing-liberal-arts-essay.

3. This paragraph draws on Michael S. Roth, *Beyond the University: Why Liberal Education Matters* (New Haven, CT: Yale University Press, 2014), 3.

4. Association of American Colleges and Universities, "What Is Liberal Education?," n.d., https://www.aacu.org/leap/what-is-liberal-education.

5. Cathy N. Davidson, *The New Education: How to Revolutionize the University to Prepare Students for a World in Flux* (New York: Basic, 2017).

6. W. E. B. Du Bois, *The Education of Black People: Ten Critiques, 1906–1960*, ed. Herbert Aptheker (Amherst: University of Massachusetts Press, 1973), 12.

7. See Roth, *Beyond the University*, 80–86.

8. John J. McDermott, ed., *The Philosophy of John Dewey* (Chicago, IL: University of Chicago Press, 1973), 464.

9. John Dewey, "Education vs. Trade-Training: Reply to David Snedden" (1915), in *The Middle Works of John Dewey*, vol. 8 (Carbondale: Southern Illinois University Press, 2008), 412. I discuss Du Bois and Dewey in regard to vocational and liberal education in *Beyond the University*, 65–66 and 164–165, respectively.

10. Victor Butterfield, "A Gift of Restlessness," commencement address at Wesleyan University, 1967.

Acknowledgments

A book like this is the product of conversations that started long before the ink hit the page. This volume began with a seed of an idea, which was brought to life through the thoughtful feedback and kind leadership of Peter Felten, who helped us at every turn. We are grateful for the intellectual and collegial generosity of the faculty and staff at Elon University, particularly the support of the Center for Teaching and Learning and the many productive writing and review sessions with the Center for Engaged Learning. Elon has been a place where pedagogical innovation is encouraged, and we are indebted to the administration whose leadership allows for the flexibility to make something new take shape. We also thank Greg Britton and the stalwart staff at Johns Hopkins University Press for their kindness and guidance. Finally, to our visionary contributors and their collaborators and students: thank you for sharing your brilliance with us.

A book like this is also the product of long nights, time spent away from family, and the hidden support of those who are always in our corner. William would like to thank his wife, Heidi, for the steady and constant support, and his kids, Joe and Miles, for the laughter, a reminder that it's lighter than we think. Phillip would like to thank his wife, Robin, and kids, Griffin and Mackie, for always being "the ice in my cream and the rock in my roll." Rebecca would like to thank her husband, Tracey. He knows why.

Redesigning
Liberal Education

Introduction
A Radical Vision for Redesigning Liberal Education

William Moner, Phillip Motley, and Rebecca Pope-Ruark

> Radical (n.). From the Latin *radix*, "the root." The call for a radical redesign of liberal education is a call to return to the core of our endeavor: the development of the fully realized human mind, equipped with the knowledge, creativity, and ethical capacities to cooperatively navigate complex social relationships within our built and natural environments.

The future of liberal education in the United States, in its current form, is fraught. Institutions are struggling to maintain viability, sustain revenue, and assert value in the face of changing demographics, dramatically increasing costs, neoliberal reimaginings of higher education as a factory to produce skilled workers, and an administrative shift away from traditional liberal arts programs and toward the funding of professional schools, "hard" sciences, technology, engineering, and mathematics. As parents and students alike question the value of higher education, smaller colleges and universities—particularly those with a well-established history in the liberal arts—have been forced to assert their own value propositions and justify their price tag compared to larger institutions, which can more efficiently compete in this environment. Headlines in the *Chronicle of Higher Education* and *Inside Higher Ed* lament the closure of these small liberal arts colleges in the face of rapid change, a trend that is set to continue as colleges and universities compete in tighter economic conditions while drawing from a shrinking applicant pool. Larger institutions are not immune to these intensifying pressures, which include the evisceration of public funding for higher education in state legislatures, dependence on tuition revenue, reduced financial aid opportunities from the federal government, and growing distrust in the ability of higher education to satisfy the demand for employable graduates.

How did we arrive at this moment, and how might institutions reassert the importance and relevance of a liberal education? What practical actions are being taken in these institutions to return to our roots in developing the skills and capacities of students to navigate complex systems and relationships? And how might we envision a future for liberal education that focuses deeply on the outcomes that will sustain students as they confront a world of rapid environmental, social, and technological change while remaining cognizant of their need to find gainful employment and also preparing them for uncertain futures?

This volume seeks to accomplish three goals in exploring this set of questions:

1. Justify the value of a liberal education as foundational to a vibrant society.
2. Present innovation in action through case studies from various institutions that redesigned their approaches to liberal education.
3. Imagine the future of liberal education through vision essays contributed by leaders in liberal education.

First, we establish a shared stance that liberal education remains valuable and vital to a thriving civic life with significant implications for a functioning democracy and society. This stance is rooted primarily in the call from the Association of American Colleges and Universities (AAC&U) for a liberal education that focuses on students' development of twenty-first-century skills, captured here as "essential learning outcomes":

- Knowledge of human cultures and the physical and natural world, focused by engagement with big questions.
- Intellectual and practical skills, including inquiry, analysis, critical and creative thinking, communication skills, information and numeric literacies, teamwork, and problem solving, extensively practiced and progressively more challenging throughout a student's progress through the curriculum.
- Personal and social responsibility, including both local and global civic knowledge and engagement, intercultural knowledge and competence, ethical reasoning and action, and foundations and skills for lifelong learning, anchored through active involvement with diverse communities and real-world challenges.
- Integrative and applied learning, including synthesis and advanced accomplishment across generalized and specialized study, demonstrated through the application of knowledge to new settings and complex problems.[1]

Our use of the AAC&U's essential learning outcomes allows for a shared understanding of what comprises a student-centric liberal education model, and these outcomes inspire our own radical vision for liberal education, offered at the end of this chapter, which unifies the spirit of this volume.

Second, we present fourteen case studies of innovative approaches to creating change in our institutions, written by authors who are working to advance and shape the future of liberal education. These authors offer both radical visions of what a liberal education should be and pragmatic, battle-tested programs and curricula that show how actionable change can be achieved in our institutional contexts.

Third, we offer vision chapters written by recognized leaders in higher education. These authors consider the vast spectrum of opportunities and challenges faced by students, faculty, staff, and administrators. In the vision chapters, the contributors prompt us to consider how our work shifts in response to artificial intelligence and machines; the role that human dispositions, mindsets, and resilience—and time—play in how we train students; pointed critiques of how the US educational system limits the development of risk-taking mindsets and truly radical innovation; and ideas for how we might bring fanciful and playful concepts of creativity and openness into our work.

At the heart of the liberal university, and our reason for assembling this volume, is the creation and production of knowledge to support the freedom of the individual—equipped with the tools and capabilities that support a democratic society—to participate meaningfully in a complex world. This notion, in today's educational environment, is prima facie radical. We begin by providing evidence that a well-designed liberal education establishes the strong roots of civil society through the work of the faculty, students, administration, and staff, who are unified by the belief that the twenty-first-century skills and essential learning outcomes enumerated above are crucial for the future of our civil society.

The Foundations of a Liberal Education

What we call a liberal education today developed in classical Greece and Rome as preparation for engaged citizenship in a free society. Martha Nussbaum argues that a liberal education in this classical Stoic sense was designed to "liberate the mind from bondage of habit and custom, producing people who can function with sensitivity and alertness as citizens of the whole world."[2] In one sense, liberal education was reserved for the wealthy and powerful, for the people—usually men with concentrated capital—who had the time and funds to learn for the sake of learning; they studied a wide range of disciplines "without regard for immediate application or benefit."[3] The liberal education of the twenty-first century, however, has been favorably reconsidered to welcome a plurality of voices to the table.

The benefits of higher education, and more specifically a liberal education, are clear. The AAC&U defines liberal education as

> an approach to learning that empowers individuals and prepares them to deal with complexity, diversity, and change. It provides students with broad

knowledge of the wider world (e.g., science, culture, and society) as well as in-depth study in a specific area of interest. A liberal education helps students develop a sense of social responsibility, as well as strong and transferable intellectual and practical skills such as communication, analytical and problem-solving skills, and a demonstrated ability to apply knowledge and skills in real-world settings.[4]

These characteristics are in high demand by employers, and a liberal education in the United States has become readily available to a wider range of people. The introduction of the GI Bill after World War II added to the college rolls, while a growing network of community and land-grant institutions offered an affordable education to oft-disenfranchised populations. Central to this approach is access to education *liberally*, to the citizenry at large, not just to the wealthy who can afford to attend elite liberal arts institutions. A truly American liberal education empowers students to become active, knowledgeable, lifelong learners dedicated to contributing to the common good of society.

Despite these benefits, it is no secret that liberal education is under attack today by politicians more concerned with training future workers than future citizens, by parents who understandably want their children to obtain well-paying jobs to justify the ever more expensive four-year degree, and by pundits who assume the word "liberal" implies the opposite of "conservative"—an obvious hot-button issue in today's climate.

Meanwhile, the skills that employers rate as most important include the very skills the AAC&U states as the benefits of liberal education. According to a Hart Research Associates study, these are "written and oral communication skills, teamwork skills, ethical decision-making, critical thinking, and the ability to apply knowledge in real-world settings."[5] Employers surveyed, however, observed that graduates lack these skills,[6] perhaps because institutions have moved the liberal arts to the periphery rather than placing them at the core. Though we hear loud arguments for vocational education in colleges and universities, we also hear that students graduating from these programs do not have the capacities—

the skills underlying twenty-first-century liberal education—to succeed upon entry into the workforce.

A joint statement by the AAC&U and the American Association of University Professors (AAUP) considers this situation a threat based on a false binary between career readiness and the goals of a well-rounded education:

> Institutions of higher education, if they are truly to serve as institutions of *higher* education, should provide more than narrow vocational training and should seek to enhance students' capacities for lifelong learning. . . . The disciplines of the liberal arts—and the overall benefit of a liberal education—are exemplary in this regard, for they foster intellectual curiosity about questions that will never be definitively settled—questions about justice, about community, about politics and culture, about difference in every sense of the word.[7]

Cathy Davidson summarizes this concept brilliantly when she posits, "The goal of higher education is greater than workforce readiness. It's *world* readiness."[8] This imperative aligns directly with the true meaning of the word "liberal" in liberal education, a message that institutions of higher education must convey to the growing cacophony of detractors in order to reclaim the narrative of value and contribution to society.

The Need for a Liberal Twenty-First-Century Education

Because of the broad competencies students learn through a liberal education, employers are increasingly hiring them for their human-centered skills. Executives in professional fields are coming out in vocal support of a liberal education, agreeing with Steve Jobs's famous argument that technology needs artistry and that a liberal arts background is essential to innovation. Many leaders of respected companies were liberal arts majors, including YouTube CEO Susan Wojcicki (history and literature), Slack founder Stewart Butterfield (philosophy and history of science), former Avon CEO Andrea Jung (English), former Disney CEO Michael Eisner (literature and theater), and former Hewlett-Packard CEO Carly Fiorina (medieval history and philosophy). *Wired, Forbes, Fast Company,* the *Atlantic*, and *Time* have all written about the value of a liberal education to all students, especially those in STEM disciplines.

In *The Fuzzy and the Techie: Why the Liberal Arts Will Rule the Digital World*, venture capitalist Scott Hartley argues that liberal arts graduates, not engineers or software developers, are coming up with the most creative innovations in the technology sector because the "fuzzies" understand people, question norms, and raise ethical concerns.[9] In essence, they have the twenty-first-century skills and habits of mind that are the core of a liberal education. Students are prepared for a future in any field, particularly fields that do not exist yet, by allowing them to develop and test their capacities for empathy, critical thinking, creative thinking, ethical reasoning, resilience, curiosity, problem framing, problem solving, collaboration, communication, and cross-cultural competence.

Northeastern University president Joseph Aoun argues in his book *Robot-Proof: Higher Education in the Age of Artificial Intelligence* that higher education must reimagine itself and prepare students via study in what he calls "humanics," an experiential learning curriculum and cocurriculum that combines technical skills with well-developed human capacities, such as empathy and creativity.[10] (The concept of humanics inspired the work featured in chapter 3 of this volume.) In the same vein, Cathy Davidson argues:

> It is safe to say that the only jobs not susceptible to automation are those that require crosscutting skills of human discernment and creativity that no robot can approximate. It's impossible to imagine that AI-powered robots could displace workers in professions that require human judgment, talent, empathy, persuasive power, leadership, or even basic human touch.... Subjective, affective human qualities cannot be replaced by machines.[11]

As these arguments suggest, liberal education is not a frivolous undertaking—despite what detractors may contend—but an inherently practical one. Wesleyan University president Michael S. Roth—the author of this volume's foreword—argues that contemporary liberal education extends from a commitment to John Dewey's idea of practical idealism.[12] Duke University professor Robert J. Thompson argues that liberal education could provide an appropriate model for developing "intellectual and personal skills with the traditional professional and technical focus on solving complex problems."[13] And Macalester College president Brian Rosenberg "believes an English or a history major may be more practical, in the long run, than a business or accounting degree."[14]

In summary, as found in the 2015 employer survey report from Hart Research Associates, employers across the board value competencies developed through a well-rounded liberal education, including "1) problem solving with people who have differing views, 2) democratic institutions and values, 3) civic capacity, 4) liberal arts and sciences, and 5) intercultural skills."[15] To help foster these competencies in our students, Davidson says we must think of the new liberal education "as a verb, one that empowers our students with better ways to live and thrive in a complicated world."[16]

Why We Should Redesign Liberal Education

In a 2016 AAC&U report, *Open and Integrative: Designing Liberal Education for the New Digital Ecosystem,* Randy Bass and Bret Eynon ask, "What could liberal education look like if we were inventing it at this moment in history?"[17] Bass and Eynon argue that the liberal education of the future should focus on engagement, community, mentorship, and integration and on being learner-centered, networked, integrative, and adaptive.[18] Higher education as a whole must be redesigned in both its approaches and the structure of its institutions to more vibrantly prepare students to be bold, empathic, community-oriented citizens who can both frame and address complex societal problems in the future. As Richard Freeland posits, "We need to take a hard, fresh look at the qualities needed for effectiveness as professionals and as citizens, to compare those qualities to the outcomes we cultivate through the arts and sciences, and to design educational formats that will empower our graduates to translate the values and skills we nurture into constructive social action."[19]

All of that requires a radical vision for the future of liberal undergraduate higher education. We offer ours here.

Our Radical Vision for Liberal Education

We focus deeply on the need for human-centered and engaged education, rooted in the classical notion of the liberal arts while confronting the vestiges of the past and the realities of the present that limit our ability to build resilient institutions for the future. "Radical" can be defined here in two senses. The first relates to the fundamental nature of a thing, with implications that reach far beyond that root. The second describes advocacy for thorough or complete social change, independence, departure from tradition, innovation, and unorthodox measures. Our radical vision calls for a return to the values that have sustained liberal education, which has endured countless crises since its origin in ancient Greece.

> A contemporary undergraduate liberal education should not be a zero-sum game among an intellectually satisfying life of the mind, social justice, community improvement, and the training necessary to achieve career and financial success. Liberal education should boldly and deliberately build student capacities for knowledge, creativity, and ethical behavior while cultivating connections and relationships between people and across disciplines. These relationships require the active involvement of faculty in designing learning environments that resist one-size-fits-all approaches.
>
> A liberal education should develop in students the confidence to explore, to advocate, to resist, to challenge and be challenged, to play, to create, to commit, and to take action. Centrally and crucially, we celebrate the agency of each student to advance their own personal learning goals and aspirations. A student's exploratory journey should be steeped in disciplinary knowledge and instill the versatility to articulate their field across disciplines and within their communities. Students should have clear means for seeking guidance and structure when they lose their way while they build confidence to try, to fail, and to remain resilient in the face of challenges and opposition.
>
> At every step, a liberal education should be the site of learning experiences that prepare students for vital engagement in their communities and

in their careers, where they will experience the fullness of an immersed, integrated, and intentional life.

Organization of the Volume

This book has two parts: fourteen innovative case studies from institutions across the country and six forward-thinking vision chapters by trendsetters in liberal education. The contributors explore how innovation is happening in liberal education, particularly with twenty-first-century outcomes in mind. How are institutions developing programs that challenge or creatively navigate entrenched structures to promote new practices? And how are institutions cultivating liberal education, in its freest sense, for the twenty-first century and beyond? Each of the authors in this collection offer their own radical vision for liberal undergraduate education.

Case Studies

The case study section of the book (chapters 1–14) presents numerous approaches to creating change in our institutions. These examples include wholesale curriculum redesigns, new approaches to general education, groundbreaking and award-winning programmatic offerings, mechanisms for welcoming populations that have traditionally been underserved, and experiments in infusing the liberal arts into professional and interdisciplinary programs. Each of these approaches places students front and center, enhances their agency, and guides their progress toward graduation and career. Many of the contributors have devised programs that radically shift how the core competencies of a liberal education can be brought into interdisciplinary spaces where ideas and research can be put into action. These authors share their willingness to confront the challenges of the twenty-first century, suggest key takeaways to inspire change in other institutions, and offer insights about the difficulties they faced when advocating for change in the risk-averse system of higher education.

Change is not easy, so each case explores the context for the innovation, the design and testing of each innovation, and the benefits and challenges associated with new initiatives, all grounded in the contributors' own radical vision for liberal education. Each chapter follows a standardized format that includes

- A radical vision statement.
- The institutional profile based on the Carnegie classification.
- A case study narrative including the rationale for change, the process, the results, and lessons learned.
- Key takeaways that will help readers to imagine what might be possible in their own contexts.

The first part of the book opens with a discussion of how institutions are adapting to shifting demographics and the inclusion of nontraditional learners by offering first-year experiences grounded in local contexts, capturing the breadth of learner characteristics. Chapter 1 describes efforts made by the University of Wisconsin-Green Bay to remain committed to a liberal mission while developing formative skills in a population of first-generation and nontraditional college students. Chapter 2 discusses how Florida International University, a Hispanic-serving institution, built linguistic and cultural characteristics into its first-year strategy in order to identify culturally learned narratives that both challenge and empower students and to design authentic curricular offerings around students' lived experiences.

The next four chapters capture grand visions for experiential and interconnected liberal education across the curriculum through large-scale redesigns, focusing on how institutions can create major changes through cooperation and the articulation of shared values across the entire campus. Northeastern's experiential liberal arts model, the subject of chapter 3, shows how alignment with an institution's presidential initiatives led to a productive redesign. Chapter 4 covers how Connecticut College reinvented its curriculum to include the liberal arts at every level while allowing students to develop an "animating question" that guides their inquiry across their journey. Chapter 5 highlights how Rollins College, through multiple iterations, brought interdisciplinary studies to the forefront of the student experience, and chapter 6 explores how the traditional Jesuit liberal education model at the College of the Holy Cross has found success and grappled with missteps as the institution has adapted that model to meet the needs of contemporary learners.

The next two cases focus on interdisciplinary experiences in fresh, new ways. Chapter 7 describes an inventive multidisciplinary and co-taught sophomore experience at Lasell University that breaks down barriers between the classroom and the community. Chapter 8 features an initiative at Brown University involving intergenerational partnerships that deliberately include student peer learning and experienced student mentorship alongside the work of faculty and staff in interdisciplinary cohort programs.

Next, we turn to three programs that model their interventions on the design thinking process, a methodology that has emerged as a way to inspire creativity and innovation. Smith College's case study (chapter 9) offers a glimpse into how design thinking is integrated throughout its institutional curriculum. Chapter 10 offers a case about Elon University's Design Thinking Studio in Social Innovation, detailing how faculty from distinct backgrounds and disciplines combined capstone work in the liberal arts, independent research, service learning, civic engagement, design thinking, and collaborative processes into one gigantic semester-long course offering. Chapter 11 describes Georgetown University's Writing Center, which shows the benefits of design thinking methods in reinvigorating how writing is understood—as an inherently interdisciplinary practice with application to all areas of learning.

The next three chapters show some ways that academic units have adapted to the rigidity of academic structures. In chapter 12, the focus is on George Mason University, which successfully integrated a liberal arts model into the core of its large business school as a way to develop the foundational knowledge demanded by employers. Elon University's German studies program, the subject of chapter 13, formed a coalition of faculty and staff from multiple programs to guide its program as it attempted to incorporate the liberal arts, world languages, sciences, communications, and business. The final case (chapter 14) traces the story of Susquehanna University, a small liberal arts institution that revamped two minor programs as a way to advance pragmatic outcomes within a setting that offers little room for robust interdisciplinary opportunities.

Vision Chapters

While each case study offers its own radical vision for the future of liberal education, the second part of the book offers perspectives from prominent thinkers and practitioners in liberal education reform and revitalization. These visions are wide-ranging, the observations of academics whose careers have been spent in pursuit of the ideal educational environment for learners. These chapters offer inspiration for the cultivation of learning environments wherein students, faculty, administrators, and institutions remain imaginative, adaptable, and open to the unknown and unknowable conditions facing us in the twenty-first century. The resilience we seek in students is necessary in our institutions, and the common thread uniting these chapters is the need to develop institutional capacities to support the dispositions and mindsets most valuable for creativity and collaboration in a time of rapid change.

Ashley Finley in chapter 15 calls for a reframing of "soft" skills, shifting them into the "core" skills that all learners should develop while in college. She shares her radical vision of how to prepare students for change while balancing the needs of the learner, the learning environment, and employers. Randy Bass follows in chapter 16 with a vision of liberal education "liberated," calling for a return to the core dispositions that will carry humans forward in light of technological change, artificial intelligence, and machine learning. He prods us to consider how the capacity for learning also applies to our institutions, which must embrace the same types of "agile, adaptive, self-reflective, and resilient" mindsets we require of our students.

William Sullivan in chapter 17 writes about the resilience of students and shares research on how classroom games like the Reacting to the Past curriculum can bring new engagement and liveliness to old and tired subjects in a format that appeals to contemporary learners. In contrast, chapter 18 by Nancy Chick and Peter Felten critiques the status-seeking behavior of busyness and implores us to slow down while encouraging our students to do the same, so that students and faculty alike can make deeper and more lasting connections with the materials and with each other.

While most contributors to this volume focus on liberal education after enrollment, Kristína Moss Gudrún Gunnarsdóttir and Meredith Twombly in chapter 19 interrogate how the admissions process drives the characteristics of students seeking a liberal education. In calling for a paradigm shift in higher education, these authors argue that admissions must play an active role in encouraging more risk taking by students, particularly those who seek to break the mold of traditional programs and wish to explore an unconventional liberal education. Last, in chapter 20, Michael Shanks and Connie Svabo offer the concept of "schol-artistry" as an action-oriented paradigm allowing for capacity building in creativity, collaboration, communication, and critique.

Each author in this collection not only believes in the value of a liberal education but also that this type of higher education should not be immune to change. In fact, liberal education must evolve with the world around us if we are to prepare our students for more than a job. If the true goal of liberal education is to help students foster the skills and mindsets required for effective and meaningful citizenship, we must adapt to the ever-changing political, economic, and social paradigms in our world. This volume showcases our radical visions in action to inspire this evolution in institutions of undergraduate higher education across the United States and beyond.

Notes

1. Association of American Colleges and Universities, "Essential Learning Outcomes," n.d., https://www.aacu.org/leap/essential-learning-outcomes.

2. Martha Nussbaum, *Cultivating Humanity: A Classical Defense of Reform in Liberal Education* (Cambridge, MA: Harvard University Press, 1998).

3. Jo Ellen Parker, "What's So 'Liberal' about Higher Ed?," *Academic Commons*, June 10, 2006, https://web.archive.org/web/20130412225525/http://www.academiccommons.org/commons/essay/parker-whats-so-liberal-about-higher-ed.

4. Association of American Colleges and Universities, "What Is Liberal Education?," n.d., https://www.aacu.org/leap/what-is-liberal-education.

5. Hart Research Associates, *Falling Short? College Learning and Career Success* (Washington, DC: Association of American Colleges and Universities, 2015), https://www.aacu.org/leap/public-opinion-research/2015-survey-falling-short.

6. Hart Research Associates, *Falling Short?*

7. Association of American Colleges and Universities, "Joint Statement on the Value of Liberal Education by AAC&U and AAUP," May 31, 2018, https://www.aacu.org/about/statements/2018/joint-statement-value-liberal-education-aacu-and-aaup.

8. Cathy N. Davidson, *The New Education: How to Revolutionize the University to Prepare Students for a World in Flux* (New York: Basic, 2017), 15.

9. Scott Hartley, *The Fuzzy and the Techie: Why the Liberal Arts Will Rule the Digital World* (Boston: Houghton Mifflin, 2017).

10. Joseph E. Aoun, *Robot-Proof: Higher Education in the Age of Artificial Intelligence* (Cambridge, MA: MIT Press, 2017).

11. Davidson, *New Education*, 139.

12. Michael S. Roth, "Against Conformity," *Inside Higher Ed*, February 22, 2018, https://www.insidehighered.com/views/2018/02/22/college-president-reflects-liberal-education-china-and-us-opinion.

13. Robert J. Thompson Jr., "A New Paradigm for Liberal Education," *Liberal Education* 100, no. 3 (2014), https://www.aacu.org/publications-research/periodicals/new-paradigm-liberal-education.

14. Quoted in Stephen Smith, "New Pressures on Liberal Education," *American Public Media*, http://americanradioworks.publicradio.org/features/tomorrows-college/english-major/pressures-liberal-education.html, accessed March 1, 2019.

15. Hart Research Associates, *Falling Short?*

16. Davidson, *New Education*, 161.

17. Randy Bass and Bret Eynon, *Open and Integrative: Designing Liberal Education for the New Digital Ecosystem* (Washington, DC: Association of American Colleges and Universities, 2016), 3.

18. Bass and Eynon, *Open and Integrative*, 6, 9.

19. Richard M. Freeland, "Liberal Education and Effective Practice: The Necessary Revolution in Undergraduate Education," *Liberal Education* 95, no. 1 (2009): 6–13.

Part One
Case Studies

Students in twenty-first-century liberal educational settings are asked to develop competencies and explore majors that will help them to define their perspective and worldview. The case studies offered in this part of the book focus on the student experience throughout the curriculum, beginning with the needs of a new generation of learners in the United States who seek a college education as the gateway to being a productive and meaningful participant in society. Two decades into the twenty-first century, higher education faces myriad concerns, and the contributors in this part of the volume confront those concerns with radical visions and pragmatic approaches to the development of students' competencies in order to facilitate success throughout their lifetime.

These chapters are clear-minded reports of the successes and pitfalls of curricular revision and program development. The contributors acknowledge that the contemporary university must balance several interwoven and often conflicting considerations in the provision of a strong foundation in liberal education.

The way we have ordered the chapters in this part is only one of many pathways through the material presented here. The reader is invited to explore these case studies in a nonlinear fashion to find the ideas that open up possibilities for their own purposes.

Chapters can be explored thematically: civic engagement (chapters 1, 2, 6, 10, 12, 13, 14), curriculum design (chapters 3, 4, 5, 7), design thinking (chapters 9, 10, 11), diversity, equity, and inclusion (chapters 1, 2), multidisciplinary learning (chapters 5, 7, 8, 9, 10, 11), problem-based learning (chapters 1, 8), professional programs (chapters 12, 13).

Chapters can also be explored by instructional level: first-year programs (chapters 1, 2, 6), a sophomore program (chapter 7), an upper-class program (chapter 10), cocurricular programs (chapters 8, 9, 11), core curriculum (chapters 3, 4, 5, 12), major- or minor-specific programs (chapters 12, 13, 14).

A tabular guide to these pathways is in appendix 2.

1 Problem-Focused Liberal Education in a First-Year Learning Community at the University of Wisconsin-Green Bay

Denise S. Bartell, Alison K. Staudinger, and David J. Voelker

Radical Vision

We reject the dominant narrative of meritocracy in higher education by recognizing the social and economic inequities underlying gaps in college access and success. We acknowledge that institutions of higher education have been designed to exclude, harm, or discipline marginalized communities and students. Taking an assets-focused approach, we center the life experiences, skills, and goals of historically underserved students to support their college success. We envision a future for liberal education that does not merely provide equity for historically underserved students but helps and encourages these students to transform higher education. We strive to empower students to become agents of change in education, to unmask college's "hidden curriculum," and to transform the educational experience into one that capitalizes on the strengths of all students. This new narrative informs our work to shift our institution and higher education more broadly toward problem-focused learning in spite of ongoing precarity.

Institutional Profile

The University of Wisconsin–Green Bay (UWGB) is a public master's-granting university that enrolls 7,200 students. It is a four-year, medium-size institution with a strong interdisciplinary focus, attended by primarily regional, nonresidential, first-generation college students.

Introduction

Gateways to Phoenix Success (GPS) is a first-year learning community rooted in mutual support and collaboration around principles of inclusion and anti-oppression. Students, instructors, staff, and other mentors build relationships through connected courses, cocurricular activities, and frequent one-on-one sessions. Rooted in theories of self-authorship and cultural competence, this approach respects students' diverse backgrounds and perspectives while facilitating the development of navigational capital and a sense of belonging in college.[1]

Designed to support students historically underserved by higher education (i.e., students of color, low-income students, and first-generation students), GPS infuses college success strategies into a yearlong intensive collaboration around big ideas and problem-focused, high-impact experiences to cultivate students' agency. We make explicit the hidden curriculum of higher education, which has intersectional implications for our students with multiple and overlapping identities, including class, race, gender, and ability. Students' and instructors' multiple identities show up in the classroom through slow community building, the affirmation of values and cultures of origin, and substantive analysis of the sociohistorical context for US education at all levels.

In the face of political threats to state-supported liberal education, we have embraced discourse about the value of accessible four-year liberal education, both interrogating it and also asking what it means for students to learn in such a state of insecurity or even work together to change both the discourse and the material conditions that sustain it. To build a bridge between accessible liberal education and the twenty-first-century world, we developed a program centered on problem-focused learning, built around shared, meaningful problems, which we approach from multiple disciplinary lenses. Thus, we envision liberal education for the twenty-first century as potentially transformative not only for students but also for society.

Case Narrative

Many of us work in higher education because we believe in the democratic potential of education. Yet often those we most hope to benefit are not served by the institutions we have built, especially as austerity policies undermine funding for public higher education. At UWGB, more than 65 percent of students come from historically underserved populations. Prior to the development of GPS, retention and graduation rates, GPAs, and engagement in high-impact practices for underserved students (USs) all lagged behind those of their peers. More important, many USs, especially students of color at UWGB, shared experiences of alienation, miscommunication, and microaggressions.

While universities often seek to attract USs to raise enrollment, they have seldom adjusted the normative assumptions undergirding higher education, especially the meritocratic notions that intellect is a fixed capacity and that all students with that capacity will succeed through individual effort. The founders of the GPS program took strategic advantage of the university's push for enrollment—in an uneasy compromise with our more radical goals of changing northeastern Wisconsin and higher education. We sought to provide a challenging liberal education experience that promotes interdisciplinary problem-focused learning for a population of students increasingly funneled into vocationally focused higher education.

We have done so in a political and economic environment that, at best, has deemphasized the value of a four-year liberal education and, at worst, has been openly hostile. Peer UW system institutions have faced the reduction or elimination of programs fundamental to liberal education. Persistent budget challenges caused by chronic underfunding have made it increasingly difficult to provide the high-impact educational experiences essential to eliminating equity gaps in college outcomes. This devaluing of a liberal education is coupled with a rhetoric—and perhaps a reality—of crisis in education, which enhances anxieties about precarity for students and instructors alike. The concept of precarity, which indicates both the threat of under- or unemployment and the attendant social, physical, and psychological effects, appropriately captures the experience of our students and, despite our relative privilege, of many instructors today.

All students can learn and thrive under the right conditions. Our job is to provide those conditions, maintaining "an unshakeable focus on student success."[2] Issues of retention and success for USs are fundamentally sociocultural, not individual or psychological.[3] Therefore, rather than blaming students for being underprepared for college, we must change the institution to meet students' needs. Foundational to the belief that all students can succeed is an asset-focused perspective; we recognize that USs possess strengths that are often overlooked. Even so, GPS recognizes that the economic and racial challenges our students face may impact the cognitive resources available for academic engagement, and we seek to restore that cognitive and emotional "bandwidth."[4]

GPS also focuses on promoting a sense of belonging on our campus and in college in general. Belonging involves students' beliefs that they are a valued member of the campus community, that they are connected to people on campus in meaningful ways, and that they matter to those people.[5] This basic need can profoundly influence the nature of students' college experiences and outcomes.

Supporting the success of USs requires actively countering flawed assumptions about the meritocratic nature of higher education, both in our students and at the institution.[6] College access and completion have more to do with privileged access to resources than with work ethic or an inherent capacity to achieve. This privilege provides not only invaluable financial resources and network ties, but also a primer on the hidden curriculum of college—the unstated norms, expectations, and values that govern the college experience.[7] We work to uncover this hidden curriculum for students (and faculty) and encourage them to engage the foundations of liberal education in order to deconstruct the rhetoric of meritocracy. Taking care to affirm students' cultural identities, we encourage them not to assimilate but to think consciously about the multiple identities they are cultivating and the conflicts that may emerge as they code-switch.[8]

Finally, GPS seeks to empower students as agents of change in their own education, on campus, and in their communities. Students begin to write their own stories through interdisciplinary problem-based learning experiences and by exploring their interests and values in classrooms open to risk. To accomplish this, we draw on visions of democratic classrooms, such as those classically developed by Paulo Freire and bell hooks, and stress the importance of students' "co-creation."[9]

Innovation Details

Although learning communities are common in contemporary higher education, the structure of GPS is unique. As a GPS student, your first year begins with a mini-seminar during orientation where you meet your faculty, peer mentors, and the twenty-five students in your GPS cohort. You might notice that the faculty and peer mentors share the role of instructor in the classroom. You meet the entire GPS group later in orientation, where you begin the work of self-exploration through a flash participatory-action-research experience that carries into the first week of classes, where you explore conceptions of the purpose of college through interviews and media analyses. During this research you engage with your family, peers, faculty, and campus staff. Your first-year seminar begins that first week of classes; it infuses essential college skills into a challenging, interdisciplinary, discussion-based course. For example, you might be enrolled in Comedy Central Civics, which integrates complex social science concepts and pop culture with statistical literacy and effective reading techniques.

You and your GPS peers also enroll in a large gateway course with high achievement gaps, like Introduction to Human Biology. You attend weekly study sessions led by undergraduate teaching assistants trained to support the development of academic agency as well as learning of the course content. With the same group of twenty-five students, along with your faculty and peer mentors, you meet again on Fridays for Twenty-First-Century Citizen, a course exploring the diverse contexts that frame learning and engaged citizenship and challenging you to examine relevant social problems from an interdisciplinary perspective. Thinking as a citizen, you explore majors, careers, and high-impact experiences. You soon start to see the hidden curriculum as your mentors honor their commitments to reciprocity and transparency not just in their assignments but also in cocurricular and civic engagement, advising experiences, and even financial literacy support.[10]

Throughout the fall, you meet regularly with your mentors, your dedicated academic advisor, tutors, and research librarians, and you visit places like the Pride, Multicultural, and Counseling Centers. You might go to the international film festival in downtown Green Bay with your peer mentor or eat dinner with your faculty mentor. You might volunteer in the community and explore other opportunities for making a difference, such as participating in student organizations.

In the second semester, you work with your classmates on a spring capstone to complete a large-scale service-learning project. You share these projects in a public showcase attended by campus and community leadership. Throughout your educational experience, you remain connected to your peer and faculty mentors, and they might encourage you to become a peer mentor or teaching assistant (TA) or help you secure an internship.

Behind the scenes, faculty and peer mentors draw on information from the student, data from early grade reports, and conversations with colleagues to understand each student's needs. All students receive individualized attention to support their college goals, and any student who begins to struggle, academically or otherwise, receives immediate assistance in the form of a personalized intervention plan, including referrals to campus or community resources. A coalition of staff across campus, including the dean of students, the Counseling and Health Center, Disability Services, the Financial Aid Department, the Learning Center (tutoring services), the Multi-Ethnic Student Affairs Office, and the Pride Center, provides a secondary support team. We have also added student-success interns: master's-level social work students who focus on the non-academic challenges that many of our students face, connecting them with campus and community resources to support their basic needs (e.g., food, housing, child care).

Faculty and peer mentors work within an intensive community of practice and support. They design together the curriculum for the common GPS courses and participate in extensive training on assets-focused, culturally competent, holistic education. Mentors meet weekly to share experiences, prepare together for the upcoming work, and strategize how best to support each student's needs. Given the high emotional workload and the steep learning curve for many faculty, this level of engagement and the supportive relationships that result are critical to the program's success.

As GPS has grown to include participants from more corners of the UWGB campus, it has become a place for conversations about systemic biases and problems in our institution and higher education in general. For example, we've learned about issues such as food insecurity, homelessness, and family crisis from our students and have created new programs to assist them. Under the rubric of Phoenix Cares, we have normalized the idea that it is OK for students to receive assistance—that help is part of belonging to a caring community. Mentors who have themselves experienced poverty, racism, classism, or other forms of oppression share their experiences with students to mitigate any imposter syndrome.

Problem-Focused Learning and Twenty-First-Century Education

Uncertainty about the political, social, and economic future of the world means that twenty-first-century education should be student- and problem-focused, the latter of which is named specifically as part of our institution's mission and identity. We begin this integrated learning in the fall courses, developing students' capacity to design and manage a collaborative, community-based learning project. We recognize that their future work, professionally and civically, will take place under unknown conditions requiring resourcefulness and interdisciplinary thinking. Students work through a series of assignments that prompt reflection on their core values and commitments, and they explore these values through experiences like volunteering, small-scale research projects on campus, major and career explorations, and high-impact experiences. For every

GPS assignment, students have the option to propose an alternative that meets their learning goals. We recognize that students may have different paths to find their purpose. These assignments often ask students to risk something. For example, we practice failure, but in a low-stakes way.

Students' co-creation culminates in the collective design and implementation of a community-based learning project in the spring GPS capstone course, in which students explore the "wicked problems" of our time.[11] These problems are not (merely) technical challenges but require students to weigh moral and ethical responsibilities, analyze political and economic implications, and map the assets they can draw on to respond to this work. To develop this project and understand problems without easy solutions, students must have knowledge as well as interdisciplinary and theoretical lenses—they must become "wicked students."[12] Then, they have to develop their deliberative and collaborative capacities to make a decision about the service project they will complete. For example, students have recorded and shared personal stories from our community, raised funds for a scholarship for students who are single parents, provided opportunities to engage and live with art in a local domestic violence shelter, and mentored youth. The project requires them to learn how to sustain group efforts, connect with professional and civic leaders, and apply their learning in the community. Not all projects are equally successful, but the program gives students the space to try, fail, regroup, and try again as a community rather than as atomistic individuals.

The ability to work in a diverse team and manage a project is essential for responding to future problems as citizens and workers. Like most high-impact practices, of which GPS is a sort of bundle, the courses require major and sustained effort as well as deepened relationships with peers and mentors, and they culminate in a public celebration at the end of the year.[13] This bundling provides a unique opportunity for students to practice the types of collaboration and interdisciplinary translation they will need in order to connect across difference in the workplace or community after college in a supportive environment.

Outcomes, Challenges, and Next Steps

GPS has taken an intentional and intensive approach to assessment in order to continually improve program outcomes and to make a successful case for resource allocation. Through this work, we know that GPS significantly improves retention for underserved students at UWGB—by as much as 18 percent through year four. GPS students also earn higher GPAs, make progress in their degree more quickly, and are significantly more likely to graduate in four years.

Beyond these more traditional metrics of success, we have compelling evidence that our students are building a stronger foundation of twenty-first-century skills during college. GPS students participate in almost three times as many high-impact practices compared to all other students at UWGB. They are significantly overrepresented as campus residence assistants, peer mentors, student ambassadors, and tutors. Our students also earn a disproportionately high percentage of university leadership awards at graduation. Perhaps most important, we estimate that there are more than 200 students (mostly from underserved backgrounds) currently at UWGB who would not otherwise be enrolled at a four-year university.

The strong findings from our assessment efforts have allowed us to significantly expand the number of students offered conditional admission, which requires GPS participation, to UWGB. As a result, the percentage of students of color served by GPS has doubled since the program's inception in 2013, and the overall population of students of color at UWGB has increased by 30 percent.

The program continues to grow due not just to these results but to the fact that it is cost-effective. GPS built on existing programs and institutional commitments, including a first-year seminar and a program providing supplemental instruction in an introductory STEM course. By bundling these programs, we have been able to maximize their impact on student success and minimize additional resource needs. Faculty mentors participate in GPS largely as part of their teaching load; we provide one additional teaching-load credit for the extensive out-of-class student contact and a small summer stipend for program development work. We also utilize undergraduate peer mentors and TAs, providing student employment and course credit for student participation, which is both cost-effective and a best practice. In all, GPS costs the university approximately $400 per student for the year, a modest sum that is more than recouped with the increased retention rate that results from the program.

One of the unexpected joys of this work has been the community of practice formed by the instructors who meet regularly to co-create the program. The shared syllabi for the common GPS courses are ever-evolving. Although it has been a challenge for some instructors to moderate their style of preparation for classes in order to work collectively, the program's directors have always been careful to leave space for academic freedom. Each class has a shared set of goals that can be approached in ways that suit the style of each faculty and peer mentor. The community of practice in GPS has also provided professional development opportunities for faculty around not only the first-year experience, but also high-impact practices, social mobility, racism, and class.[14] And for many instructors, the peer mentor relationship has been one of the most meaningful mentoring experiences.

One reason these communities have been so vital for sustaining us in our work has been the pressures mentioned above, which also frame this volume: precarity means that the creative responses of community building take on new meaning despite the labor involved. Still, we know that many students who need this support are not yet getting it on our own campus, and there have been ongoing challenges to secure the necessary resources to fund and operate the program and to prevent participants from burning out. Moving forward, we must address a growing staffing challenge. The UWGB campus has four colleges, but virtually all of the GPS faculty have come from the College of Arts, Humanities, and Social Sciences. The programs that support GPS are in some cases fairly small with limited faculty resources. Providing faculty for GPS often occurs at the expense of courses key to the college's programs, while other colleges have been allowed to opt out of participating in this institutional initiative. This creates further precarity for the core liberal education programs at our institution.

Concluding Thoughts, Next Steps

We in Wisconsin know firsthand the pressure that disinvestment in public education puts on students to understand college as mere job training. At the same time, the political and economic challenges that have prompted these reactionary responses of austerity cannot be solved by students who understand themselves narrowly, but instead require a civic community built through problem-focused learning.

With GPS, we set out to design a program to change the educational experience for underserved students and ended up creating an experience that empowered faculty, staff, and students to be agents of change at our institution and beyond. GPS students have created meal donation projects to address food insecurity and served as campus leaders challenging the institution to better serve its students. Faculty and staff have become advocates for taking a more intersectional approach to student success, influencing campus policies and practices and modeling the type of thinking we need to respond to crisis in a new way. Since 2013, our university has become more focused on supporting equity and student success through holistic, engaged liberal education. But the most important payoff is seeing how current and former GPS students have become stakeholders in their education and active members of our university and community.

KEY TAKEAWAYS

Take an assets-based approach to students. Rather than seeing underserved students as unprepared for college, explore how their life experiences, home communities, goals, and ambitions can empower them to succeed.

Build on existing programs. Determine what existing programs and initiatives can be woven into an integrated program to support underserved first-year students.

Identify and recruit faculty and staff who are committed to student success in an intentional and holistic way. This pioneer cohort of participants can develop the program and recruit additional participants.

Recognize and compensate faculty and staff for additional labor. Recognize participation in the program as important teaching but also as institutional development. Use course credits and stipends to reward participation. Advocate for counting this work toward tenure and promotion or other reviews. Consider the disparate service loads for nontenured instructors, tenure-track instructors, and instructors of color.

Involve advanced students as peer mentors. Whenever possible, recruit and train peer mentors who are from the same underserved groups served by the program. Once the program is established, use program alumni as peer mentors.

Build a truly collaborative team. A successful program will improve because of grassroots ideas and feedback. Participants will need to feel supported in this challenging work.

Collect data to document success stories and areas that need improvement. These data are critical for garnering support from administrators and buy-in from parents and students.

Notes

1. M. Baxter Magolda, "The Activity of Meaning Making: A Holistic Perspective on College Student Development," *Journal of College Student Development* 50, no. 6 (2009): 621-639; George D. Kuh and Patrick G. Love, "A Cultural Perspective on Student Departure," in *Reworking the Student Departure Puzzle*, ed. John M. Braxton (Nashville, TN: Vanderbilt University Press, 2000), 196-212; Terrell K. Strayhorn, *College Students' Sense of Belonging: A Key to Educational Success for All Students* (New York: Routledge, 2012).

2. George D. Kuh et al., *What Matters to Student Success: A Review of the Literature* (Washington, DC: National Postsecondary Education Cooperative Report, 2006).

3. William G. Tierney, "An Anthropological Analysis of Student Participation in College," *Journal of Higher Education* 63, no. 6 (1992): 603-618.

4. Cia Verschelden, *Bandwidth Recovery: Helping Students Reclaim Cognitive Resources Lost to Poverty, Racism, and Social Marginalization* (Sterling, VA: Stylus, 2017).

5. Nancy K. Schlossberg, "Marginality and Mattering: Key Issues in Building Community," *New Directions for Student Services* 48 (1989): 5-15; Strayhorn, *College Students' Sense of Belonging*.

6. Alexander W. Astin, *Are You Smart Enough? How Colleges' Obsession with Smartness Shortchanges Students* (Sterling, VA: Stylus, 2016).

7. Buffy Smith in Charlie Tyson, "The Hidden Curriculum," *Inside Higher Ed*, August 4, 2014, https://www.insidehighered.com/news/2014/08/04/book-argues-mentoring-programs-should-try-unveil-colleges-hidden-curriculum.

8. Tierney, "Anthropological Analysis."

9. Harry C. Boyte, "Public Work: Civic Populism versus Technocracy in Higher Education," in *Agent of Democracy: Higher Education and the HEX Journey*, ed. David W. Brown and Deborah Witte (Dayton, OH: Kettering Foundation Press, 2008), 79-102.

10. Mary-Ann Winkelmes et al., "A Teaching Intervention That Increases Underserved College Students' Success," *Peer Review* 18, nos. 1-2 (2016): 31-36.

11. Horst Rittel and Melvin Webber, "Dilemmas in a General Theory of Planning," *Policy Sciences* 4 (1973): 155-159.

12. Paul Hanstedt, *Creating Wicked Students: Designing Courses for a Complex World* (Sterling, VA: Stylus, 2018).

13. George D. Kuh and Ken O'Donnell, *Ensuring Quality and Taking High-Impact Practices to Scale* (Washington, DC: Association of American Colleges and Universities, 2013).

14. Denise S. Bartell and Caroline Boswell, "Developing the Whole Teacher: Collaborative Engagement as Faculty Development within a First-Year Experience Program," *Journal of Faculty Development* (September 2019).

2 Attending to Local Context, Culture, and Language at Florida International University

Isis Artze-Vega, Phillip M. Carter, and Heather Russell

Radical Vision

Our vision reclaims the liberal arts as a liberating force for students, evoking W. E. B. Du Bois's conviction that liberal education is an essential tool for emancipation.[1] Our view of twenty-first-century education is grounded in a commitment to engaging our diverse student body and the curricular opportunities they make possible. Partnering with students, we produce, disseminate, and build culturally responsive and sustaining materials and take the time to identify culturally learned narratives that both challenge and empower students. Principally, we harness the power of context to create curricular experiences that are authentic for our diverse student body. Our vision for the future of higher education—and liberal education in particular—is rooted in creating a place where pedagogical and curricular praxis is self-reflexively designed to meet the needs of culturally, linguistically, and ethnically diverse student bodies, and where multilingualism, multiculturalism, and equity are centerpieces of our ethos and efforts.

Institutional Profile

Florida International University (FIU) is the fourth-largest public university in the United States, enrolling 56,000 students; it is the largest Hispanic-serving university in the continental United States; and it is

Florida International University

designated by the Carnegie Foundation for the Advancement of Teaching as a research 1 institution (highest research activity).

Introduction

"Our demography is our destiny," Florida International University president Mark B. Rosenberg often affirms. From 2015 to 2019, on average, demographic student data at FIU have been as follows: 67 percent Latinx, 13.7 percent black, and 51 percent Pell Grant recipients. FIU's Latinx and black student body is also diverse in terms of national origin, reflective of Miami's ethnic and racial diversity. Thus, we approach liberal education with a sense of urgency—there is so much at stake for our students. We see that their learning experiences and degrees materially and tangibly change their lives and those of their families and communities.[2] As a large, urban research university in South Florida and the country's largest Hispanic-serving university, we are also keenly aware of the significance of our work to the national landscape: Latinx college enrollments are projected to surge 27 percent by 2022, and nearly 500 institutions have been designated as Hispanic-serving institutions (HSIs). We are thus driven by the responsibility and opportunity to imagine what it means to truly *serve* Hispanic students while maintaining a commitment to equitable outcomes for all students.

For several years, FIU engaged in deep self-reflection, exploring this very question: how best to serve our students. Our analyses revealed fissures in our conventional approaches, a comprehensive discussion of which is beyond the scope of this case study. One central recognition, however, was that we were not leveraging our ethnic, racial, linguistic, and cultural diversity as strengths. We needed to develop a purposive, asset-based diversity model to drive our university's mission, our undergraduate education's learning outcomes, and our student success goals—in direct contrast to the prevailing deficit-based discourse around student success. South Florida, Miami, and FIU are already among the most diverse places in the United States, but we asked ourselves, how might we as an institution of higher education do diversity better? How could we create a space where diversity signifies something meaningful for our varied constituents? With respect to the goals of liberal education, how might we help students develop a sense of social responsibility as well as the skills they will need to thrive in a future characterized by technological innovation and global uncertainty?

In our case, this has meant working to develop a taxonomy of difference that attends to our South Florida context to help students develop twenty-first-century skills, implement new curricula and instructional practices, and recognize and leverage students' cultural wealth and experiential ways of knowing. In so doing, we have found that unfettered by the master narratives created about their specific socioeconomic and cultural circumstances, students excel. In this case narrative, we explore these themes through specific course-level innovations situated in institutional and departmental contexts. Although our examples come from FIU's English Department, we imagine these conversations to be cross-disciplinary and translatable to a variety of disciplinary, institutional, and regional contexts.

Case Narrative

"Hispanic" students were first mentioned nationally in 1992, when the US Congress voted to reauthorize the Higher Education Act and created the designation "Hispanic-serving." Thereafter, accredited colleges and universities have been designated Hispanic-serving if at least 25 percent of full-time-equivalent undergraduate enrollments are Hispanic. The designation is, therefore, based on enrollment, not on any historical, curricular, or philosophical orientation to Hispanic students, and no legislation clarifies what it means to be Hispanic-serving. At the same time, students from low socioeconomic and underserved backgrounds conventionally have chosen professional fields of study, instead of the arts and sciences, especially once they transfer from community college to a university.[3] And yet, by 2025 most graduates will enter a workforce in which machines will process data, perform technological functions, and compute scientific calculations more efficiently and accurately than humans can.

Meanwhile, diversity and inclusion initiatives and efforts to revitalize the liberal arts have been conceived separately. Indeed, twenty-first-century skills are often discussed absent of context or relevance to specific student groups. Finally, we recognize the gap that often persists between a theoretical commitment to an asset-based approach, on the one hand, and implementing these commitments in actual praxis, on the other. Our response: university-wide initiatives and partnerships that uphold our epistemological and pedagogical commitment to engage our diverse student body and the curricular opportunities they make possible.

Innovation Details

We have designed initiatives to help students understand and navigate the university, with a particular emphasis on demystifying the humanities. First, we have cultivated partnerships with external organizations that have helped us implement various aspects of our vision. Our long-standing partnership with the Andrew W. Mellon Foundation, for example, has supported three distinct humanities-focused projects. One of them funds efforts to align curricula for students who transfer from Miami Dade College to FIU after earning an associate's degree. It also provides a summer "bridge" program, advising and internship opportunities, and mentorship by successful humanities graduates, and it helps students find their way to fulfilling careers through the customization of an existing career assessment tool.

Once students are enrolled at FIU, a second project promotes active, learning-centered, culturally responsive teaching in our humanities classrooms and engages faculty in reimagining humanities classrooms and curricula. Finally, the HSI Pathways to the Professoriate program seeks to address the underrepresentation of Latinx people in the professoriate by providing mentorship for diverse undergraduates interested in pursuing scholarly careers, including individualized guidance on student research projects. The first cohort to complete the program in the spring of 2018 had a 100 percent successful placement in top graduate programs.

To complement the external support, we have examined our own internal practices and updated our institutional reward structures to reflect our commitment to context and diversity. To this end, we have articulated a vision of teaching excellence characterized by learning-centeredness, evidence-based practice, and cultural responsiveness. Evaluations of teaching will eventually reflect these values.

Ultimately, students' most immediate experience of the vision we have set forth thus far takes place daily in the context of the classroom. This is why we think seriously about course design in terms of both updating existing courses to include diverse materials tailored to local contexts and constructing new courses that challenge and empower students. In short, we are making curricular changes to create lasting change. For instance, the Writing and Rhetoric program has successfully redesigned our first-year composition courses in a process guided by asset-based principles. Notably, language difference is posited as a strength; instructors are not gatekeepers but proceed from the assumption that all students can succeed; the curriculum is project-focused and collaborative; there is more reflection on learning about learning; and activities and assessments are more focused on twenty-first-century literacies with students producing multimedia writing projects and not just traditional essays.

In a similar vein, the literature program embarked on the creation of a textbook for Introduction to Literature, with selections from Miami and FIU authors together with literary classics. As Russell writes in the introduction:

> In creating this textbook, we wanted to affirm the literatures and voices of where we are . . . : South Florida. We have authors . . . in this book who graduated, as you will, from FIU. . . . We wanted to put stories—maybe like the ones you heard from your Abuelos and Tanties—alongside Ernest Hemingway and Walt Whitman. . . . Reading this LIT 1000 textbook, the product of a great deal of hard work by faculty who believe in you and want you richly to experience literature in all of its diversity and cultural richness,

is hopefully your first but not your last deep dive into the wondrous possibilities of literary study.[4]

Statements like these invite student readers into our vision, demystifying our process, aims, and values. Similarly, individual faculty have redesigned their courses in concert with the emancipatory vision set forth in this chapter.

Course Innovation Number 1: Reclaiming Grammar

Like many public, land-grant, and minority-serving institutions, FIU offers a Modern English Grammar course. This type of course is rarely offered in English Departments at private universities or elite public institutions because grammar courses were originally intended for those imagined to need grammatical remediation. However, often these courses were not giving students what they needed: information for future teachers, perspectives on grammar in writing, information about the grammar of nonstandard varieties of English, and perspectives on the grammar of translanguaging and other bilingual speech varieties.[5] In minority-serving institutions, where students live out the effects of disaffirming language ideologies on a daily basis, the value of these kinds of courses has been very much in question.[6] As Carter points out, for many students "Modern English Grammar constitutes the only encounter with the linguistic study of language in an entire undergraduate curriculum and may therefore provide the only occasion to engage students critically with basic information about the types of language found in their homes and communities."[7] In response to these critiques, we radically updated the course, making room for instruction and critical conversations about the structure of English language variations, particularly in the local community and educational contexts.

Although critical teaching rarely takes place in courses on grammar, sociolinguistic research on language attitudes among FIU students shows that those with Latinx backgrounds exhibit negative attitudes toward non-European varieties of Spanish, perceive of Spanish less favorably than English, and report negative feelings about language mixing or "Spanglish," even when they admit to using it.[8] Since language is so tightly linked to self-concept, which is so tied to academic achievement, we realized that shifting our students' perspectives on grammar was just as important—and far more empowering—than teaching about grammar in the abstract.

As we have done in the writing program and in the introduction to literature textbook, we now describe our perspective on the course in plain language up front, and we frame it as critical questions: What is grammar? What does it mean to talk about "good" and "bad" grammar? Who benefits and suffers from such distinctions? And where do notions of "grammatical correctness" come from? During the first week of the redesigned course, we historicize grammar through a survey of the history of the English language. Beyond typical historical moments of note, we add such dates as 1825, 1953, and 1959, years that point to key moments in US Latinx history in which Spanish, English, and their speakers came in close contact: the granting of land to English speakers in Mexico, the Puerto Rican Great Migration to New York City, and the end of the Cuban Revolution. The historicizing of English grammar and the explicit inclusion of Latinx people on the timeline militate against the view that English and its grammar "belong" to any particular group or "come from" a single time and place. Students are, therefore, able to see themselves inside the language, its history, and its grammar.

As the course moves to the linguistic analysis of the structures of modern English, we retain the framing of grammar as fluid and susceptible to historical and cultural influences. We invite students to discover how grammatical structures evolved over time, often comparing English to other languages spoken by our students, such as Spanish, Portuguese, and French. We later consider how English is changing in Miami. After examining Spanglish versions of two fairy tales, students discover that Spanglish, although grammatically flexible, has its own grammar.[9] Through this analysis, students are empowered to see their language practices as valuable and worthy of study, which demonstrates the liberating force of liberal education. At the end of the course, students work in teams to create podcasts about language in Miami, an assignment that positions them to be authorities on the variety of primary languages in their community.

We posit that courses (across the curriculum) inherited from historically white colleges and universities may implicitly disenfranchise ethnic- and language-minority students. These courses should be rethought and repurposed with intention, lest further generations of students learn that a prerequisite for scholastic success is divestment from their home language, culture, and identity.

Course Innovation Number 2: Heritage Language Instruction

Constructing the liberal arts of the future always starts in local contexts, and at the institutional level this means analyzing both strengths and areas for growth. At FIU, our students' multilingualism is an undeniable strength, but it cannot be taken for granted or assumed to be sustainable without nourishment. When we think about what our students need from their liberal arts education in order to be successful after graduation, Spanish-language skills top the list. But when we look at research conducted by linguists on the intergenerational maintenance of Spanish in South Florida, we worry. Countless studies show that Spanish proficiency is being lost over time, including among Cuban Americans, where its retention has traditionally been highest.[10] This is true even though bilingual ability is highly valued in South Florida and comes with an economic advantage.[11]

To build on the strengths of the home language, many Latinx students need courses tailored specifically to their gifts and needs. These courses include heritage language (HL) instruction, a pedagogy designed for learners who already have a cultural connection and some proficiency in the language studied.[12] HL learners differ from second-language learners, the assumed audience for most postsecondary language classes, in that they have unique linguistic skills, experiences, and orientations. In the United States, the Spanish HL education movement began in the 1970s and expanded alongside the widespread growth of the US Latinx population during the 1980s and 1990s as administrators, teachers, and policy makers sought to respond to the educational needs of this population.[13]

HL courses are entirely asset-based and tightly woven with issues of social justice. Many Latinx students see their Spanish as a burden, rather than as a gift or an asset. Some students feel ashamed for being illiterate in Spanish, or for having learned a variety they perceive to be illegitimate, or for having learned it "poorly." Properly designed HL courses attend to these issues. Unfortunately, Latinx college students are generally underserved by HL courses, including at HSIs, which may assume that students have sufficiently acquired the language at home. At FIU, the Department of Modern Languages currently offers only two courses for heritage learners, which in the spring of 2015 enrolled only 178 students. As noted, FIU is the largest HSI in the United States, and roughly two-thirds of our students are Latinx-identified. While not all in that group can be classified as Spanish HL speakers (some are English monolinguals, others Spanish-dominant bilinguals), the majority of them are. This means that in the fall of 2014, there were roughly 27,000 undergraduate HL speakers of Spanish on campus, likely the largest Spanish HL student body in the world. In spite of this, we estimate that less than .01 percent of HL Spanish speakers on campus receive instruction designed specifically for their needs.

We have advocated for the expansion of HL course offerings at FIU in several ways. Though our labor is not yet complete, we present our efforts as a model for readers hoping to create or advocate for HL courses at their home institutions. First, we contributed to our university's strategic planning process, aiming to educate our colleagues about the differences between foreign language and HL instruction and to make sure that HL instruction had pride of place in our strategic plan. Second, we created a Heritage Language Planning Committee, which helped disseminate information to the relevant stakeholders and departments. Third, we invited experts on HL instruction to campus to offer talks and workshops on best practices in HL teaching and program building. Finally, we worked with the Center for Teaching and Learning to disseminate ideas about how to incorporate heritage languages into classrooms across the curriculum. These practices included offering extra credit for learning basic disciplinary content and vocabulary in a heritage language, inviting students to use HLs in class discussions, and asking students how to describe a course concept in their HL.

Concluding Thoughts, Next Steps

We will continue to work on moving FIU toward becoming a center for excellence in heritage language instruction. We will be engaged in assessing the impact of our various curricular and pedagogical redesigns. We are piloting a new project designed by two members of the English Department, who aim to design an English major using the principles articulated in Joseph Aoun's groundbreaking work on higher education in the age of artificial intelligence.[14] As the economy becomes ever more automated, skills associated with "human ingenuity" will become increasingly valued and valuable.

Our faculty also will pilot a project to create "a streamlined English major with an eye towards bridging the 'skills gap' between what business prizes and what universities teach,"[15] which is rooted in the principles of liberal education described here. The strengths of our student body and our investment in liberal education through diversity, multilingualism, and interdisciplinarity will ensure not only that our students are included in the changing economy, but that they will be leading the change.

KEY TAKEAWAYS

Examine how courses and curricula are redesigned. Courses *cannot* only be driven by conventional disciplinary content; course designers should check to make sure they are not inadvertently relying on and transmitting perspectives and assumptions that are damaging to students. Instead, begin by asking how courses and assignments empower students.

Commit to multilingualism. Language skills are a centerpiece of twenty-first-century liberal education. Acknowledging and valuing nonstandard varieties of English across curricula, providing dedicated and specialized spaces to utilize and build on heritage languages, and offering options to study other languages—including less commonly taught languages—will be essential to advancing language skills and cultural literacy.

Get to know your student body. The faculty and administration should understand and affirm the identities of their students; have an informed sense of the meaning of designations such as "first generation," "DACA student," and "Pell Grant recipient"; distinguish in policy and discourse their understanding of race, ethnicity, and culture as related but distinct categories; and recognize how social, political, cultural, and historical contexts shape students' multiple identities differently.

Notes

1. W. E. B. Du Bois, *The Souls of Black Folk* (1903), http://www.gutenberg.org/files/408/408-h/408-h.htm.

2. We also recognize how color complicates the discussion since many of our Latinx students benefit from white privilege. See Rob Wile, "Haitian, Jamaican or American . . . If You're Black in Miami, Odds Are You're Struggling," February 25, 2019, https://www.miamiherald.com/news/business/article226732184.html.

3. K. A. Goyette and A. L. Mullen, "Who Studies the Arts and Sciences? Social Background and the Choice and Consequences of Undergraduate Field of Study," *Journal of Higher Education* 77, no. 3 (2006): 497-538.

4. H. Russell, "Welcome Letter from Chair," in *Norton Introduction to Literature: FIU Edition*, ed. Amy Huseby (New York: Norton, 2018), 1.

5. O. Garcia, "U.S. Spanish and Education: Global and Local Intersections," *Review of Research in Education* 38 (2004): 58-80.

6. M. Silverstein, "Monoglot 'Standard' in America: Standardization and Metaphors of Linguistic Hegemony," in *The Matrix of Language: Contemporary Linguistic Anthropology*, ed. Donald Brenneis and Ronald Macauley (Boulder, CO: Westview, 1996), 284-306; R. Lippi-Green, "Accent, Standard Language Ideology, and Discriminatory Pretext in the Courts," *Language in Society* 23, no. 2 (1994): 163-198.

7. P. M. Carter, "Critical Language Study and Modern English Grammar in Context," *American Speech* 90, no. 2 (2015): 246-266, 246-247.

8. P. M. Carter and S. Calleasano, "The Social Meaning of Spanish in Miami: Dialect Perceptions and Implications for Socioeconomic Class, Income, and

Employment," *Latino Studies* 16 (2018): 65-90; P. M. Carter and A. Lynch, "Multilingual Miami: Current Trends in Sociolinguistic Research," *Language and Linguistics Compass* 9 (2015): 369-385; P. M. Carter, L. López Valdez, and N. Sims, "Narrativizing Miami: Discursive Tropes about Spanish in the Speech of Miami Bilinguals." Paper delivered at the Spanish in the United States and in Contact with Other Languages conference, March 2015, New York.

9. A. J. Toribio, "Spanish-English Code-Switching among U.S. Latinos," *International Journal of Sociology of Language* 158 (2002): 89-119.

10. B. Zurer Pearson and A. McGee, "Language Choice in Hispanic-Background Junior High School Students in Miami: A 1988 Update," in *Spanish in the United States: Linguistic Contact and Diversity*, ed. Ana Roca and John Lipski (Berlin, Germany: Mouton de Gruyter, 2013).

11. H. López Morales, *Los cubanos de Miami: Lengua y sociedad* (Miami, FL: Universal, 2003); A. Lynch, "Spanish-Speaking Miami in Sociolinguistic Perspective," in *Research on Spanish in the United States*, ed. Ana Roca (Somerville, MA: Cascadilla, 2000), 271-283; A. Roca, "Language Maintenance and Language Shift in the Cuban American Community of Miami: The 1990s and Beyond," in *Language Planning*, ed. David F. Marshall (Philadelphia, PA: John Benjamins, 1991), 245-257; T. Boswell, *The Cubanization and Hispanicization of Metropolitan Miami* (Miami, FL: Cuban American National Council, 1994); S. Fradd, T*he Economic Impact of Spanish-Language Proficiency in Metropolitan Miami* (Miami, FL: Greater Miami Chamber of Commerce and the Cuban American National Council, 1996); D. McGuirk, "An Ethnolinguistic Analysis of Hispanics in Miami-Dade County," PhD diss., Florida International University, 2004.

12. T. G. Wiley, "On Defining Heritage Languages and Their Speakers," in *Heritage Languages in America: Preserving a National Resource*, ed. J. K. Peyton, D. A. Ranard, and S. McGinnis (Washington, DC: Center for Applied Linguistics, and McHenry, IL: Delta Systems, 2001), 29-36.

13. S. Beaudrie and M. Fairclough, eds., *Spanish as a Heritage Language in the United States: State of the Field* (Washington, DC: Georgetown University Press, 2012).

14. Joseph Aoun, *Robot-Proof: Higher Education in the Age of Artificial Intelligence* (Cambridge, MA: MIT Press, 2017).

15. M. Creeden and P. Feigenbaum, "Project Proposal: 21st Century English" (Florida International University, 2018), in authors' possession.

3 The Experiential Liberal Arts
An Integrative Model for Twenty-First-Century Education at Northeastern University

Chris W. Gallagher and Uta G. Poiger

Radical Vision

The future of liberal education is experiential and integrative. In order to be responsible and adaptive global citizens in a rapidly changing world, learners must be able to apply and transform knowledge and skills, such as creativity, ethical reasoning, cultural agility, entrepreneurship, and systems thinking, across a range of contexts. In an era of technological ubiquity, artificial intelligence, and automation, twenty-first-century learners must integrate their distinctly human capacities with technological proficiencies. The future of liberal arts disciplines and colleges lies in integrating technological proficiencies into our educational models and integrating ourselves into broader visions of twenty-first-century education. For our students' sake and our own, we need to give up our defensive postures, collaborate with our colleagues in STEM and professional fields, and focus on offering all students a holistic education that fuses the human and the technological.

Institutional Profile

Northeastern University is a private, not-for-profit doctoral university designated as a research 1 institution by Carnegie and enrolling approximately 18,000 undergraduate and 15,000 graduate students. It is a large, four-year institution with a highly residential campus in Boston with a classification in community engagement and is building a global university network with current sites in London, Toronto, Vancouver, Seattle, San Francisco, and Charlotte.

Introduction

The grand challenges of the twenty-first-century—from climate change to cyberterrorism to nuclear proliferation to the rise of authoritarian populism—are complex and systems-embedded. In order to address them, we need professionals and citizens who can cope adaptively with ambiguity and change, who can collaborate on the human and the technological aspects of these challenges, and who can address them in their local and global manifestations. The most compelling value proposition for liberal education in the twenty-first century is that it should teach the knowledge and skills necessary to confront the grand challenges of our time. At Northeastern University, we call it the Age of Humanics— "an age that integrates and elevates our human and technological capacities to meet the global challenge of our time: building sustainable human communities."[1] Liberal learning and the liberal arts are critical to this vision not only because they represent the "human" in humanics, but also because in the twenty-first century, the human and the technological are inextricable.

This chapter centers on the experiential liberal arts, an education model developed by Northeastern's College of Social Sciences and Humanities. The experiential liberal arts informed humanics and developed alongside it. It is not a particular program or practice, but rather a college-wide model. At the heart of this model are three key integrations: (1) rigorous study of culture, society, and ethics with experiential learning; (2) traditional liberal arts capacities with new digital proficiencies; and (3) local with global engagement. The experiential liberal arts has helped our liberal arts college transform the student experience, spur curriculum innovation, forge a shared college identity, and play a key role in our institution's ambitions.

Case Narrative

The College of Social Sciences and Humanities (CSSH) was formed during a 2010 institutional restructuring that created smaller, more nimble colleges that would operate in a hybrid responsibility-center management budget model. Traditionally, Northeastern had been best known for experiential learning, engineering, and business. It had undergone a dramatic transformation in the preceding years, becoming an ambitious research university committed to use-inspired research on security, health, and sustainability. In this context, many CSSH faculty wondered how diverse disciplines, including English, criminal justice, and economics, could unite and thrive in their new institutional home.

At the same time, CSSH faced a host of internal and external challenges that nearly all liberal arts colleges did and still do: declining enrollments, especially in the humanities; stubborn coverage models of curriculum; disciplines struggling to make sense of vast amounts of unstructured data; rapidly changing employment and citizenship demands; and public skepticism about the value of liberal education. Two questions guided the college's journey in the years that followed:

- How can we forge a shared educational model that will prepare students to act effectively, adaptively, and ethically in a rapidly changing world?
- How can we use this model to galvanize our CSSH colleagues and students and assert the relevance of the liberal arts and liberal education to the university's mission?

Our chief goal was to develop an education model consistent with our vision of a twenty-first-century liberal education. We wanted to highlight the integration of humanistic, social scientific, and technological skills that we believe will be critical for virtually everyone in the years ahead. At the same time, we wanted to invite faculty and students across disciplines to help shape the new college's shared mission and identity. Finally, as our institution's academic planning process got under way, we saw an opportunity to assert the integral nature of the liberal arts and liberal learning to Northeastern's evolving vision for 2025.

Our primary inspiration was the experiential work already happening in our college and across our university. Experiential learning dates back more than a century at Northeastern. Almost all students complete at least one co-op, which is a six-month research and work experience in one of a broad range of organizations: corporations, research institutes, NGOs, and governmental agencies. Most students complete two. They are prepared and guided to reflect on their learning by college-based co-op coordinators, who also work with employers to craft meaningful experiences. Many students also take advantage of Dialogue of Civilizations programs: faculty-led summer study abroad experiences that engage with communities around the globe. Students routinely conduct use-inspired research in labs, research centers, and community spaces. They engage in service learning and study abroad. They are active in clubs and organizations. One goal of the experiential liberal arts is to ensure that these experiences are interwoven with, rather than supplemental to, students' academic studies. We believe that critical twenty-first-century liberal learning skills—including adaptability, cross-cultural communication, and networking—can be achieved only by intertwining learning in classes with learning in other contexts.

In addition to breaking down walls between classrooms and other contexts, the experiential liberal arts challenges the boundaries between liberal arts disciplines and STEM and professional disciplines, between liberal education and "practical" education, and between the human and the technological. We have been inspired by the integrative visions of higher education leaders like Amy Gutmann and Joseph Aoun, our university's president.[2] Our thinking has also been shaped by national and international discussions of the digital and public humanities promoted by the National Endowment for the Humanities, the Andrew W. Mellon Foundation, the American Historical Association, and the Modern Language Association as well as integrative initiatives, such as the Teagle Foundation's Liberal Arts and the Professions.[3]

The "virtuous circle" of experiential learning.

Innovation Details

The experiential liberal arts model has been conceived and developed collaboratively. As a new dean, Uta Poiger engaged faculty and department and program leaders in a process of identifying areas of strategic focus for the college. The resulting focuses—integrating resilience and sustainability; cultural transformations, governance, and globalization; and big data and digital methods in the humanities and social sciences—demonstrated the experiential and integrative commitments of our college. From there, the authors of this chapter drafted a white paper on what we began calling the "experiential liberal arts." This document articulated an integrative conceptual framework and demonstrated the relevance and impact of the humanities and social sciences through examples of faculty and students developing and sharing expertise with and for various publics in a variety of media.

The experiential liberal arts embraces the idea that "learning happens everywhere," but it posits that the key to preparing learners to act effectively and ethically in a rapidly changing world is helping them apply and transform their knowledge and skills across contexts. We designed what we call the "virtuous circle" (see the figure) to represent the cyclical nature of experiential learning. The experiential liberal arts builds on this understanding of learning to promote three interrelated integrations:

1. *The integration of the rigorous study of society, culture, politics, and ethics with experiential learning.* In our model, experiential learning is not just the application of theories learned in classrooms; the experiential liberal arts is a holistic approach to learning that encompasses all learning contexts. Students are, after all, *experiencing* society, culture, politics, and ethics both inside and outside the classroom, on and off campus, and our goal is to help students study these key subjects wherever they are experienced. The theories, frameworks, and methods learned by students in classrooms are made even more rigorous by their application and transformation in other spaces, whether through a co-op, undergraduate research, service learning, or study abroad. As the virtuous circle suggests, we expect students (and faculty) to bring their new understandings back to their classrooms, which then prepare them for further learning and discovery elsewhere.
2. *The integration of familiar liberal arts capacities, such as ethical reasoning and social and cultural analysis, with new proficiencies, such as text mining and network analysis.* Today, technology reaches into every corner of our lives, and we all work at human-technological and physical-digital interfaces. There is a critical need to bring humanistic and social scientific thinking to bear on technology—and to bring technological, specifically computational, thinking to bear on the humanities and social sciences. We see this integration as an opportunity to deepen students' engagement with humanistic and social scientific inquiry and content. For instance, English majors use computational tools, theories, and perspectives to pursue both age-old critical questions and new questions that data mining of large digital corpora makes possible. They come to understand how

texts and textual practices have always been shaped by technologies. They arrive at deeper insights into, for example, the evolving conceptions and ethics of "intellectual property" over time through the combination of humanistic and technological lenses.
3. *The integration of local and global engagement.* Experiential learning takes Northeastern students into the city of Boston and across the globe. But the experiential liberal arts is less about *where* students study (although this is important) than about developing a mindset that is attuned to both the local and global implications of *what* they are studying and experiencing. Increasingly, we are abandoning domestic-abroad distinctions and encouraging all of our students, whether they are studying or working in Boston, London, Shanghai, or Lusaka, to consider how their topics (and perhaps methods) are shaped by local circumstances and conditions *and* by broader global forces. We encourage students to study the interplay of the global and the local, no matter where or what they study.

The white paper provided a common language for what we were already doing and articulated a vision for how we could move forward together. But without the engagement of faculty, students, staff, alumni, and parents, it would have been just words on a page. Our department chairs further developed the experiential liberal arts in planning a presentation to our provost, adding their own formulations and examples. A faculty working group developed a curriculum framework that provides conceptual scaffolding for every CSSH student's experience throughout their undergraduate career. Each department and program developed multimedia, web-based, searchable student pathway profiles.[4] College-wide student leadership groups, the CSSH alumni council, and parent groups served as think tanks, providing invaluable feedback on the developing model. Our communications and advancement teams formulated our college's brand around the experiential liberal arts so that our external constituents, including prospective students and donors, would understand how and why we value liberal learning.

While it is conceived as ever-evolving, the experiential liberal arts has already produced a number of positive results, including the following:

A Transformed Student Experience

Our model encourages students to carve their own pathways, and no two CSSH students follow the same trajectory. Still, there is a family resemblance. Our students are achieving postsecondary success through the integrations at the heart of the experiential liberal arts. Two of our graduates demonstrate what this looks like.

Whether studying contemporary cinematic interpretations of Shakespeare or the uses of Asian literature in children's television shows, English major and media production minor Bella Hendricks says she was able to "combine [her] interests in new media and more traditional literary studies in really productive ways" throughout her undergraduate career. In addition to essays, she submitted videos and computer code as final projects in her classes. Using digital tools, she says, "helps you understand the media you're dealing with in a new and modern, relevant way." At the same time, critically analyzing literature gave her skills to apply to her own work, making her "a better creator of media." Hendricks extended and refined the analytical and creative skills she learned in her classes outside the classroom. For her two co-ops—at a music conservatory and an ad agency—she helped produce web content and live events. She also volunteered as a television production assistant for a citywide initiative helping local nonprofits to support neighborhood beautification projects. Hendricks's undergraduate experience integrated liberal learning and professional learning, the humanistic and the technological, classrooms and the wider world. She is now a marketing coordinator at an architectural firm.

Aja Watkins, a combined philosophy and math major with a minor in law and public policy, says that she "was able to use many of the mathematical tools [she] was learning when answering philosophical questions—and [she] was able to apply a philosophical frame of mind to [her] coursework." She regularly viewed one discipline through the lens of another, whether using her Ethics and Evolutionary Games course to test mathematical models or using the analytical tools of philosophy to critique prevailing theories in ecological economics. Watkins became interested in issues of educational opportunity through her co-op with a youth organization and her work on a state ballot initiative on charter schools. The latter experience led her to design an interdisciplinary honors thesis in which she combined her philosophical training with her mathematical skills. She built an interactive simulation model that shows users the consequences of different policy decisions around school choice. This model could have been developed only by someone with Watkins's interdisciplinary background in philosophy, economics, math, and public policy. As Watkins put it, the project "served as the perfect culmination of [her] education-related work experiences and [her] coursework." Watkins is now pursuing a PhD in philosophy at Boston University.

As different as Hendricks's and Watkins's interests and trajectories have been, they both integrated their classroom work with learning beyond the university, and they combined and synthesized familiar liberal arts capacities with new proficiencies. They developed broad perspectives and deep expertise, leaving their undergraduate experiences well prepared for the challenges ahead of them.

Curricular Innovation

The experiential liberal arts has catalyzed curricular innovations at the undergraduate and graduate levels, including combined majors and interdisciplinary minors, the experiential liberal arts curriculum framework, a graduate certificate in digital humanities, and the expansion of experiential learning in our master's and PhD programs. CSSH faculty have developed partnerships with our computer sciences colleagues to generate interdisciplinary courses (e.g., Bostonography: Texts, Maps, and Networks), minors (e.g., Digital Methods, Culture, and Society), and computer science majors combined with criminal justice, economics, English, history, philosophy, political science, or sociology.

These innovations are paying dividends. Our combined majors have been extremely popular. In 2017, 2018, and 2019, more than half of our first-year students enrolled in one of our sixty combined majors. At the same time, we have experienced some unintended consequences. For example, courses like Bostonography and Literature and Digital Diversity, designed to attract CSSH majors into computational thinking and further coursework with computation, have instead attracted majors from other colleges, especially the Khoury College of Computer Sciences. While we are delighted about the engagement of computer science majors with our intellectual frameworks, we seek opportunities to involve all students, including those in CSSH, in the integration of digital and liberal learning.

To this end, with philanthropic support, we are developing modules that model the integration of liberal arts and technological capacities in core courses for our majors that do not signal "digital technology" in their titles. This effort, which we have dubbed the "digital integration initiative," was spurred by a 2017 external review of the college and by our students, who have told us in surveys that the combination of liberal arts capacities and digital proficiencies becomes particularly critical when they go into the broader world during their co-ops.

Increasingly, CSSH faculty are developing courses and modules that are integrated into the curricula of other colleges. For example, colleagues in philosophy with expertise in information ethics are developing integrative modules on ethics and computing challenges for an introductory course for a new master's program in artificial intelligence, while a colleague in sociology has developed assignments that use social sciences and humanities data and questions for an introductory-level course on data science. Happily, this latter course has drawn our CSSH majors in higher numbers than the initial innovations did.

A Shared College Identity

The experiential liberal arts has become the hallmark of the College of Social Sciences and Humanities. Offering a compelling value proposition for liberal learning and the liberal arts, it invites faculty, students, and staff in our diverse departments and programs into a shared intellectual and academic enterprise. At the same time, it has helped us align our research, educational, hiring, funding, and outreach priorities.

One surprising but welcome result has been the vigor of our undergraduate students' embrace of the experiential liberal arts and the shared identity it offers them despite their diverse majors. We had not realized how hungry our students were to identify with their college—not just their major—as they felt their business or engineering peers did. In a university traditionally not known for the liberal arts or liberal learning, we were particularly pleased to host and cosponsor with the AAC&U a fall 2016 summit of higher education leaders called "The Liberal Arts Imperative in the Digital Age."[5] That our university administration supported—indeed, urged—this initiative speaks volumes about our institution's commitment to the college, to liberal arts, and to liberal learning. The summit also established Northeastern as a contributor to national and international discussions of twenty-first-century liberal education.

An Integral Role in The University's Planning
Process and Vision

The shared college identity was crucial in asserting the college's role in our university's academic planning process. Many faculty, students, and staff in the College of Social Sciences and Humanities, convinced that the experiential liberal arts had to be a critical component of any vision of the future of the university, participated in and led working groups as part of this process. The vision that emerged reimagines the university as a series of globally networked intercultural hubs, transcending traditional institutional boundaries to create "networks of humans and intelligent machines collaborating to build communities that are connected and creative, resilient and entrepreneurial."[6]

Northeastern University's notion of humanics endorses the twenty-first-century skills articulated in this volume, including critical and creative thinking, ethical reasoning, civic responsibility, networking, and cross-cultural competence. It recognizes these skills as *distinctly human*—as the very capacities that will make students "robot-proof," as Aoun puts it, in the wake of the automation of broad swaths of the workforce. Additionally, it insists that liberal learning cannot be conceptualized as a separate sphere: it must be integrated with the study and practice of technology. Only then can we ensure humane, ethical conceptualizations and uses of technology and data and prepare students to navigate dynamic and unpredictable personal, professional, and civic landscapes. In short, humanics cannot thrive without the humanities and social sciences, and our university cannot achieve its ambitions without CSSH.

Concluding Thoughts, Next Steps

Some readers may worry that we dilute the force of the liberal arts by adding the qualifier "experiential" or that we risk losing the defining character of liberal education if it is subsumed under a broader formulation such as humanics. These are reasonable concerns, but ultimately we do not share them. We see these integrations as opportunities to strengthen both our appeal to students and the broader public and the education we offer. Integrating does not mean subsuming; it means combining into a new whole that is greater than the sum of its parts.

Our priority in the coming years is to continue to assess our experiential liberal arts model. Programs and departments in the college are incorporating experiential and integrative learning into their program assessments. We are exploring a range of methods—portfolios, student pathway visualizations, employer surveys, student interviews—to investigate the role that the experiential liberal arts plays in students' learning.

For example, we provide students many opportunities throughout their undergraduate careers to engage in mindful reflection, from goal-setting activities in their introductory seminars to guided reflections while they are on co-op to integrative capstone projects. Many students also participate in Northeastern's Self-Authored Integrated Learning (SAIL) platform, which allows them to plan, capture, track, and visualize their learning over time and across learning contexts.[7] Christopher Gallagher is completing a longitudinal interview study started in 2014 on the transformative effects of the experiential liberal arts on students. We have a treasure trove of data on student learning, and we are building assessments to collect, triangulate, analyze, and use those data. We are particularly interested in longitudinal assessments; for example, we will be tracking if and how student paths adjust as a result of digital integration.

KEY TAKEAWAYS

Develop an educational model that leverages the strengths of your college and offers a compelling value proposition for liberal education in the twenty-first century. Liberal arts colleges, whether freestanding or part of a comprehensive university, need a conceptual framework rooted in twenty-first-century skills and the assembled expertise of their faculty to articulate (in both senses of that word) those programs and practices. We have found that such a framework both accelerates and lends coherence to innovations that might otherwise be difficult to sustain. It also keeps the focus on the transformation of the student experience.

Invite broad participation in the development of your educational model. Collaboratively designing and refining the model provides an opportunity for diverse colleagues to become part of a shared, college-wide enterprise. A key challenge for many in liberal arts colleges is to encourage colleagues to replace complaints about marginalization with affirmative, unapologetic, and specific articulations of the value of the liberal arts and liberal learning.

Use the educational model to forge a shared college framework. The advantages of forging a shared identity are many. Faculty are more likely to perceive themselves as part of a shared project; current students are more likely to feel that they, like their colleagues in professional schools, have a college home; prospective students are more likely to see themselves as part of a describable community; administrators are more likely to perceive and reward the contributions of the college to the institution; and donors are more likely to understand and appreciate the college mission.

Integrate learning assessment into the educational model. We can see some results in the pathways of outstanding students, and robust, systematic assessment will strengthen our case. We recommend building an assessment and evaluation plan into the initial design of your educational model so that you can track its impact on students' experiences from the beginning.

Seek opportunities to integrate your educational model into broader institutional initiatives. Faculty and students in liberal arts colleges within comprehensive universities often feel marginalized, but colleges with strong educational models can play critical roles in institutional initiatives, especially strategic planning, and in intertwining education, research, and engagement beyond the university. Every liberal arts college should be asserting the centrality of liberal education to any responsible twenty-first-century academic plan and institutional vision.

Notes

1. Northeastern University, "Academic Plan: Northeastern 2025," September 30, 2016, https://www.northeastern.edu/academic-plan/plan.

2. Amy Gutmann, "What Makes a University Education Worthwhile?," in *The Aims of Higher Education: Problems of Morality and Justice*, ed. Harry Brighouse and Michael McPherson (Chicago, IL: University of Chicago Press, 2015), 7-25; Joseph Aoun, *Robot-Proof: Higher Education in the Age of Artificial Intelligence* (Cambridge, MA: MIT Press, 2017).

3. See https://www.neh.gov/grants/odh/digital-humanities-advancement-grants; https://mellon.org/initiatives/architecture-urbanism-and-humanities/resources/tag/digital-humanities; https://www.historians.org/about-aha-and-membership/aha-history-and-archives/historical-archives/public-history-public-historians-and-the-american-historical-association; https://action.mla.org/tag/public-humanities/; http://www.teaglefoundation.org/Grants-Initiatives/Current-Initiatives-Listing/Liberal-Arts-and-the-Professions/RFP.

4. College of Social Sciences and Humanities, "CSSH Student Pathways," n.d., https://www.northeastern.edu/cssh/pathways.

5. https://www.northeastern.edu/liberalarts.

6. Northeastern University, "Academic Plan: Northeastern 2025."

7. https://sail.northeastern.edu.

4 Creating Connections
An Intentional, Integrated Liberal Education at Connecticut College

Michael Reder and Ann Schenk

Radical Vision

The future of liberal education depends on the development of curricular structures that foreground self-directed learning and integrative experiences both inside and outside of the classroom. A twenty-first-century liberal education should foster in students a passionate curiosity about issues our world faces, help them devise their own transdisciplinary learning journey based on that curiosity, and ask them to test and apply their learning in real-world scenarios. The curriculum should help students understand connections between and among the liberal arts and sciences and support them in developing the habits of mind to intentionally integrate their courses and activities throughout their undergraduate years. Such an education should require *all* students to participate in a school's highest-impact learning experiences. Creating an effective liberal education will involve the entire campus—students, faculty, administrators, and staff—and must also be informed by extensive evidence about student learning and experiences.

Institutional Profile

Connecticut College, located in New London, is a four-year highly residential, selective, private, not-for-profit baccalaureate college enrolling 1,800 students. Its mission is to "educate students to put the liberal arts into action as citizens in a global society."[1]

Connecticut College

Introduction

The Connecticut College Connections curriculum is an interdisciplinary, inquiry-driven education that requires students to intentionally place their academic priorities in the broader context of the liberal arts in a way that is both personally meaningful and relevant to the global society in which we live. In the first year, students are introduced to the liberal arts in their broader context, and in the sophomore year they are asked to propose their own unique "animating question." This question is intended to be a focusing element in their continuing studies, serving as a guide to and an eventual unifying element of their education. Students refine or even redefine their questions as they continue their coursework and are supported creatively and intellectually in their pursuit of answers through both curricular and cocurricular components.

Connections contains several elements that are unique: topically focused first-year seminars (FYSs) that are team-advised and serve as an extended introduction to liberal education and to the college as a whole; reimagined 100-level introductory courses that intentionally connect the topic of the course to other disciplines (ConnCourses); and multiyear, inquiry-driven Integrative Pathways that help students frame their personalized animating question through a series of curricular and cocurricular activities. Integrative Pathways culminate in an all-college symposium in which students critically synthesize their studies and share the story of their individualized education. The four-year curriculum is designed to lead students to connect the liberal arts courses they take across disciplines to their chosen major(s) and to their own interests and lives, and to apply the entirety of their education to both local and global communities through community learning, study away, and funded internships.

Connections is innovative both in the way in which it was created—using extensive evidence about student learning and with broad campus participation—and in requiring all students to engage in the most impactful learning experiences. The design process relied on evidence related to high-impact practices, how learning works, and our own research into student, faculty, and staff experiences on campus. We strategically built on the college's existing resources of strong faculty and administrative leadership, an excellent Office of Institutional Research, a well-supported faculty Center for Teaching & Learning, and a robust tradition of shared governance.

Case Narrative

The general education program that was in place prior to Connections required courses from a variety of different disciplines without any clear reason or coherence, and it was not perceived by students as an exciting opportunity to enjoy the breadth of the liberal arts. Instead, students routinely approached our outdated distribution requirements as obstacles to get past as early as possible while on the way to completing the "real work" of their major. Both students and faculty often viewed them as little more than a checklist of required courses that students had to fulfill, preferably before the end of their sophomore year. In an effort to increase students' engagement in the liberal arts and create a deeply integrated and distinctive educational experience, we embarked on a multiyear process of curriculum redesign.

Focus groups held with students revealed that, in common with the experience of many first-year college students across institutional types, their college courses were less work than they had expected. Many students talked about receiving high grades despite doing very little work outside of class. While the lack of work required to receive excellent grades reflected a national trend,[2] we wanted to ensure that our students had the highest quality learning experiences. Data from the Wabash National Study of Liberal Arts Education (WNS) confirmed that our first-year students were not working as hard nor were they as intellectually challenged as we wanted them to be.[3] When compared to similar selective, small liberal arts institutions, we scored lower than average on questions related to "academic challenge and effort" and "high faculty expectations." Students' level of "academic motivation"—their willingness to work hard in a course to learn the material (regardless of whether that would improve their grade) or to do more reading than required to learn more about a topic—decreased over the course of their first year. Based on our results on the WNS, we undertook a college-wide, multi-year Academic Challenge Initiative during which we held myriad cross-campus conversations about how we could improve our students' experiences and learning. In addition to improving our students' overall experiences related to intellectual challenge and academic rigor, those conversations eventually led to our three-year Curriculum reVision process, which included faculty, staff, alumni, and students. Revamping students' first-year experiences and then reimagining their curricular and cocurricular experiences throughout their remaining three years were central to our efforts.

Another key WNS finding involved the variation among student experiences within each school in the study. The WNS revealed that differences in the frequency of experiences that contribute to learning for students within any given institution are greater than the variations between institutions. In other words, at each college or university in the WNS, regardless of type—open-access community colleges, large state schools, highly selective private colleges and universities—the variation in learning experiences for students at the same institution is greater than the average difference in learning experiences between institutions. In other words, our schools offer more than one education: at the same school, some students have a large number of good experiences, and others receive significantly fewer. We sought to eliminate this disparity at Connecticut College.

We identified and examined the curricular and cocurricular experiences that best exemplify our vision of liberal education. These include community engagement, travel and study abroad, independent research with a faculty member, personalized advising and mentoring, college leadership positions, deeply engaging with a new language and culture, internships, and senior culminating projects. Our institutional researcher sorted these into three categories: optional and limited in access; optional and unlimited in access; and required. We quickly realized that only a small concentration of high-achieving students—what some of us termed "web page students"—had a lot of those key experiences. This finding convinced us that our new curriculum should require of all students as many of the high-impact curricular and cocurricular experiences as possible.

Connecticut College has four interdisciplinary academic centers that offer certificate programs that can enhance any academic major and where students experience the best education that Connecticut College has to offer. Each academic center has a different focus: arts and technology; public policy and community action; international studies; and the environment. Certificate students complete specialized coursework, a funded internship, and a closely advised and sophisticated senior integrative project, which typically applies their major field of study to transdisciplinary issues. The challenge we faced was that only 15-20 percent of our students complete such a certificate. They are an "optional and limited" commodity: students must apply, and because they are resource-intensive programs, admission is highly competitive. Most students never consider applying to a certificate program because they are involved in other activities or are not inclined to take on the extra work. In our new curriculum, we have aimed to leverage the excellence of the centers into our general curriculum.

The Process: "It Takes a Campus"

Creating the Connections curriculum involved dozens of cross-campus conversations about the ultimate goals of a liberal education and how we could best improve our students' experiences and learning. Connecticut College decided to develop a required curriculum that would help students achieve the following learning outcomes:

- Intellectual and creative inquiry within and beyond the major.
- Integrative problem-solving capacities.
- Appreciation of different modes of intellectual inquiry and the complexity of cultural understanding.
- Nuanced understanding of how studies within a disciplinary major fit into a larger intellectual and social context.

- Capacity to turn learning into practice and practice into learning through engagement with local and global communities and to apply a critical and ethically informed lens to all their learning.

Faculty working groups began to construct potential models for curricula that were informed by nationally recognized high-impact practices that lead to significant student learning, including the AAC&U's LEAP (Liberal Education and America's Promise) and its suggested high-impact practices, the Wabash National Study, the National Survey of Student Engagement (NSSE) measurements, and the latest information about how students learn best, including the neuropsychology of learning and emotional connection in learning.[4] Local evidence included our students' experiences as detailed in the WNS's effective practices scales and extensive conversations with both faculty members and students. A wide variety of staff colleagues, including those working in residential and student life, career services, information services, counseling, athletics, and academic support, joined in discussing the creation of our new curriculum.

Faculty and staff piloted the various components of Connections in the order in which incoming students would experience them, allowing us to roll out our new curriculum over the course of several years. We began by adding team advising to our first-year seminars. At the same time, a faculty working group piloted the first 100-level interdisciplinary ConnCourses and developed criteria for other faculty to follow. Finally, a faculty and staff working group designed the structure for the Integrative Pathways that scaled up key elements of our academic centers.

The faculty Center for Teaching & Learning cosponsored discussions and workshops focused on defining the components of the Connections program and on considering how to effectively design and teach new courses within it. Institutional researchers gathered evidence and data about student, faculty, and staff experiences. The Office of the Dean of the College collaborated with other groups to secure funding and to guide the rollout. Admissions and college relations groups worked on materials for recruits, students, parents, and alumni. The Office of the Dean of the

Faculty worked to ensure that departments had proper staffing and resources and that faculty involved in the program were properly recognized. The wide engagement of faculty, staff, and students throughout the process created a broad sense of ownership of the new curriculum.

The Results: What and Why

The concept of "full participation" now structures our entire educational experience. It provides a framework that embraces students, faculty, and all campus community members, and it keeps us "focused on creating institutions that enable people, whatever their identity, background, or institutional position, to thrive, realize their capabilities, engage meaningfully in institutional life, and contribute to the flourishing of others."[5]

The three most distinctive curricular components of Connections are

- *First-year seminars.* Team-advised topical seminars that introduce student to the mission and meaning of Connecticut College's liberal education.
- *ConnCourses.* Introductory-level disciplinary courses that place the subject within the context of the liberal arts.
- *Integrative Pathways.* Inquiry-based multicourse sequences that engage a variety of disciplines. Integrative pathways are framed by an individualized animating question that students develop starting in the sophomore year and refine throughout their education, concluding with a public presentation at an all-campus symposium.

These key curricular structures of Connections deliberately require liberal arts thinking, which is introduced in FYSs and ConnCourses, individualized through the student's animating question, developed through the Integrative Pathway, and celebrated during the senior symposium.

The small, discussion-based first-year seminars are designed to provide entering students with the opportunity to learn about subjects in their professors' areas of expertise in the context of the liberal arts mission. All FYSs are designated as writing-intensive courses, providing a solid foundation for college writing; there is also a second required writing-intensive course later in their four-year education. Each seminar professor acts as the academic advisor to the fifteen or so students in the seminar, and a staff advisor, a career advisor, and two or three student advisors join the faculty advisor to form the seminar advising team. The team works together to help first-year students transition to college life and to college-level work, and it models for students the twenty-first-century skill of collaboration across constituencies.

One of the three weekly seminar meetings is designated for interactive experiences that partner with other FYSs or for events that engage the broader community. In addition, custom modules are offered to the entire advising team, including required workshops; optional modules on topics like time management, study skills, and media literacy; information on programs like prevention of sexual violence; exploration of identity- and power-related issues; and enrichment opportunities like mindfulness and meditation. All FYSs have engagement funds for experiential learning, social events, programming, and non-class gatherings, and 65 percent of the FYSs went off campus in the fall of 2018 to do activities ranging from traveling to the Metropolitan Museum in New York to bowling at the local bowling alley.

Team advising in FYSs is a key and distinctive feature of the program. Each seminar has two or three sophomore student advisors assigned to it, which provides a near-peer source of information both for incoming students and for faculty members. Serving as a student advisor provides a leadership development opportunity and, we believe, helps with the retention of those students from their first to their second year. Staff advisors are drawn from diverse roles across campus and have included campus security personnel, administrative assistants, professional staff, and senior administrators. Many staff advisors are encouraged to attend the seminar whenever it meets and to participate in its design.

The idea for ConnCourses emerged from discussions with students and with faculty members who taught 100-level courses. Although faculty enthusiasm for sharing their discipline and engagement with students is the hallmark of a small liberal arts college, we learned that faculty often did not enjoy teaching those introductory courses. Our old 100-level courses were typically designed to be an overall introduction to a major or discipline, but most students merely were seeking a general education distribution requirement and never took another course in that department. It is no wonder that these larger-than-average courses were not enjoyable for faculty to teach or students to take.

In ConnCourses, students explore a particular discipline and its connections to the other liberal arts and sciences. Intentionally diverse in perspective, these introductory courses examine how knowledge is constructed in a specific field of study and then ask students to connect those ideas and concepts to their own interests and to the world around them. Although typically developed by individual faculty members, all ConnCourses are workshopped by an interdisciplinary group of faculty using a specially designed rubric. These courses cultivate an integrative approach to learning and problem solving, and they prepare students for the work they are expected to do while in college. Examples of the many ConnCourses include Mona Lisa to Instagram (art history); The Meaning of Dinosaurs (philosophy); Incentives and Society: Shit Rolls Down Hill (economics); and The Invention of Adolescence (literature). ConnCourses are popular: the number of faculty offering them and students wanting to take them has increased every semester they have been offered.

Both FYSs and ConnCourses indirectly begin the process of developing an animating question by explicitly engaging students with the aims of a liberal arts education and the importance of transdisciplinary thinking. Faculty model what it means to ask worthwhile, difficult questions and how to revise and explore such questions, preparing students to propose their own animating question in the second semester of their sophomore year.

Integrative Pathways enhance traditional majors by asking students to narrate the story of their own individual liberal arts education within a broad intellectual framework. Every Integrative Pathway is organized around a central theme intended to appeal to students with diverse disciplinary interests; there are no pathways designed for a particular major.

The pathway helps students frame an individualized animating question that is meaningful to them, which in turn provides a focus for students' coursework, study away, and internships. The thirteen Integrative Pathways we currently offer are Bodies/Embodiment; Cities and Schools; Creativity; Entrepreneurship, Social Innovation, Value, and Change; Data Information and Society; Eye of the Mind: Interrogating the Liberal Arts; Global Capitalism; Media, Rhetoric, and Communication; Migrations, Displacements, and (Im)Mobilities; Peace and Conflict; Power/Knowledge; Public Health; and Social Justice and Sustainability: Developing Resilient Communities Locally and Globally. Pathways still in development include Science and Morality and one focusing on food.

Each Integrative Pathway consists of four principal components:

- *Thematic inquiry.* Every student must take a designated course, typically in the spring semester of the sophomore year, that examines the approaches and major themes of that specific pathway. Students work with classmates, faculty, and staff advisors to define their animating question.
- *Curricular itinerary.* These three courses, taken in a variety of departments and disciplines, allow students to explore the theme of their pathway. Rather than using a disambiguated general education courses checklist, students intentionally choose courses that help them consider and refine their animating question. Students select courses from five modes of inquiry: creative expression; critical interpretation and analysis; quantitative and formal reasoning; scientific inquiry and analysis; and social and historical inquiry.
- *Global/local engagement.* Each pathway requires students to take their learning off campus in one or more local, national, or international contexts, such as study away, an internship, or community-based learning.
- *Senior reflection.* During the fall of the senior year, students attend a pathway-specific senior reflection seminar in which they complete an integrative culminating project. A critical goal of this seminar is for students to clearly and concisely tell the story of their entire

education to a variety of audiences, explaining how their animating question has developed and how their curricular and cocurricular experiences have shaped their education and postgraduate plans. This component culminates in an all-college symposium later in the fall semester where students share their responses to their animating questions with the wider college community.

The pathway model does not move away from majors or the disciplines. If anything, it helps students appreciate what disciplines beyond their major can contribute to their own field. Integrative Pathways lead students to apply a variety of ideas, approaches to knowledge, and skills to real-world problems, helping them think broadly about the liberal arts and their role as an educated citizen.

Concluding Thoughts, Next Steps

We are rolling out Connections in phases as new classes enter, and we are finding it to be increasingly effective with each successive year. Although faculty and staff are learning to better and more succinctly articulate the key components of Connections to students and parents, the process is sometimes confusing because different entering classes have different graduation requirements and options until the transition is complete. Because Connections is driven by student interests, academic advising has been enhanced, and there is increased support for both faculty and staff to advise more effectively. As we write this chapter, some pathways are still in development and others are at capacity, so they are not yet a requirement for all students. More than 60 percent of the class of 2021 have joined a pathway or a center, and ten different thematic inquiry courses were taught in the spring of 2019. During the fall of 2019 we offered our first set of senior reflection seminars and held our first all-campus symposium, both of which had been piloted by a small group of students the previous year.

In spite of the success and the general widespread support for our new curriculum, there has been some faculty anxiety about the impact of Connections on departmental majors and staffing, as well as what our changed curricular requirements will mean for new faculty lines and hiring.

Our students' experiences of their courses in the first year now seem overwhelmingly positive: 91 percent of students entering in 2018 (class of 2022) described their mentoring relationship with their advising team as "strong" or "somewhat strong," and 88 percent said that their FYS met or exceeded their expectations. Perhaps most significant, data show that incoming first-year students are increasingly enthusiastic about our curriculum. While only 44 percent of the entering class of 2020 (in the fall of 2016) felt positively about Connections, that improved to 63 percent for the entering class of 2021, to 71 percent for the class of 2022, and to 76 percent for the class of 2023. More than 90 percent of the entering class of 2023 reported that Connections was an important factor in their decision to enroll, with more than half saying that our new curriculum was "very important."

Beyond creating a curriculum that is appealing to entering students and parents and has garnered national attention,[6] the process of revision brought the Connecticut College campus together to collaborate in an unprecedented manner. Designing and implementing our new curriculum created opportunities for faculty and staff to think more intentionally about their teaching, course design, and program structures. Similar to what Connections now asks of our students, we articulated big questions about the liberal arts, how we integrate our education, and what drives us as individuals. Perhaps most important, we created a distinctive curriculum that lives up to its name, forming important, intentional connections among and between faculty, staff, and students.[7]

KEY TAKEAWAYS

Use evidence about effective teaching practices and student experiences. Look to nationally recognized information, seminars, and workshops about effective experiences and high-impact practices (AAC&U, NSSE) and to the extensive body of literature about how students learn most effectively (WNS, NSSE). Study your own campus as well. Use student and faculty focus groups to learn how to make compelling changes.

Have faculty lead the process with active staff participation and administrative support. True curricular revision takes years, not months, in order to create something for the decades to come. Administrative leaders need to carefully calibrate their involvement and know when to push and when to step back and let others lead. An extensive revision of the four-year curriculum cannot be implemented without the enthusiastic commitment of a majority of the campus community. The process is best led by faculty members, particularly those who are well respected as scholars, teachers, and leaders. Remember that the insights of staff who work with students are invaluable to the process, and staff inclusion can help create wide buy-in and ownership.

Stay local and aligned with your mission and values. While you can certainly learn a great deal from peer schools and those who have undertaken the process of change already, your educational changes or innovations need to develop from your own institution's strengths, values, and mission. What "signature experiences" does your campus offer to students? Strive to increase the frequency and distribution of the distinctive educational experiences you offer that lead to significant student learning. Leverage your campus's strengths and utilize existing committee structures and offices to initiate the process and keep it going.

Notes

1. For information about Connecticut College's mission and values, see https://www.conncoll.edu/at-a-glance/mission--values.

2. Richard Arum and Josipa Roska, *Academically Adrift: Limited Learning on College Campuses* (Chicago, IL: University of Chicago Press, 2011).

3. See https://centerofinquiry.org/wabash-national-study-of-liberal-arts-education.

4. See, for example, Susan Ambrose et al., *How Learning Works: Seven Research-Based Principles for Smart Teaching* (San Francisco, CA: Jossey-Bass, 2010); James Zull, *The Art of Changing the Brain: Enriching the Practice of Teaching by Exploring the Biology of Learning* (Sterling, VA: Stylus, 2002).

5. Susan Sturm et al., "Full Participation: Building the Architecture for Diversity and Public Engagement in Higher Education," Columbia University

Law School, Center for Institutional and Social Change, 2011, http://imaginingamerica.org/wp-content/uploads/2015/07/fullparticipation.pdf.

6. Connecticut College's Connections curriculum is featured in three articles from a themed issue of AAC&U's *Peer Review* titled "The LEAP Challenge: Engaging in Capstones and Signature Work," 20, no. 2 (Spring 2018). Further details appear in Maxine Joselow, "Fostering Connections," *Inside Higher Ed*, June 30, 2016, https://www.insidehighered.com/news/2016/06/30/connecticut-college-revamps-gen-ed; and Dan Berrett, "General Education Gets an 'Integrative Learning' Makeover," *Chronicle of Higher Education*, August 8, 2016, http://www.chronicle.com/article/General-Education-Gets-an/237384.

7. For more information about Connections, our Academic Challenge Initiative, our Curriculum reVision process, or the Center for Teaching & Learning's involvement in Connections, contact Michael Reder at reder@conncoll.edu.

5 Building a Developmental, Interdisciplinary General Education Curriculum for the Future
Foundations in the Liberal Arts at Rollins College

Emily Russell, Susan Rundell Singer, and Toni Strollo Holbrook

Radical Vision

Knowing that twenty-first-century problems won't be solved in isolation, we envision a liberal education that is not merely multidisciplinary, but interdisciplinary, one that grows with students. A foundational model for liberal education promotes sustained progress by using multiple disciplinary lenses and by examining central themes, such as innovations, environments, enduring questions, cultural collisions, and identities. This move is a student-centered choice that challenges and requires faculty to grow outside of their strict disciplinary training. The success of this vision requires a campus culture of improvement. Iteration must be built into the design process, and faculty development opportunities should become a conduit for pedagogical exchange and growth. To create innovative learning communities for students, we need to create intentional faculty communities as well.

Institutional Profile

Founded in 1885, Rollins is Florida's oldest college. It has a small, highly residential, four-year undergraduate program, an evening degree program, and a graduate school of business. Enrollment totals more than 3,200 students, 2,000 of whom are traditional, residential undergraduates. Rollins maintains an average 10:1 student-faculty ratio, retains 85 percent of entering students, and holds an additional classification in community engagement.

Introduction

In 2014, Rollins College embarked on an ambitious plan to reimagine its general education curriculum. The innovation of the Foundations program lies in a series of five thematically linked developmental and integrative seminars. The college's previous decades-old curriculum carried students to courses across the disciplines, but students rarely made connections between those classes. Faculty wanted to design a program that would be responsive to complex global problems and to make explicit to students the ways in which a diverse and integrated disciplinary tool kit would be relevant to real world demands. General education, then, should not be isolated in the first semesters; students spiral back to these courses alongside their major and elective curricula and come to understand more deeply the value of breadth in a liberal education.

Students complete sequenced Foundations seminars, and each course offers a different disciplinary way of knowing to the examination of a unifying question or problem. The sequence culminates in an interdisciplinary 300-level practicum. Each Foundations course level has a unique learning outcome drawn from the Association of American Colleges and Universities' (AAC&U) Liberal Education and America's Promise (LEAP) initiative. By designing courses around the learning outcomes of critical thinking, written communication, and information literacy, faculty synthesize disciplinary perspectives with a foundation of transferable skills. Core competency classes and a first-year seminar complement courses within thematic clusters. Through this constellation, the college seeks to deliver on the promise of its mission to liberally educate students for global citizenship and responsible leadership.

However, the original structure of the program was not enough to facilitate interdisciplinary connections for students. With support from the Andrew W. Mellon Foundation, the college now uses multiple mechanisms to deliver and assess the curriculum, creating opportunities for faculty to regularly collaborate with colleagues across campus. Instead of thinking within the confines of majors, faculty ask instead, "What do we want all students to learn?" and "How can we best teach that?" In the new program, faculty participate in a series of pedagogy workshops, colloquiums, and assessment teams. Through these collaborative opportunities, we address the full scope and scale of the program: its overall architecture, individual course redesign, and how students engage these skills outside of the classroom.

Rollins is proud of its history of educational innovation, rooted in John Dewey's work of the 1930s. Faculty speak enthusiastically about the experimental culture on campus, especially the opportunities to lead international field studies and teach community engagement courses. By building collaborative, interdisciplinary faculty development into our general education program, we have been able to construct a critical mass around the innovative work done by individual instructors. From exchanging thoughtful assignments to bringing together groups of students for guest lectures and campus events, we have been able to share the work of our most enterprising faculty. Through these very intentional efforts, we extend and sustain our culture of innovation.

Case Narrative

The Rollins commitment to experiential learning, innovation, and real-world relevance creates experimentation in our classrooms, but this spirit also has animated our decade-spanning project to reimagine general education. In this sense, we offer a hopeful counterexample to the trend highlighted by Robert Zemsky, Gregory Wegner, and Ann Duffield in *Making Sense of the College Curriculum*, who found that while faculty have been quick to embrace a revolution in pedagogy over the past several decades, that passion has failed to translate into significant curricular change.[1]

After graduating the first cohort of students from the Foundations program in the spring of 2018, we offer a case study that describes four phases of curricular innovation: (1) seeking change, (2) design and pilot, (3) implementation, and (4) refinement/iteration. In sharing lessons learned, we hope to offer a pragmatic and optimistic account for other schools seeking to restructure their curricula to meet the demands of twenty-first-century liberal education.

Phase 1. Seeking Change

In 2005, the faculty of Rollins College began exploring the possibility of curricular renewal. For more than twenty years, the college had been operating under a distribution model of general education colloquially referred to as "alphabet soup." Students moved through the program collecting twelve letter requirements—including L for literature, C for non-Western cultures, and V for values. Both students and advisors often thought of the program as a process of box checking and would schedule courses to "get this one out of the way." Although a distributive model of general education is common and enduring, few Rollins faculty felt a strong sense of ownership of the program. When surveyed in 2005, two-thirds of faculty respondents thought that the "current general education program was not meeting the needs of our students," and it was determined that a change was in order.

From the very beginning, the process of curricular renewal at Rollins sought broad faculty input, and the work was channeled through faculty governance. The Curriculum Committee created ad hoc subcommittees and summer study groups, and it worked with the Office of the President to support a colloquy called "Liberal Education and Social Responsibility in a Global Community." This colloquy drew national thought leaders, including Jaron Lanier, Steven Pinker, and Maya Angelou, to campus. As the college moved from the research to the design phase, the steering committee reported in 2012 that "in some form, over 70 of the faculty [have] worked on the curriculum renewal process."[2]

The faculty landed on two central goals for any new general education curriculum. First, the curriculum should be developmental. First-year students are at a different intellectual and social developmental stage compared to students completing their fourth year of college. Hence, a curriculum should distinguish between introductory 100-level courses and more advanced 400-level courses, and students should move through their general education experience sequentially to match their intellectual growth.

Second, the curriculum should encourage students to integrate knowledge across multiple disciplines. It should be inherently interdisciplinary and require students to connect knowledge from different fields in order to prepare them for real-world problem solving after graduation.[3]

Phase 2. Design and Pilot

The Rollins Plan (RP) was a pilot program for a revised general education. Beginning in 2009-2010, students completed seven courses sequenced across four years, beginning with an introductory course and ending with a senior year capstone. Students completed courses in four divisions (expressive arts, social sciences, humanities, and natural sciences). Courses were organized into two thematic tracks: "revolutions" and "global challenges: Florida and beyond." Asking students to choose courses by theme allowed the college to achieve a secondary goal of building cohorts among both students and faculty. Finally, Rollins was eager to connect its local efforts to national movements in higher education; the course sequence was designed to both introduce and reinforce all fifteen LEAP learning outcomes developed by the AAC&U.

Many of the intended advantages of the new curriculum were immediately felt by participating faculty and students. Students interviewed "described themselves as 'less likely to forget what they learned because of how they have learned,' leading them to a new 'awareness,' 'growth of awareness,' and abilities to integrate across disciplines."[4] Faculty teaching in the pilot program reported:

> I have learned a lot about teaching from participating in the RP. I have had to consciously focus on teaching technical material in a nontechnical way. I have become better at avoiding jargon and getting to the heart of issues I want to discuss. I have spent more time thinking about assessment of learning. I have become better at asking students to connect what they are learning in this class to what they are learning in other classes.

> I love the fact that all of these students are juniors, so the high expectations for writing and discussion are upheld by most students. . . . It is nice this [general education] course is not a hodgepodge of freshmen through seniors who have not shared any common academic experiences.[5]

Running a small pilot parallel to the conventional alphabet-soup track, however, brought challenges. The RP program experienced significant student attrition. By the third semester, fifty of the eighty-nine students who began the program had withdrawn, with many citing a lack of choice, conflicts with major classes, and a perception that it was easier to complete requirements outside of the RP. While it revealed important areas for revision, the limited pilot may have stalled campus-wide enthusiasm for the project of curricular revision (since only a fraction of faculty taught in the program), and there were drawbacks that were caused by the small scope. The problems of the RP were also visible to the broader student body; when the revised program was unveiled in 2012, the front page of the student newspaper announced "Dawn of the Gen Ed Dead."

As we detail in the following two sections, a more productive approach for institutions might be to fully initiate a new program that has regular review and revision built into expectations of the first few years of implementation. We would not recommend the pilot approach to other schools embarking on a general education redesign. While the program we adopted after the RP pilot was able to take advantage of some lessons learned, the cost in time and enthusiasm was great.

Phase 3. Implementation

With the class of 2018, we initiated the Rollins Foundations in the Liberal Arts (rFLA) program. In the fall of their first year, students selected a "neighborhood," our name for thematically organized intellectual communities (with a nod to our most famous alumnus, Mr. Rogers). In this first iteration, rFLA consisted of ten required courses: one first-year seminar, four competency courses (writing, foreign language, health and wellness, and mathematical thinking), and five sequenced neighborhood courses that culminated in an interdisciplinary capstone. Where the RP sought to include all fifteen LEAP learning outcomes, neighborhood courses focused on five key transferable skills: critical thinking, written communication, information literacy, ethical reasoning, and integrative learning. These seminars tied disciplinary ways of knowing to skills that were named and reinforced across courses. A report by the National Academies of Sciences, Engineering, and Medicine argues that transfer of knowledge is most successful when we extend learning beyond narrow contexts, provide opportunities for students to be mindful of themselves as learners and thinkers, and apply concepts to real-world problems.[6] Our purposeful revision of the curriculum sought to build these principles into a constellation of integrative coursework.

The Rollins faculty's decision to move away from a distributive model of general education was a bold and student-centered choice. Under the alphabet-soup structure, nonmajor students would take introductory or elective classes that were largely designed for majors. Our conscientious faculty would work to engage all students, but learning goals for courses were largely disciplinary and sought to progress students from one major course to the next. This model had distinct advantages, especially for smaller programs, which could offer more elective courses by counting on students seeking general education requirements to fill seats. The content of courses could be comfortably in the faculty member's area of expertise, with no mandate toward interdisciplinarity.

The faculty vote to adopt rFLA, however, was largely embraced as an opportunity to seek new modes of course design and instruction. All courses offered in the Foundations program needed to be designed from scratch: proposals were submitted to a subcommittee of academic affairs that outlined how the course would meet both the learning outcomes and the themes of the program. Two years into the program's adoption, one faculty member reflected on the opportunities for new thinking provided by teaching outside the major: "[rFLA] allows courses to be less content-driven and to provide more scope for foundational skills and big picture thinking, both of which our students desperately need in their early years. If I was trying to hit all of these elements in a normal course, I wouldn't have time to draw attention to the bigger picture as much."[7] Central to this comment are an attention to the question of what students need (as opposed to what faculty are primarily trained in) and the conviction that transferable skills, developmental instruction, and integrative thinking are the answer.

Of course, faculty typically arrive on a liberal arts campus with highly specialized graduate training, and the departmental structure often serves to reinforce disciplinary boundaries. In order to facilitate interdisciplinary connections for students, we needed to create opportunities for faculty to regularly collaborate with colleagues across campus. As a requirement of the rFLA program, faculty participate throughout the year in monthly pedagogy workshops and colloquiums. On our campus with about 200 undergraduate faculty, a typical faculty development workshop will draw between 10 and 20 participants; rFLA faculty workshops regularly include more than 60 attendees. A small team of faculty conducts student learning outcomes assessment during the summer and reports results to the faculty each fall.

The mandate for course redesign and workshop participation made intensive demands on faculty time, and such an ambitious program required a commensurate commitment of institutional resources. With support from a five-year grant from the Andrew W. Mellon Foundation, Rollins funds these efforts with stipends to faculty teaching in the rFLA program. Although a direct expression of institutional commitment, the stipend model of support has several drawbacks: (1) the generous stipends offered at the beginning of the program were unsustainable even with external grant support, and they have been scaled back in years since; (2) a stipend can make teaching in general education seem transactional, rather than being viewed as an opportunity for innovation and creativity; and (3) stipends can quickly come to be regarded as entitlements, and it can be hard to maintain expectations for participation in faculty development while simultaneously cutting back on compensation.

Phase 4. Refinement/Iteration: A Culture of Improvement

Since the inception of rFLA, the college has used both faculty governance and regular rFLA faculty meetings to seek continuous program and student learning outcome (SLO) improvements. Through collaborative opportunities, faculty have taken on the full scope of the program: SLO assessment results, overall architecture, syllabus redesign, and shared assignments and classroom exercises. After more than a year of intensive revision to the program's policies and structure (labeled rFLA 2.0), one lesson learned is that while such changes are important, building a strong culture of assessment and faculty development provides tools for continuous improvement that persist after the subcommittees dissolve and the catalog is published.

We learned a tremendous amount about the drawbacks and successes of the program in the early years of its full implementation. To assess the rFLA program, we surveyed students and faculty; collaborated with an external reviewer, Dr. Kris De Welde; and analyzed patterns of staffing and student enrollment. The majority of students surveyed were positive about the program, valuing it as an opportunity to expand their knowledge, achieve a well-rounded education, and gain important skills (especially writing, reading, and critical thinking).[8] One faculty member wrote to De Welde, "The Neighborhoods also allow faculty to collectively design, implement, and reflect on best pedagogical practices across disciplines. There are few spaces on campus where this level of discussion has been possible in the past."[9]

Splitting students into thematic cohorts can be an innovative approach for a twenty-first-century education that is integrative and focused on global problems. It can also provide an opportunity for building community, a feature that we found had mixed results among students: some students felt connected to their neighborhood and enjoyed seeing the same classmates across courses, while others never really found that cohesion. More conceptually, the selection of themes revealed faculty ambivalence, which may be at the heart of the thematic project itself. In our litmus test for a "good theme," faculty struggled to balance the need to have a theme broad enough that most faculty, from all divisions of the college, could design a course around it, but not so broad that it would lose coherence. Specificity, on the other hand, was a drawback for students who felt they were taking five versions of the same course.

As we sought to achieve the integrative learning that was central to the goals of curricular revision, we discovered that we may have been relying too heavily on course sequencing and a shared theme to deliver this promise. Without reflective assignments, shared core readings, and consistent course-level discussions about other classes taken, a theme is insufficient to achieve interdisciplinary learning. While students were ambivalent about their cohort experiences, faculty were enthusiastic about the interdisciplinary communities that were built into the program. We have opened thematic pathways for students, and we have retained these themes as an opportunity to bring faculty together to find alternative ways to support integrative learning.

Concluding Thoughts, Next Steps

Through rFLA faculty communities, we created the space to develop, encourage, and mature a culture of continuous improvement in general education. Faculty teaching in rFLA operate with an expectation that meetings will focus on programmatic questions and the sharing of pedagogical strategies. For example, we will develop a more intentional delivery of diversity and inclusion, rethink links to our first-year seminar, and offer workshops on how to teach writing, facilitating tough topics, or reading in different disciplinary modes. These meetings also represent an opportunity for the faculty and administrators most deeply involved in assessments of student learning to make a case about the value of assessment to skeptical colleagues. Almost every campus hears a chorus of concerns about "the tail wagging the dog" or "teaching to the test" in conversations about assessment and rubrics. At Rollins, we've found some success by reminding faculty that by adopting AAC&U's Valid Assessment of Learning in Undergraduate Education (VALUE) rubrics for our core learning outcomes, we have an opportunity to look outside our campus and compare our results to those of similar institutions.

At the same time, narrowing the scope of learning outcomes has allowed us to host a truly campus-wide conversation with a shared vocabulary and common goals. Our developmental program, where each learning outcome is introduced and then reinforced in a later class, means that we can track student cohort or individual progress over time. By making the conversation about student learning more rigorous and sophisticated, we are primed for a much richer local conversation about how we are preparing students for global citizenship and responsible leadership—our mission promise to students.[10]

KEY TAKEAWAYS

Build in faculty development and interdisciplinary community. Dedicate resources to faculty development, and make these development activities a requirement of teaching in the program. Emphasize peer-to-peer exchange.

Offer students and faculty opportunities to articulate the value of liberal arts education. It's not enough for students and faculty to know *what* classes are required; they should also know *why* the curriculum is designed in this way. Use advising discussions, on-campus interviews, the last day of classes, or mock interviews at presentations to ask students, "How does what you've learned here prepare you for life after graduation?"

Look to tools beyond the curricular structure. In the design phase, it's easy to get bogged down in course sequencing and policies. A robust culture of faculty development coupled with a meaningful culture of assessment allows for workshops on assignment design, student learning outcomes, classroom exercises, and new programming. Various approaches can be quickly adopted, revised, or discarded, and they can spread in a grassroots fashion.

Create space for grassroots change. By year three of the rFLA program, almost all faculty teaching information literacy were using a robust version of an annotated bibliography assignment, which was designed around the VALUE rubrics and prompted student reflection on their research progress. This shared assignment spread through word of mouth and was painlessly adopted without a mandate from the program director or dean.

Place local work in national context. Tying learning outcomes and program design to broader conversations led by groups like the AAC&U supports an evidence-driven approach to curricular design and concomitant continuous improvements to student learning. When innovative ideas become commonplace to a local audience, external reviewers or snapshots of the national landscape can be energizing.

Distribute leadership among faculty. At the minimum, consider a compensated faculty director or rotating administrator drawn from the faculty. Additional faculty coordinators can serve as advocates for the program, especially in the early years. Establish a regular cycle for these roles to draw in new voices and share ownership of the program.

Use program gains to aid broader changes on campus. Learning outcomes assessment for the rFLA program created a micro-climate for faculty conversations about assessment, which quickly spilled over to the college's demonstration of learning (programmatic assessment of majors) efforts. Use these assessment micro-climates as a springboard to deepen the campus culture of assessment.

Notes

1. Robert Zemsky, Gregory R. Wegner, and Ann J. Duffield, *Making Sense of the College Curriculum: Faculty Stories of Change, Conflict, and Accommodation* (New Brunswick, NJ: Rutgers University Press, 2018).

2. Judy Schmalstig et al., "RP [Rollins Plan] Steering Committee Report to Academic Affairs Committee" (2012), unpublished report in authors' possession.

3. Schmalstig et al., "RP Steering Committee Report."

4. Peggy Maki, "External Evaluation of the Rollins Plan Pilot Curriculum" (November 30, 2011), 5, unpublished report in authors' possession.

5. Schmalstig et al., "RP Steering Committee Report," 11.

6. National Academies of Sciences, Engineering, and Medicine, *How People Learn II: Learners, Contexts, and Cultures* (Washington, DC: National Academies Press, 2018), doi.org/10.17226/24783.

7. Kris De Welde, "External Evaluation of the Rollins College Foundation in the Liberal Arts: Final Report" (February 16, 2018), 7, unpublished report in authors' possession.

8. Emily Russell, "Summary of Qualitative Student Survey Results" (February 19, 2018), unpublished report in authors' possession.

9. De Welde, "External Evaluation," 5.

10. As this chapter demonstrates, the revision of general education at Rollins was a decade-spanning project that involved hundreds of faculty, staff, and students. We do, however, want to acknowledge the particular implementation efforts of Claire Strom, Gloria Cook, Mark Anderson, Gabriel Barreneche, Ashley Kistler, Jana Mathews, Jennifer Cavenaugh, Robin Mateo, Tiffany Griffin, James Zimmerman, Tricia Zelaya-Leon, and Janette Smith.

6 Exploring the Borderlands
Using Interdisciplinarity to Build Civic Literacy at the College of the Holy Cross

Laurie Ann Britt-Smith

Radical Vision

At the College of the Holy Cross, we challenge the claim that those new to the academy cannot engage in the complex conversations required for the development of civic literacy (knowledge about how to actively participate in the functions of one's community). We favor an interdisciplinary approach for all students across the first year of study, which sets the foundation for cultivating twenty-first-century competencies. Integrating intellectual development with ethical and social considerations allows students to negotiate meaning and knowledge as part of a whole rather than siloed into random categories created by institutions. This combats the growing vocationalization of higher education. Once students are made aware of the complexity of being active and engaged citizens, the claim that one can perform a job without consequence becomes void. First-year students need to begin fostering an adult identity that includes civic professionalism: a commitment to a career and a life governed by knowledge, practice, and a sense of responsibility for the good of society, not just the individual.

Institutional Profile

The College of the Holy Cross in Worcester, Massachusetts, is a not-for-profit, private baccalaureate college with an enrollment of 3,000 full-time students. Founded in 1843, it is a four-year Jesuit, Catholic, and primarily residential institution with a liberal arts and science focus.

Introduction

From middle school onward, students are inundated with messages that focus on ever-future goals of personal and career-based achievement. Many institutions of higher learning have fallen into a pattern of promoting professionalized end goals, often cutting back on general education requirements in order to meet the rising demands of outside accreditation requirements, leaving little time for reflection on what is going on outside of the track of one's chosen major. This is troubling for all liberal arts schools, but particularly for those deeply invested in a mission to produce educated citizens who work toward the common good.

As early as 1992, members of the Holy Cross faculty recognized a societal shift in thinking about the liberal arts and the role of higher education, and they purposely began the process of developing a first-year curriculum that became the Montserrat program in 2007. Intentionally fostering civic literacy through interdisciplinary work reclaims the earlier goals of a liberal arts education, which prioritize helping students make sense of the world and discern their place within it by cultivating wise judgment, or practical wisdom, alongside academic knowledge. Additionally, this program encourages the development of the cognitive nimbleness and creativity that are hallmarks of twenty-first-century skills. Students learn to bring appropriate knowledge to bear on specific circumstances, helping the people affected by those circumstances to understand why this particular knowledge serves this circumstance best.[1] When guided toward projects that have community consequences, these powerfully engaged, flexible, discipline-based civic literacies have implications beyond the classroom, and they absolutely can be developed during the first year of college.

Case Narrative

Although there are many lenses through which to examine the Montserrat program, one of the most helpful in understanding the potential of this type of pedagogy is civic literacy and the development of civic professionalism. Civic engagement requires that institutions confront their tendency toward isolation, challenging them to design programs that break down disciplinary silos and that include voices from the community, particularly those actively working toward socially positive goals.[2] Civic professionalism as a goal of undergraduate liberal education embraces the pursuit of practical wisdom as a fundamental purpose. Through classroom learning, mentoring by practitioners, and ethical reflection, students are provided with academic knowledge, practical skills, and an "educated conscience"—all of which are necessary for successful negotiation of twenty-first-century literacies.[3]

Writing across the curriculum (WAC) work is vital to the development of civic professionalism, or practical wisdom, because it allows students the opportunity to draw on their academic knowledge across disciplines as they encounter new circumstances. Scholars such as Rose and Weiser, Coogan, Jolliffe, Flower and Heath, and others have called for and explored a WAC/WID (writing in the disciplines) approach to service learning and civic engagement.[4] The governing presumption in these models is that it is rare for students new to the academy to visit complicated sites of social engagement and truly understand what they are seeing. Indeed, community-based and service-learning classes can turn into a form of poverty tourism, which simply reinforces stereotypes and worldviews that previously existed. However, with an institutional commitment to providing an integrated experience for students that breaks down academic and social boundaries, it is possible to develop civic literacy in the first year because of an element of learning identified as "new disciplinarity."[5]

New disciplinarity is a means to examine the borderlands created when two or more areas of specialized learning come together so that students can creatively enact projects while drawing on all of their disciplinary knowledge to address new issues and create solutions.[6] Although developed for discussion of the sciences, this concept has implications for all interdisciplinary work. According to this theory of learning, when disciplinary experts enter into these borderlands, their forms of knowledge do not simply fuse together because "elasticity" is a central facet of all discipline-based projects. One's primary referent/identity remains, and so borderlands create a temporary, fertile space for cognitive and social growth based on the opportunity to explore and "engage with alternative specialties" in order to produce original questions and dynamic experiments and projects.[7]

The first challenge in creating the Montserrat program was to balance pedagogical innovation with the Jesuit and liberal arts traditions that form the foundation of the institution. There is an expectation that students will be exposed to conversations that allow them to develop a complexity of intellectual thought informed by ethical considerations, as well as a mastery of *eloquentia perfecta*—a characteristic of the Jesuit rhetorical tradition that, as adapted to twenty-first-century learning, is extremely flexible and allows for a liberal education that defies disciplinary borders. This rhetorical tradition requires that individuals be mindful of relationship, purpose, and message, so that any form of communication, regardless of genre or medium, is accurate, graceful while also firm, and most important, beneficial to the speaker or writer and to the audience. Also reflective of its pedagogical tradition, Holy Cross does not have a written or oral communication requirement in its general education curriculum. Providing this kind of instruction as students develop during their course of study has always been considered a shared responsibility.

Unfortunately, the continual external push toward specialization in the disciplines can work against the inclusion of intentionally cross-disciplinary developmental space in a curriculum. Creating and continuing this program is an act of resistance. Belonging to no single department, it is meant to build community and increase student curiosity about learning, connecting coursework to their experiences and expectations. The program is not perfect. Our past is still very much part of our present, as it is with all liberal arts colleges. However, ten years of assessment of this program—and the success of the college and our alumni—tell us we must be doing something from which others can learn.

The Montserrat invitation for students is "challenge, explore, reflect, discover." The name reflects the school's Jesuit identity and the intention of the program. Montserrat is the place where Ignatius of Loyola (founder of the Jesuits) had a moment of insight and transformation that began his lifelong journey to champion individual spiritual and educational development in the service of others. As the former program director, Stephanie Yuhl, states, "When you come to Holy Cross it should be the beginning of a transformational experience for you."[8] Over the last several years, various faculty committees have created goals for the program that identify not just the intellectual skills necessary to succeed at the school, but also the values that students will need to become contemplative yet active participants in society. The challenge, Yuhl continues, is to "create opportunities for first-year students to encounter the values in really intensive ways off the bat, right from their first moments of being part of the Holy Cross community."[9]

Over the course of their first year, all students earn a credit for the required Montserrat class plus a subject area credit in the general education curriculum, which is determined by the faculty member's area of expertise. In order to develop their borderlands, faculty from across the college combine into one of six thematic clusters: contemporary challenges, core human questions, the divine, global society, the natural world, and the self. Professors in each cluster teach one or two sections, with each section capped at eighteen students. The instructors write a collaborative description of the inquiry questions and thematic study for that year's cluster, and each writes a description of their own individual course and how it connects to the overall theme. Faculty also organize cocurricular readings and events that develop each cluster's annual theme, providing social and experience-based learning that extends beyond the classroom.

Students have some degree of agency in their preparation for the program. They review these descriptions and identify six sections of possible interest. Then, an extensive process places them into their specific Montserrat class and also into their dormitory. Borrowing from models of learning communities and special-interest housing, students live with others in their clusters, and often classmates will be floormates, if not roommates. Living in an intentional community allows students to have commonalities for discussion and also to have time to study together, form organic peer response groups for writing, or work on group projects. Matthew Cedeno, class of 2022, reflecting on the importance of this facet of the program, stated, "I had a really positive experience with Montserrat. Both my roommates and professor as well as my classmates really helped me transition to life at Holy Cross quite seamlessly. Apart from being one thousand miles away from home, I had to balance my academics and athletics. I was fortunate enough to have had two great roommates who made the transition period much easier."[10]

Another key to the success of this program is the articulation of specific writing goals. Although these goals focus on evidence of academic skill, they are informed by a mindset that reflects the necessity of twenty-first-century skills: "Montserrat faculty members seek to cultivate in students a vital shift in their ways of learning, one that reflects the values of a liberal arts education. Through many kinds of writing, students are encouraged to become thoughtful and analytical producers of knowledge, not just consumers and reproducers of information."[11] The individual goals focus on good writing across the curriculum, yet the individual classes are also informed by the disciplinary expertise of a particular professor. In these borderlands, knowledge, vocabulary, and rhetorical strategies from multiple discourses develop independently and then are integrated in order to produce sophisticated arguments and projects that can be modified to suit different audiences.

Although there are multiple ways for cross-disciplinary engagement to occur, the most common is across each cluster. For example, when the contemporary challenges cluster, consisting of professors from anthropology, history, political science, philosophy, and English/writing, met to create their borderlands around the theme "burning walls, building bridges: community and otherness," those disciplines informed each other. Launching from the common reading of *Brave New World*, each professor integrated the novel into their class syllabus, making the text relevant to the particular disciplinary discussion going on plus attending to the larger conversation of the cluster. As smaller disciplinary readings came to the table, the potential for the integration of civic awareness grew.

Unfortunately, all professors were not equally able or willing to bend their material to the common conversation, nor were they equally willing to allow increased student agency in assignments or activities. This created resentment between course sections as students began to compare notes, and their participation in this cluster's common events waned significantly by the end of the year. This is not unusual for first-year programs that rely solely on common readings and events to try to spark growth. Deeper student engagement and agency can, and really must, occur within as well as across clusters.

A more successful variation of interdisciplinary collaboration occurred when a biology professor and a religious studies professor in the self cluster linked through the topic of HIV/AIDS. Students examined the ethical questions surrounding the epidemic before turning to the virology of it. Mary Roche, the professor of religious studies, was very enthusiastic about the experience of working across disciplines, especially across the humanities-science divide. She reported, "First-year students were challenged to gain confidence in talking about the epidemic, about sexual issues, about justice and privilege in a spirit of intellectual inquiry. We all are asked to examine some assumptions and biases that may be working on or just below the surface of how we think and respond to HIV and AIDS."[12]

The professor of biology, Ann Sheehy, designed the second semester of the self cluster to deliver the content necessary for a natural science credit, writing in her syllabus, "Many aspects of the social, political, and cultural impact that the HIV pandemic is having on the global community will be discussed, but ultimately your success in this course will depend on your ability to understand the fundamental *science* of HIV."[13] The assigned projects required students to do much more than just regurgitate knowledge. Working in the borderlands between the disciplines, they first produced grant proposals that demonstrated knowledge of the ethical and civic concerns of the epidemic as well as showcased their knowledge of the science and the scientific method of research. Next, they created posters, a common genre in science writing, but students had to draw from their practical wisdom to identify their audience, present their scientific knowledge in a way that would appeal to that audience, and write a reflection on the rhetorical elements of the poster: the who, what, and why.

While a few students chose the safety of a traditional science conference poster, the majority addressed specific groups in the larger community, showing an awareness of how the science they were studying in the classroom affected those outside of it. Mining knowledge gained during the fall semester, they identified nonprofit and activist groups with which they could possibly share their scientific information and produced pieces that would engage and inform those audiences. Sheehy remarked, "Even the science [students] took risks with the art elements and combined their skills to produce truly original work that reflected sophistication on multiple levels." When asked about the work the students produced, Roche said, "I was especially gratified to see the work that students had done at the end of the year—it was amazing—and I think that they drew on a number of elements from the fall in doing that work, seeing that 'battle' being waged by science is also informed by the value commitments of scientists whether they be religious, philosophical or humanistic."[14] A further step toward creating true civic literacy would have been to take these posters to the public, but time is always a factor. Assessment shows that a number of students follow up on their first-year projects, seeking additional opportunities to enter these borderlands through community activism and summer research projects.

A final example of the application of twenty-first-century skills is on permanent display as a public art piece attached to the Holy Cross library. In the spring of 2016, a tile mural called *Lungs of the Planet* was installed as part of a rooftop garden. Showcasing interdisciplinary knowledge and expressing environmental issues, it was created by 120 students in the natural world cluster in a collaboration with the Visual Arts Department and community art organizations. The mural is eight feet high and twelve feet wide and depicts a pair of lungs with trachea that transform into tree branches, which support various flowers and birds. The background is made up of colorful tiles portraying blossoms, fruit, animals, and chemical diagrams to symbolize the cycle of life. It joined an older piece, *Civitas Branching*, which was created as a collaborative project with an art center in the neighborhood. Both pieces demonstrate how the careful cultivation of cross-disciplinary work and creative elasticity can bloom into something practical and wise—an enduring symbol of civic literacy for those who created it and those who will follow as members of the campus and local community.

Concluding Thoughts, Next Steps

Students envisioning general education classes as interferences to endure rather than as opportunities to develop is a nearly universal issue in postsecondary education. Like many required general education programs, Montserrat is often maligned by first-year students as a waste of time and not counting for anything. A primary reason for this is that they have absorbed the consumerist mindset and resist anything that challenges the belief that if you take a course it must at least count for one of those pesky gen ed requirements, and gen ed courses are not as valuable as the courses taken for your major. The suspicion that the second semester is a waste is ironically increased by courses like those offered by Professors Roche and Sheehy. As powerful as the collaboration is, the students can only claim one subject area as being fulfilled. Having to pick credit for either religious studies or science creates the impression that the other half of the class does not matter because it does not count toward their gen ed requirements.

Part of this student perception could be addressed with clearer communication about curricular requirements. Our students are generally unaware that many institutions require writing and oral communication courses. Their Montserrat section is meant to cover those courses plus offer an additional gen ed content area requirement credit. Because of this, the content material that would be covered in one class in general education is spread over two semesters, which allows for much more depth in their writing, research, and conversation about the topic; however, that does not address why only one subject area can count. This frustrating rule reflects the reality that innovation in higher education is always in tension with enduring models of how credit is counted both internally and by external accreditation agencies.

Like many liberal education institutions, Holy Cross is conducting a review and revision of its general education requirements. There is a recognition that there must be a change in how we account for learning. The Montserrat program is a driving factor in that conversation. Assessment of the program—focused on the development of digital and information literacies, communication literacies, and civic literacies—is also ongoing. Hopefully with data in hand, Holy Cross can make the program stronger without requirements that damage what should be a robust effort across disciplines. As should be the case, one innovation will lead to many more. As our campus discusses how to strengthen the program and make evaluation of it fairer and representative of the work we want our students to do, we are inevitably going to reconsider the entire idea of what constitutes general education in the twenty-first century.

That process will take several years to complete. In the here and now, the most powerful ally any institution can have is its students. When trying to make sense of what is directly confronting them, students are very receptive to their peers, and so it is vital to build in practices that allow student voices to communicate the value of the program. When asked about her experience in Montserrat, Maddy Downey, class of 2021, replied:

> Originally, I was unaware that the semesters would be broken up into two different sections taught by two different professors; however, I am grateful that this was the case. I loved being able to learn how both [professors] approached similar subjects given their differing backgrounds and teaching styles. . . . In my opinion, my academic experience benefited greatly from having the opportunity to learn from two different professors with two distinct voices.[15]

Another student, Olivia Ferrik, class of 2020, reported that her section included working at a local center with adult refugees. The Montserrat program pushed her to "step outside of my comfort zone and form relationships with people I may not have otherwise."[16] She returned to the center to tutor grade school students as a sophomore. Caitlin Keaveny, class of 2021, was also deeply affected by her experience. Her section was a history course that discussed both the founding fathers and modern social justice issues. The course also included community-based learning with a local group that assists children of immigrants. She said, "The class challenged me . . . and gave me lasting memories and relationships which I will continue to value well after my time here at Holy Cross."[17] These are just a few examples that provide powerful qualitative evidence of learning that is valuable for the student.

The gift of a liberal arts education has always been the sophisticated ability to think critically and deeply about a given subject so that students can apply those skills to vocations that promote the greater good. There must be a way to preserve the best of that tradition while also preparing students to navigate a world that appears to reward only those educated on specialized tracks that lead to narrow, self-involved futures. The greatest skill we give our students is the ability to resist being tracked and categorized, to resist labels for themselves and others.

Engaging in cross-disciplinary conversations starting with the first year of the college experience is a vital step toward empowering students to be more than a particular major in service to a specific career goal. They need the opportunity to discover who they are as individuals and where their interests and talents can lead them. Curricula in the liberal arts must include the development of wise judgment and practical wisdom—two characteristics that can only develop in spaces where there is time to explore different perspectives and engage with conversations beyond the familiar and comfortable. When done well, Montserrat and programs like it provide that space and foster empowerment of the individual in community and for community.

KEY TAKEAWAYS

Articulate what makes your institution unique. Explore the intentions of your specific college or university. Interrogate your mission statement. Use these ideals to get a commitment from the institution for program development and implementation.

Allow for the organic development of program goals. Develop a multi-year plan for implementing your vision based on those goals.

Collaborate. Break down the borders between disciplines and between the academic and student life at your institution.

Appeal to the expertise of the community. Take advantage of existing faculty in everything from directing the program and clusters to designing learning experiences, while also allowing for freedom in individual instructor's curricular decisions.

Expect pushback from students. It's difficult to reprogram the expectation that every experience has to have a credit-bearing or major track equivalent.

Bring in models to help with the counterprogramming. Current students; young, successful, civically minded professionals; and older alumni all have roles to play.

Notes

1. William M. Sullivan, "Knowledge and Judgment in Practice as the Twin Aims of Learning," in *Transforming Undergraduate Education: Theory That Compels and Practices That Succeed*, ed. Donald W. Harward (Lanham, MD: Rowman and Littlefield, 2012), 141.

2. Harry Boyte and Eric Fretz, "Civic Professionalism," *Journal of Higher Education Outreach and Engagement* 14, no. 2 (2010): 67-90.

3. William M. Sullivan, "Markets vs. Professions: Value Added?," *Daedalus* 134, no. 3 (2005): 19-26, 21.

4. Shirley K. Rose and Irwin Weiser, "Introduction: The WPA as Citizen-Educator," in *Going Public: What Writing Programs Learn from Engagement*, ed. Shirley K. Rose and Irwin Weiser (Logan: Utah State University Press, 2010),

1-14; David Coogan, "Community Literacy as Civic Dialogue," *Community Literacy Journal* 1, no. 1 (2006): 96-108; David A. Jolliffe, "Writing across the Curriculum and Service Learning: Kairos, Genre, and Collaboration," in *WAC for the New Millennium: Strategies for Continuing Writing-across-the-Curriculum Programs*, ed. Susan H. McLeod et al. (Urbana, IL: National Council of Teachers of English, 2001), 86-108; Linda Flower and Shirley Brice Heath, "Drawing on the Local: Collaboration and Community Expertise," *Language and Learning across the Disciplines* 4, no. 3 (2000): 43-55.

5. Anne Marcovich and Terry Shinn, "Where Is Disciplinarity Going? Meeting on the Borderland," *Social Science Information* 50 (2011): 582-606.

6. Anne Ruggles Gere, Anna V. Knutson, and Ryan McCarthy, "Rewriting Disciplines: STEM Students' Longitudinal Approaches to Writing in (and across) the Disciplines," *Across the Disciplines* 15, no. 3 (2018): 63-75.

7. Marcovich and Shinn, "Where Is Disciplinarity Going?," 584.

8. Quoted in Christopher Amenta, "Ten Years in Montserrat," *Holy Cross Magazine* 52, no. 1 (2018): 38-45, 41.

9. Amenta, "Ten Years in Montserrat," 40.

10. Quoted in Jane Carlton, "A Tour Guide's Guide to Holy Cross," College of the Holy Cross, July 3, 2019, https://news.holycross.edu/blog/2019/07/03/a-tour-guides-guide-to-holy-cross.

11. "Montserrat First-Year Writing Goals," faculty handout, College of the Holy Cross, adopted Spring 2015.

12. Mary Roche, personal communication, June 13, 2016.

13. Ann Sheehy, course syllabus, MONT Self Cluster 106S-01, Spring 2015, in author's possession.

14. Mary Roche and Ann Sheehy, interview, College of the Holy Cross, May 11, 2016.

15. Madeline Downey, personal communication, December 2, 2018.

16. Quoted in Amenta, "Ten Years in Montserrat," 44.

17. Quoted in Carlton, "A Tour Guide's Guide to Holy Cross."

7 Redesigning Learning through Multidisciplinary Teaching
Voices from a Sophomore Core Experience at Lasell University

Michael J. Daley, Dennis A. Frey Jr., and Catherine Zeek

Radical Vision

Our radical vision for liberal education follows Immanuel Kant's clarion call, *sapere aude* (dare to know).[1] The twenty-first century brings new priorities regarding the nature of knowledge and its development through education. These knowledge priorities extend beyond kinds of information to understanding sources and the uses of information across fields and media, shifting the locus of learning from an outside authority to the student's own intellect. Higher education curricula must integrate traditional liberal arts with professionally focused experiences in order to prepare students "to deal with complexity, diversity, and change."[2]

Institutional Profile

Lasell University (established in 1851) is a liberal arts institution enrolling about 1,700 undergraduates in professional programs and traditional arts and sciences fields.

Introduction

In 2014-2015, Lasell University faculty unveiled a redesigned core curriculum based on our Connected Learning pedagogy, an approach that develops and integrates ideas, concepts, and direct experiences through action; it combines projects, simulations, and real-world situations with direct, critical reflection. Faculty include these components in every course so that students further develop and apply the knowledge and skills learned in the classroom. The redesign created a set of inquiry-based experiences through which students build crosscutting skills, integrate multiple disciplinary perspectives, and collaborate with others from diverse socioeconomic, ethnic, and professional backgrounds. Through its vertical design, the core curriculum engages students in progressively more complex experiences, with core learning outcomes woven through both core and major courses. Early courses introduce crosscutting communication, problem solving, collaboration, and inquiry skills, as well as historical, scientific, psychosocial, and aesthetic ways of thinking; later courses focus on synthesis and the application of core and major skills.

In this chapter, we discuss how one innovation, a co-taught sophomore-year course called the multidisciplinary course (MDSC), engages students in applying these skills to vexing societal issues. In the process, students become critically self-aware and confident in making new knowledge. The MDSC is a project-based experience that engages students in critical thinking about complex societal issues, such as climate change, economic inequality, social injustices, and community design. Given the persistence of these big and often ill-defined problems, it is impossible to come at them from one way of thinking, hence two faculty members from distinct areas co-teach this three-credit course. Through extensive modeling and mentoring, the faculty team works with students to apply and develop a variety of twenty-first-century skills as the entire learning community grapples with the complex problem at the center of the investigation. In addition to building key competencies, the MDSCs integrate the liberal-arts-based core curriculum and the pre-professional curricula found in most of Lasell's majors, immersing students in the twenty-first-century skills essential to their professional and social contexts. For second-year students in particular, this experience, taken in either the fall or spring, serves as a crucial milestone in the transition from passive to active and authentic learning, from siloed disciplinary learning to multidisciplinary inquiry, and from the traditional classroom to a civically engaged community.

Case Narrative

During the 2010-2011 academic year, an internal program review of our decade-old general education curriculum noted three key issues. Students and faculty tended to view general education as a checklist of arbitrary requirements unrelated to their majors or to each other. As a result, students often failed to value or systematically develop key crosscutting skills observed in other research, such as communication, collaboration, critical thinking, problem solving, and ethical behavior.[3] Finally, because the courses lacked common design parameters or learning outcomes, faculty found it impossible to gather and assess evidence of our program's impact.

Faculty launched a process of self-study and curriculum redesign, leading to the adoption in 2014 of the Lasell core curriculum, an integrative, interdisciplinary curriculum that combines employer priorities, professional expectations, and high-impact pedagogies. Its three broad goals are to develop and enhance the students' intellectual skills; to explore and appreciate the knowledge perspectives of liberal learning; and to demonstrate students' abilities of synthesis and application. These goals and their respective outcomes are embedded throughout core and major-specific courses, and expectations increase in complexity across the students' four-year programs.

Given the community-wide support for this endeavor, it is unsurprising that there have been multiple sources of inspiration and motivation. We asked key participants in the development to reflect via email on this question: "From your lens how do you describe the MDSC program as part of a twenty-first-century curriculum?" Lasell's provost and vice president for academic affairs, James Ostrow, drew on John Dewey's foundational work, *Democracy and Education*, as he reflected on our mission of implementing Connected Learning for our students through the MDSC:

> How can the things we have students do in the interest of learning have lasting value in their experience, or matter more than things "received and left

behind"?[4] This is a fundamental problem to solve—one might call it the experiential equalizer of all differences in curricular content or pedagogical method. If whatever we teach has no or little duration in value for the student beyond providing evidence of understanding something to a professor, then variations in curricular content obviously have diminished significance.

The things we teach—painting, history, biology, management, design, the care and training of others, philosophy—are in themselves, prior to their conversion into things to be taught, means of understanding. . . . Of course, one must acquire these tools—the question is the degree of association between their acquisition and actual use, or their value in the student experience as anchored in their original purpose.[5]

The foundational concept for the MDSC program therefore builds on the integration of conceptual knowledge by challenging students to apply that knowledge as a tool to solve—or at least approach and comprehend—big, messy problems. Based on the theory of situated cognition, the tools become helpful only insomuch as students are given the opportunity to use them in the culture and context framed by members of the community.[6] Moreover, members of the community promote student learning through teaching practices that include modeling, coaching, scaffolding, articulation, reflection, and exploration as described in cognitive apprenticeship theory.[7] Informed by these theories, the design of the MDSC program creates purposeful opportunities for co-teaching faculty to help students acquire and integrate cognitive and metacognitive strategies to engage with messy, ill-defined, and/or unknown problems. Faculty experts from multiple disciplinary domains acculturate students to the epistemes and contexts of their fields, expanding students' conceptual understandings and worldviews.

Inspired by our university-wide commitment to Connected Learning and motivated by the desire to invite our students into that epistemic community, Lasell's faculty design team purposefully placed this innovation in the sophomore year. For a variety of reasons, the second year of a college education represents a key point in student development. Various scholars have argued that the second-year experience can be challenging for students since a general dissatisfaction or disillusionment with college sets in, perhaps leading to the "sophomore slump."[8] To be sure, academic performance can slide during the second year, but more disconcerting is the general malaise that can afflict second-year students as they begin to employ their newfound critical abilities to question everything, especially their path through the institution. This general trend for sophomores may be explained in part by the fact that many of the high-impact, first-year support structures at many colleges and universities do not persist into the second year.[9] Recognizing that we at Lasell had fallen into this trap—a raft of high-impact practices,[10] like first-year seminars and professional advising, for our first-year students abruptly ended after the second semester—we now extend that support structure into later years. Grounding our co-taught project-based courses in the theories of cognitive apprenticeship and situated cognition, the MDSC program thus maintains the intellectual connectedness of our students during a critical year of development.

Our innovation also grew from the efforts to bring our general education plan more fully in line with our Connected Learning pedagogy. Thus, Lasell's redesigned core curriculum prioritizes integrative, inquiry-based, and interdisciplinary learning through a series of sequential signature cohort experiences. This developmental arc starts with the first-year seminar (FYS103), continues with the sophomore multidisciplinary course (MDSC203), includes an applied ethics course (PHIL302) in the junior year, incorporates at least one internship in the major, and culminates in a senior capstone course. In many of our majors, the capstone spans the full senior year and integrates experiences in the field, the major, and the core. Among these varied cohort experiences, the multidisciplinary course in the second year remains the most unusual in structure.

The faculty responsible for developing this experience kept the intentional developmental arc at the forefront of their design. They wanted to allow for multiple sections of the MDSC that would reflect many different societal issues. Therefore, the first step was to create a common set of parameters so that the entire cohort of sophomores would be guaranteed a similar experience of multidisciplinary inquiry. They came up with the following purposefully broad parameters, which allow for inquiry into a wide range of themes and approaches:

- The course engages students in thinking about a real-world problem from multiple perspectives. Perspectives include positions of academic discipline, profession, race, gender, economic status, nationality, and other labels of identity.
- A co-taught structure best supports the desired student learning outcomes in interdisciplinarity.
- Active learning, group assignments, and projects are the dominant form of pedagogy. The course emphasizes social learning and the co-construction of new understanding and knowledge.
- Projects should be shared with the Lasell community.

The first prototype of the MDSC—Persuading People, Preserving Planet—was offered in the fall of 2011 and continues to be offered each year, most recently fully online. Co-taught by faculty from environmental studies and psychology, this topic engages students in understanding the problems of creating sustainability and the challenges of changing habits. Since that first prototype course, twenty other topics have been developed and taught by faculty teams representing all five of Lasell's schools, exploring issues of power, privilege, and social and environmental justice.

The MDSC begins with a messy, persistent problem or issue that can only be understood and addressed through interaction among multiple disciplines. Thus, the first step is to create an epistemic community committed to active learning by all participants about this complex problem. Here, the hope is that our students will be empowered "to learn how problems are solved [or at least problematized] with deliberation, creativity, resilience, and collaboration" so that they may participate authoritatively "in a messy world" and "to their fullest capacity as a human being."[11] Touching on this need for multiple perspectives and meaningful experiences, Ostrow argues:

I believe that it is impossible to preserve the relevance and integrity of the distinctive strengths of academic disciplines within contemporary education without an interdisciplinary platform. Why is this the case? The complexity of the modern world coupled with the rapidly changing nature of "information" means that wherever the specialized character of disciplines translates into separation and isolation, the contents and methods of each of the disciplines are rendered irrelevant for nonspecialists—or anyone beyond the enclosed circle.[12]

In order to avoid the irrelevance of an "enclosed circle," our MDSCs bring together practitioners of different disciplines who lead and model the exploration of persistent problems, like environmental sustainability, injustice, racism, and sexism, through collaborative inquiry. Two faculty members who have taught this experience multiple times—Deborah Baldizar and Karin Raye—offer these comments about this multidisciplinary approach:

As colleagues from different backgrounds (visual arts and justice studies) we strive to create a team-teaching environment designed to promote openminded collaboration and a willingness to challenge personal beliefs through respectful dialogue. We seek to model, through our own learning and growth, the importance of skill mastery outside our own expertise and respect for other perspectives and modes of analysis that differ from our own.... Our goal as professors is to teach students to engage in problem-solving exercises designed to build confidence, foster creativity, celebrate honesty and resilience, and enhance transferable skills that apply to all fields of study.[13]

Faculty teams often represent quite different disciplines, which intentionally shifts the focus from content expertise to the ways in which inquiry is conducted. One student, Armando Machado Jr. (class of 2018), picked up on this, noting that being "taught by two professors from two very different fields was my favorite part of [the MDSC] Wood in the World . . . because it combined science, history, and information gathering on the Lasell campus."[14] When that content-to-process shift is combined with a reliance on project-based learning, the MDSC results in a learning community that demands the active engagement of all involved. As explained by Christina Tomasik (class of 2020), who took MDSC203, Social Justice: Race and Space, "It helped to show me just how important it is to have these frank, uncomfortable, and often 'messy' conversations with people from all different sides of the issue, to help understand different viewpoints and debunk some of the toxic myths that exist about race."[15]

A second key component for sophomores grappling with big, perplexing issues is understanding the flexibility and perseverance needed to think and act across traditional lines. Through thoughtful course design and carefully structured project-based learning experiences, faculty help students build that capacity. The aforementioned faculty team of Baldizar and Raye describe the design of their course, Challenging Injustice through Art and Creativity, this way:

> Studying the Universal Declaration of Human Rights (justice studies) and the Elements and Principles of Design (art) provides the foundation and scaffolding necessary to approach each assignment. As a class, we evaluate each artist using historical, human rights and aesthetic analyses encouraging students to hear, contemplate and respectfully discuss their peers' diverse and sometimes conflicting perspectives.
>
> In our Lego Project . . . [we] ask, "what social issue would move you to act?" and "how can you convey that message artistically?" Students are asked to adopt a growth mindset and utilize their creativity and perseverance to create a sculpture out of Legos that visually communicates a social justice issue they feel strongly about and wish to educate about.
>
> As a result of the trial and error/problem-solving approach necessary to complete each assignment and to fulfill project expectations, students embrace critical analysis and learn to examine issues and problems from multiple perspectives and angles. They critique each other and their own work, cull through various choices, decide how to combine and synthesize the material into a coherent visual message, and present it to the class.[16]

The careful scaffolding of project-based learning and a focus on real-world problems make it possible for students to develop the ethical and social skills necessary for living in the twenty-first century. As Tomasik points out, students must engage with people and perspectives that they had not previously encountered, sometimes hearing "shocking stories for the first time" and discovering "very different approaches to potential solutions."[17] They become "more aware of the effect" that interdependencies have across communities and among individuals.[18]

Finally, the multidisciplinary experience compels students to synthesize and apply their new knowledge to the big, messy problems that perplex human societies. The ability to synthesize and apply inquiry methods to intellectual problems is an important twenty-first-century skill. While all disciplines employ inquiry methods, seldom are students taught how to stretch the application of these methods to ambiguous societal problems. Conversely, many general education frameworks present liberal arts ways of knowing in a traditional checklist style, which does not provide students with the opportunity to make connections and apply the methods to bigger issues. By modeling and supporting thinking from multiple disciplinary perspectives, faculty compel students to retrieve information, to spot its relevance and applications, and to synthesize and apply it to the problems.

Tomasik reflects on the sometimes awkward experience of applying what she learned in class to a practical setting:

> After a grueling semester of confronting our own biases and diving into a variety of primary sources, the class culminated in the final project, which aimed to not only get students out of the privileged bubble we often live in but encouraged us to transcend the safe space we created in the class, while incorporating all of the information and skills we'd acquired throughout the semester. In the first part of the project, we opened a dialogue about discrimination on campus by holding a series of interviews with people we might not otherwise talk to about race and encouraged them to discuss their experiences with it, personally or otherwise.
>
> [The MDSC] equips students with the skills to discover the greatness in themselves through investigation and the authentic discovery of new knowledge through projects and experiences.[19]

The MDSCs are specifically structured and designed to provide students with opportunities to apply multiple ways of knowing in attempts to understand the world; to wrestle with messy, ill-defined problems; to collaborate with colleagues from diverse backgrounds and disciplines; and to communicate in varied formats and media with a range of audiences. This purposeful design and the timing of the course during the sophomore year after several foundational courses are important since they often do not happen in other courses or in a traditional checklist-style general education curriculum. The skills that the MDSC emphasizes are exactly the skills that will support students' success in their junior and senior years, when they encounter advanced content and concepts in their majors, apply for and complete internships, and develop capstone projects that demonstrate their professional competence. While all higher education course topics are multifaceted, our encouragement of students to apply multiple ways of knowing to problems provides a key component for a contemporary undergraduate liberal education.

Concluding Thoughts, Next Steps

Although perspectives from multiple people—a senior administrator, former students, and a faculty team—are presented here, they share much in common. For instance, all of them highlight the ways in which multidisciplinary project-based learning leads to deeper understanding not only of the big, messy issue at hand, but also about one's own intellect and how to apply that to one's surroundings in meaningful, integrative ways. This required, co-taught experience for all sophomores at Lasell intentionally and explicitly synthesizes the intellectual and applied skills that define twenty-first-century liberal learning. The MDSC innovation also blends social and ethical skills, both of which are needed as students confront challenges that have perplexed and will indubitably continue to perplex human societies. By challenging our students in their second year with this cohort experience, we hope that they discover something about themselves, their communities, and their world that will inspire them for the next stages of immersion and integration in their major-specific programs. If we get it right, they will be able to integrate more fully the crosscutting skills of liberal learning with their profession, thus launching them into a successful career and a life of learning.

KEY TAKEAWAYS

Approach professional development *ad sapientiam* **(rather than** *ad nauseam***).** Get stakeholders together to brainstorm, plan, discuss, debrief, evaluate, and redesign on a regular basis, so that best teaching practices can emerge, evolve, and enlighten. Even at institutions with limited resources, these types of professional development opportunities remain critical.

Democratize the classroom. Embrace epistemological modesty: no one can know everything, especially when the theme being explored is a huge, intractable problem. Toss the institutional authority and power dynamics overboard.

Practice scholarly yoga. Engage everyone in the practices of intellectual flexibility and open-mindedness. After all, inquiry starts with being curious and wanting to know more about something. Make explicit the fundamental need for flexibility and for mindfulness.

Experiment fearlessly. Encourage everyone to experiment without fear of failure. Indeed, "where you succeed will never matter so much as where you fail."[20] We learn much more about ourselves, our abilities, and our understanding when we confront challenging material without obsessing about success or failure.

Prioritize process, but content still matters. Deep, collaborative inquiry can occur only with meaningful content. If there is no content and all process, then the work won't have any meaning for those involved in the exploration.

Create time and space to play. Use the classroom and other experiences to play with thinking and inquiry, while reminding everyone involved that playful inquiry is transformative. As argued by Marc Bekoff, "play is the site of invention and creativity, the site of metamorphosis of same into other, just as much for beings as for meanings."[21]

Mash up those twenty-first-century skills. In constructing students' experience, focus on the ways in which assignments, projects, and outcomes build on their intellectual, applied, ethical, and social skills. Do not compartmentalize or silo those skills from each other. Instead, mash them up intentionally and explicitly so that students learn to recognize the nuances and complexities of the world around them.

Notes

1. Immanuel Kant, *Perpetual Peace and Other Essays*, trans. Ted Humphrey (Indianapolis, IN: Hackett, 1983), 2.

2. Association of American Colleges and Universities, "What Is Liberal Education?," n.d., https://www.aacu.org/leap/what-is-liberal-education.

3. R. Crutcher et al., *College Learning for the New Global Century: A Report from the National Leadership Council for Liberal Education and America's Promise* (Washington, DC: Association of American Colleges and Universities, 2007).

4. John Dewey, *Democracy and Education* (New York: Macmillan, 1916), 187.

5. James Ostrow, email, July 12, 2018.

6. John Seely Brown, Allan Collins, and Paul Duguid, "Situated Cognition and the Culture of Learning," *Educational Researcher* 18, no. 1 (1989): 32-42.

7. Allan Collins, John Seely Brown, and Susan E. Newman, "Cognitive Apprenticeship: Teaching the Craft of Reading, Writing and Mathematics," *Thinking: The Journal of Philosophy for Children* 8, no. 1 (1988): 2-10.

8. M. B. Freedman, "The Passage through College," *Journal of Social Issues* 12 (1956): 13-27; M. A. Schaller, "Wandering and Wondering: Traversing the Uneven Terrain of the Second College Year," *About Campus* 10, no. 3 (2005): 17-24; Althea J. Sterling, "Student Experiences in the Second Year: Advancing Strategies for Success beyond the First Year of College," *Strategic Enrollment Management Quarterly* 5, no. 4 (2018): 136-149.

9. C. Sanchez-Leguelinel, "Supporting Slumping Sophomores: Programmatic Peer Initiatives Designed to Enhance Retention in the Crucial Second Year of College," *College Student Journal* 42 (2008): 637-646.

10. George D. Kuh, *High-Impact Educational Practices: What They Are, Who Has Access to Them, and Why They Matter* (Washington, DC: Association of American Colleges and Universities, 2008).

11. Paul Hanstedt, *Creating Wicked Students: Designing Courses for a Complex World* (Sterling, VA: Stylus, 2018), 6.

12. Ostrow, email, July 12, 2018.

13. Deborah Baldizar and Karin Raye, email, July 11, 2018.

14. Armando Machado Jr., email, July 12, 2018.

15. Christina Tomasik, email, July 8, 2018.

16. Baldizar and Raye, email, July 11, 2018.

17. Tomasik, email, July 8, 2018.

18. Tomasik, email, July 8, 2018.

19. Tomasik, email, July 8, 2018.

20. Karen J. Fowler, *We Are All Completely beside Ourselves* (New York: Putnam's, 2013), 80.

21. Quoted in Vinciane Despret, *What Would Animals Say if We Asked the Right Questions?*, trans. Brett Buchanan (Minneapolis: University of Minnesota Press, 2016), 80.

8   Intergenerational Partnerships to Support Liberal Learning Goals at Brown University

Mary C. Wright, Maud S. Mandel, Jessica Metzler, and Christina Smith

Radical Vision

All courses should serve as sites to help students develop key twenty-first-century competencies, such as communication and analytical skills. We believe this vision is best anchored through the cultivation of teaching teams, where undergraduates, graduate students, and faculty work in partnership to deconstruct teaching hierarchies and promote student agency in the learning process. This approach calls for meaningful student participation in all stages of a course. Through these efforts, students—as teachers and learners—will more fully and self-reflectively develop analytical and communication skills, becoming better prepared for a multiplicity of postgraduation paths. Further, instructors will use evidence-based teaching approaches to create course and curricular structures that support students to be the "architects of their own course of study,"[1] with the freedom and flexibility to design their own educational path.

Institutional Profile

Brown University in Providence, Rhode Island, is a private, not-for-profit, research 1 doctoral university enrolling approximately 7,000 undergraduates and 3,000 graduate and professional students as of the fall of 2019. It is a four-year, medium-size Ivy League university.

Introduction

The Learning Collaborative is a new initiative at Brown University designed to foster students' learning of twenty-first-century skills, such as writing and problem solving, through peer-to-peer teaching and robust support for student-faculty course design and teaching partnerships. Building on the Writing Fellows program, founded in 1982, the Learning Collaborative now houses both a Problem-Solving Fellows program and a Research Fellows component, all with complementary faculty development initiatives. Our assessment of the two sample programs presented here suggests that they benefit faculty teaching and student learning.

Case Narrative

David Scobey describes a "Copernican moment" in higher education, leading to a "Liberal Education 2.0" in which "knowing how to learn from, learn with, work with, and argue with a wide array of significant others" are key outcomes.[2] For students seeking a liberal education, this moment creates new pressures to learn twenty-first-century skills, such as communication and problem solving, which are increasingly seen as critical outcomes of a college education.[3] For academic staff, there are related and equally seismic pressures: calls for more democratic or collaborative relationships among instructor, learner, and course material, and increasing pressures on the traditional academic curriculum "from the growing body of experiential modes of learning."[4]

How can the academy best respond to these calls? Many universities are addressing this challenge through central learning outcomes aligned with a series of undergraduate requirements. Instead, Brown University's open curriculum allows for an innovative decentered approach, drawing on the university's core strengths, namely the self-directed nature of the curriculum and the distinctively high proportion (approximately 50 percent by graduation) of undergraduates in teaching and mentorship roles.

In 2014, Maud S. Mandel, dean of the college at that time, proposed that Brown should "make a significant investment in undergirding the acquisition of core competencies by expanding institutional support for writing, reading, data analysis, problem solving, and communication skills . . . [through training] peer educators to help fellow students develop the competencies they will need after Brown."[5] Research was later added to this list. These six areas were selected in response to Dean Mandel's vision that students could improve these key skills ("learning how," in Scobey's words) while pursuing their interests in regular academic courses that are part of an open liberal arts curriculum (i.e., "learning what").

In 2016 the Sheridan Center for Teaching and Learning began to develop the Learning Collaborative. This initiative builds on the Writing Fellows program by offering professional development and training for a cohort of undergraduates, who then offer formative feedback on writing in partnership with faculty.[6] Problem solving was the first new area of the Learning Collaborative, selected because it aligns with the work that many of our undergraduate TAs are already doing; continues an Association of American Universities grant in this area; and is an ideal mix of skill-based competencies and holistic student development.

All Learning Collaborative areas are examples of Students as Partners (SaP) initiatives, a term used to signify collaborative initiatives with students, faculty, and staff "contribut[ing] equally, although not necessarily in the same ways, to curricular or pedagogical conceptualization, decision-making, implementation, investigation, or analysis."[7] Within the framework of the Learning Collaborative, we conceptualize SaP as intergenerational teaching teams to more fully acknowledge the faculty, graduate student, and undergraduate triad.

A foundational principle of the Learning Collaborative is that teaching others is one of the most powerful ways to learn.[8] Further, peer teaching is a promising strategy to help close achievement gaps and increase students' well-being, performance, and retention.[9] Although peer teaching can achieve these aims, it is important to note that the Learning Collaborative is not a remedial initiative. Our goal is to have all undergraduates participate and improve their core skills, whether they are a fellow or a student in one of these courses. This initiative is innovative for targeting crosscutting liberal arts skill areas in the core academic curriculum, promoting student learning through peer teaching, and taking an ecological approach by building in faculty development.

Structure and Distinctiveness

The Brown Learning Collaborative consists of three core components:

- Expanding undergraduate teaching fellows programs in key competency areas (e.g., writing, problem solving, research, data analysis), which are supported by a rigorous academic course on the theory and practice of teaching each skill.
- Pairing fellows with faculty and TAs (in the context of a course) to create intergenerational teaching teams.
- Developing faculty and TA course design programs in the same competency areas in order to offer evidence-based professional development to instructors and help them create environments to foster student learning and teaching partnerships.

While building on the Writing Fellows program and other SaP initiatives, the Learning Collaborative goes beyond that model in several key ways. First, most SaP initiatives at other institutions are small scale, with fewer than six students, and for both SaP and high-impact practices, most take place in the cocurriculum.[10] The ambition of the Learning Collaborative is to scale up student teaching and learning of twenty-first-century skills to encompass most, if not all, courses in the university. Further, research suggests that deeper-level study skills, such as metacognition, are best taught in the context of a course because many aspects of this learning are domain-specific.[11] Therefore, the work of the fellows takes place in the context of partnership with faculty in academic courses across the disciplines.

Another important difference is that all Learning Collaborative areas have a parallel program of workshops, institutes, and seminars on course design, which are aimed at addressing the structural changes needed to foster the teaching of twenty-first-century skills. This part of the program is aimed at faculty, but instructors are encouraged to participate with graduate student or undergraduate collaborators, and many do.

The sections below detail two areas from the Learning Collaborative: writing and problem solving. One example focuses on the Problem-Solving Fellows, the first new student-focused area of the Learning Collaborative. The second example focuses on the writing across the curriculum seminar, the first new course design program for faculty. In both cases, the evaluation plan aligns with many frameworks that suggest measuring the scope of participation, immediate participant reaction (e.g., program satisfaction and intent to apply ideas), change in participants' teaching reflection or practices, and evidence of impact on student learning outcomes and experiences.[12] Both projects were deemed exempt from or not regulated by IRB review.

Problem Solving

Executives, human resources managers, college presidents, faculty, and students express a consensus that problem solving is one of the most important outcomes of a college education.[13] Most faculty report encouraging their students to seek solutions to problems, explain problems to others, or seek alternative solutions to problems.[14] However, only a scant majority of college seniors report that they are well prepared to be effective problem solvers—and fewer than a quarter of employers perceive graduating students to be competent at this key skill.[15]

Design of the Undergraduate Fellows Course

In 2018, Christina Smith (Sheridan Center and engineering) developed a course, The Theory and Practice of Problem Solving, for the Problem-Solving Fellows (PSFs) program. This course was first offered in the spring of 2018 with five students serving as STEM undergraduate TAs (UTAs); an additional twenty-two enrolled in the fall of 2018 and the spring of 2019. (Of the twenty-seven PSFs, 15 percent were students from historically underrepresented groups, and 19 percent were first-generation college students.) The course is designed to help students become effective problem solvers through their teaching. PSFs are introduced to learning theory frameworks, learning strategies, evidence-based instructional practices, and the problem-solving process. These concepts are applied to the context of the students' teaching through activities in class, writing a teaching statement, conducting peer observations of teaching, conducting a self-study think-aloud,[16] developing concept maps, and completing an end-of-course project focused on improving teaching and/or problem solving at Brown. Students reflect in class and are asked to write a one- to two-page reflection for each assignment in order to practice metacognition.

Each class meeting includes a discussion of the reading, an activity that focuses on the students' experiences, and a reflection. For example, for the topic of critical thinking, students read a chapter on critical thinking and critical perspectives prior to the class,[17] and in class they are asked how they define critical thinking and its relationships to epistemology and problem types. Students dissect a current homework problem by sharing a simplified version of their problem, identifying what assumptions they made in order to start working on the problem, and at least one question that challenged those assumptions. They go through a similar exercise regarding their teaching assumptions. Students ask questions that challenge their peers' problem and/or teaching assumptions. The class session concludes with a reflection on how to facilitate critical thinking and with identifying one thing to change in their teaching the following week.

Assessment

There are three key ways that the PSF program is being assessed:

1. *Immediate perception of usefulness and plans to apply ideas from the program.* In an end-of-term course evaluation, one student said, "The course, overall, helped me develop my metacognitive skills to such a larger extent that I believe it is the reason for my success in my really difficult courses. It also employed [sic] us with a number of new mindsets and teaching strategies to utilize as TAs and possibly future educators." Another student said, "I learned about epistemology

and other frameworks for discussing learning, as well as practical ways to create an environment conducive to learning."
2. *Participant work products.* Students' reflections regarding how their beliefs around teaching and learning had changed throughout the course included the methods they use to accomplish their teaching goals; an awareness of the norms, beliefs, and practices in science and their relation to diversity in STEM; understanding the relationship between culture, fixed and growth mindsets, educational background, and question types; and how to teach students to be confident in their ability to learn on their own. Students reflected that it is important to establish a culture of trial and error for students when solving problems and that the methods they use when solving problems could help or hinder progress.
3. *Student self-assessment of learning gains.* Fellows and students in introductory chemistry courses were asked about their problem-solving approaches, using a series of validated surveys. Overall, while chemistry students' ($n = 40$) problem-solving tactics increased some (+ 9 percent), PSFs ($n = 5$) showed larger gains (+ 24 percent). We acknowledge the small sample sizes and nonrandom assignment (because of the educational nature of this program), but these are promising results that suggest strong future impacts of this initiative.

As the program grows, we plan to collect other measures of problem solving. In addition to this feedback, another exciting outcome of the course is that returning PSFs are collaborating with Dr. Smith to offer a university-wide orientation for UTAs, which expands the reach of the program. We are also looking to expand the pool of students taking the course from primarily UTAs to other peer educators on campus.

Writing across the Curriculum Seminar
Although nearly all faculty at four-year institutions indicate that it is important for students to learn how to write effectively (93 percent), less than a majority regularly ask for multiple drafts of written work (34 percent) or provide feedback on drafts (49 percent)—teaching methods

known to improve student writing.[18] Thus, while student fellows programs are a critical component of the Learning Collaborative, it is equally important that we offer support for faculty and graduate student instructors in the Learning Collaborative's key areas.

The first of these programs for faculty is focused on writing. Although many colleges and universities have writing across the curriculum programs, our model allows students to participate in the course design process with faculty, and it is integrated with the Writing Fellows program, allowing us to realize the vision of intergenerational teaching teams.

Design of the Seminar

In 2017, Jessica Metzler at the Sheridan Center launched the writing across the curriculum seminar (WACS), a yearlong program that provides support for faculty to design, develop, and teach a course that supports writing in their discipline. The program combines an intensive two-day seminar on writing pedagogy and course design with a supportive peer community and individual consultations and feedback. The seminar includes an introduction to the principles of writing across the curriculum and writing to learn, and it provides participants with tools and techniques to integrate writing into their courses (e.g., scaffolding effective writing assignment sequences), develop writing exercises, and respond to students' writing. Follow-up support is given through collecting early student feedback when the new or revised course is first taught, peer teaching discussions, and individual consultations.[19] Faculty are encouraged to participate with a graduate student or undergraduate student co-designer (and receive funds to pay this collaborator), and participants receive priority for a writing fellow.

Assessment

In 2017–2018, six faculty teams (six faculty members and two graduate students in total) completed the WACS, designing and teaching courses that integrated student writing as a core component to help students learn either the subject matter, disciplinary writing conventions, or both.

Four of these faculty members then taught courses in collaboration with undergraduate writing fellows in an intergenerational teaching partnership. Three faculty came from STEM disciplines, and three were in the social sciences. (An additional cohort of five faculty, one graduate student, and one undergraduate student began the WACS in June 2018.) Three measures of effectiveness were collected:

1. *Immediate perception of usefulness and plans to apply program ideas.* At the end of the seminar, all participants completed a survey. In the feedback, all participants agreed that the two-day intensive course design seminar was effective, and they noted a range of positive outcomes. "Being able to work concretely on my course was especially useful," wrote one participant. Another reported feeling "excited to provide feedback on drafts/steps in the scaffolding process to help students build their writing skills," while one described their experience in the following way: "I simply had no clue how to do this before."
2. *Participant work products.* Pre- and post-syllabi were collected from faculty participants in the seminar, except when the course was new, and reported changes were documented during follow-up consultations. Among faculty participants, changes made to syllabi mirrored the central objectives of the seminar. Examples of syllabi revisions included incorporating writing as a central pedagogical goal of the course, adding course design components around peer feedback, and adding a plagiarism statement. Faculty who did not change their syllabi described changes to their practice (e.g., adding in-class peer review activities or writing exercises).
3. *Student feedback.* Early student feedback offered an additional corroborative perspective on these changes. Most participants opted to engage in early student feedback, and student-identified key strengths of the courses were consistent with emphases of the seminar, such as providing scaffolded assignments, concrete guidance for writing, opportunities for low-stakes writing, and opportunities for peer feedback.

These assessment data suggest that a program that offers foundational pedagogy instruction and follow-up support for evidence-based writing practices within a WAC framework is an effective model for supporting faculty across disciplines in their goal to improve student writing.[20]

Concluding Thoughts, Next Steps

In 2018–2019, with support from a Howard Hughes Medical Institute grant, the Learning Collaborative added a new area focused on building research skills. Specifically, this initiative offers a faculty development series around course-based undergraduate research experiences. These are designed to scale up the benefits of one-to-one research experiences through authentic, discovery-based classes, generally in STEM.[21] In the spring of 2020, we also will start a data science fellows program and a course design institute.

Brown University has an open curriculum, so it is often said that our students can be the architects of their own education. The Learning Collaborative seeks to enable students not only to be the architects of their *own* education but also to help peers reach *their* learning goals.

KEY TAKEAWAYS

Begin with a needs assessment. In the case of the Learning Collaborative, focus group feedback was collected through multiple presentations to Brown University administrators, faculty, staff, and alumni and from more than eighty STEM UTAs and students of UTAs. These discussions were very helpful for understanding the level of support for the initiative and how to build the Learning Collaborative.

Embed significant faculty, student, and staff input into the process. With each new competency area, the Sheridan Center hosts a working group (i.e., a finite committee) to gather input into critical issues, such as program design, timing, and assessment. At times, the planning committee meetings also become professional learning communities, which is a key element in sustaining larger-scale innovation, such as when participants share ideas about how they teach core skills like writing or problem solving.[22]

Define the core identity of the model. At the start, because of the large number of curricular peer mentoring programs on our campus, it was helpful to define the elements of the Learning Collaborative that are essential to the model. This has helped maintain the core identity of the program. In turn, other aspects of the program that are not part of this core definition—such as hiring of fellows or the specific format of faculty development programs—can be adapted to fit different contexts.

Pace expansion. Each new area of the Learning Collaborative has required careful planning, cultivation, and assessment. Therefore, the recommended pace for adding new areas is no more than one per year.

Plan for "carrots." Busy faculty and students need incentives to consider adding something more to their plate. It is essential to think about what will motivate them to participate in a new initiative.

Notes

1. Brown University, "Operational Plan for Building Brown's Excellence," September 15, 2015, https://brown.edu/web/documents/provost/Operational_Plan_FINAL_PUBLIC_2015.09.15.pdf.

2. David M. Scobey, "A Copernican Moment: On the Revolutions in Higher Education," in *Transforming Undergraduate Education: Theory That Compels and Practices That Succeed*, ed. Donald W. Harward (Lanham, MD: Rowman and Littlefield, 2012), 37-49, 47.

3. Derek Bok, *The Struggle to Reform Our Colleges* (Princeton, NJ: Princeton University Press, 2017); Matthew T. Hora, Ross J. Benbow, and Amanda K. Oleson, *Beyond the Skills Gap: Preparing College Students for Life and Work* (Cambridge, MA: Harvard University Press, 2016).

4. Randy Bass, "Disrupting Ourselves: The Problem of Learning in Higher Education," *Educause Review*, March 21, 2012, https://er.educause.edu/articles/2012/3/disrupting-ourselves-the-problem-of-learning-in-higher-education, 24; Mary C. Wright, Debra R. Lohe, and Deandra Little, "The Role of a Center for Teaching and Learning in a De-Centered Educational World," *Change* 50, no. 6 (2018): 38-44.

5. Brown University, "Operational Plan," 37.

6. Tori Haring-Smith, "Changing Students' Attitudes: Writing Fellows Programs," in *Writing across the Curriculum: A Guide to Developing Programs*, ed. Susan H. McLeod and Margot Soven (Newbury Park, CA: Sage, 2000), 123-131.

7. Alison Cook-Sather, Catherine Bovill, and Peter Felten, *Engaging Students as Partners in Learning and Teaching: A Guide for Faculty* (San Francisco, CA: Jossey-Bass, 2014), 6-7.

8. Helvi Koch and Nadine Spörer, "Students Improve in Reading Comprehension by Learning How to Teach Reading Strategies: An Evidence-Based Approach for Teacher Education," *Psychology Learning and Teaching* 16, no. 2 (2017): 197-211; Kristi Lundstrom and Wendy Baker, "To Give Is Better than to Receive: The Benefits of Peer Review to the Reviewer's Own Writing," *Journal of Second Language Writing* 18, no. 1 (2009): 30-43.

9. Julia J. Snyder et al., "Peer-Led Team Learning Helps Minority Students Succeed," *PLOS Biology* 14, no. 3 (2016): e1002398; Denise Drane, Marina Micari, and Gregory Light, "Students as Teachers: Effectiveness of a Peer-Led STEM Learning Programme over 10 Years," *Educational Research and Evaluation* 20, no. 3 (2014): 210-230; Jana M. Hanson et al., "Evaluating the Influence of Peer Learning on Psychological Well-Being," *Teaching in Higher Education* 21, no. 2 (2016): 191-206.

10. Bass, "Disrupting Ourselves"; Lucy Mercer-Mapstone et al., "A Systematic Review of Students as Partners in Higher Education," *International Journal for Students as Partners* 1, no. 1 (2017), https://mulpress.mcmaster.ca/ijsap/article/view/3119.

11. John Hattie, John Biggs, and Nola Purdie, "Effects of Learning Skills Interventions on Student Learning: A Meta-Analysis," *Review of Educational Research* 66, no. 2 (1996): 99-136; Matthew T. Hora, Ross J. Benbow, and Bailey Smolarek, "Re-thinking Soft Skills and Student Employability: A New Paradigm for Undergraduate Education," *Change* 50, no. 6 (2018): 30-37.

12. Suzanne Hines, "Evaluating Centers for Teaching and Learning: A Field-Tested Model," *To Improve the Academy* 36, no. 2 (2017): 89-100; Carolin Kreber and Paula Brook, "Impact Evaluation of Educational Development Programmes," *International Journal for Academic Development* 6 (2001): 96-108.

13. Hart Research Associates, "Fulfilling the American Dream: Liberal Education and the Future of Work," July 2018, https://www.aacu.org/sites/default/files/files/LEAP/2018EmployerResearchReport.pdf; Bok, *Struggle to Reform*; Hora, Benbow, and Oleson, *Beyond the Skills Gap*; Honor J. Passow and Christian H. Passow, "What Competencies Should Undergraduate Engineering

Programs Emphasize? A Systematic Review," *Journal of Engineering Education* 106, no. 3 (2017): 475-526.

14. Kevin Eagan et al., *Undergraduate Teaching Faculty: The 2013-2014 HERI Faculty Survey* (Los Angeles: Higher Education Research Institute, University of California, 2014).

15. Hart Research Associates, "Fulfilling the American Dream."

16. John Cowan, "The Potential of Cognitive Think-Aloud Protocols for Educational Action-Research," *Active Learning in Higher Education*, October 29, 2017, https://journals.sagepub.com/doi/full/10.1177/1469787417735614.

17. Sharan B. Merriam and Laura L. Bierema, *Adult Learning: Linking Theory and Practice* (San Francisco, CA: Jossey-Bass, 2014).

18. Eagan et al., *Undergraduate Teaching Faculty*; Nancy Sommers, *Responding to Student Writers* (Boston: Bedford/St. Martin's, 2013); Nancy Sommers, "Revision Strategies of Student Writers and Experienced Adult Writers," *College Composition and Communication* 31, no. 4 (1980): 378-388.

19. Donald H. Wulff and Jody D. Nyquist, "Using Qualitative Methods to Generate Data for Instructional Improvement," *To Improve the Academy* 5 (1986): 37-46.

20. Thank you to Dr. Marc Lo, University of Pennsylvania, for distributing and analyzing the survey data referred to in this chapter.

21. Lisa C. Auchincloss et al., "Assessment of Course-Based Undergraduate Research Experiences: A Meeting Report," *CBE: Life Sciences Education* 13 (2014): 29-40; Nancy H. Hensel, ed., *Course-Based Undergraduate Research: Educational Equity and High-Impact Practice* (Sterling, VA: Stylus, 2018).

22. Adrianna Kezar, "What Is the Best Way to Achieve Broader Reach of Improved Practices in Higher Education?," *Innovative Higher Education* 36 (2011): 235-247.

9 The Design Thinking Initiative at Smith College

Borjana Mikic

Radical Vision

What if all students viewed themselves as designers? What if all students were given the opportunity to actively participate in designing solutions to address society's challenges? What if they were given the time and space to develop the necessary mindsets and skill sets for such work? From our educational systems to our voting processes to the communities we live, work, and learn in, everything in our human-made world is designed. The impact of designers is profound, and yet only a very small segment of our population views itself as having the right to claim the identity of designer. At Smith College, our radical vision for the future of liberal education is that all students be given the opportunity to develop into designers, and we propose that design thinking may be an ideal pedagogy of practice for twenty-first-century capacity building in the liberal arts.[1]

Institutional Profile

Smith College in Northampton, Massachusetts, is a private, not-for-profit baccalaureate college enrolling approximately 3,000 students. It is a four-year, small, highly residential, predominantly undergraduate women's college.

Introduction

Herbert Simon defines design as "devis[ing] courses of action aimed at changing existing situations into preferred ones."[2] Implicit in this definition is the ability to ask, with critique and compassion, preferred by whom? For academic institutions, such as Smith College, which aim to educate leaders capable of "developing solutions to society's problems,"[3] cultivating students' capacity to design with intention and compassion will be critical to realizing our stated mission.

In this case study, I tell the story of the Design Thinking Initiative at Smith College and outline how the processes, methods, and mindsets of design thinking map to the twenty-first-century competencies that are in high demand. The initiative is a multiyear experiment aimed at enabling the capacity of all students to develop and activate their agency as designers of their educational paths, their lives, and the world around them. In this chapter, I outline our approach to advancing liberal arts capacities through the initiative by describing our approaches to the development of experimental spaces to support our work, stand-alone interdisciplinary courses in design thinking, faculty development and curricular enhancement efforts, and broader institutional synergies through staff engagement. Finally, I conclude with our current understanding of transferable lessons learned for other institutions seeking to engage in this type of transformational approach to liberal education.

Case Narrative

The mission of Smith College is to educate women of promise for lives of distinction and purpose, with a further goal of educating engaged global citizens and leaders to address society's challenges. If we accept Simon's definition of design,[4] then educating students to develop the necessary capacities to address society's challenges requires that we educate them to think like designers (that is, to devise courses of action that move society from existing problematic conditions to some preferred resolution of these challenges). Such a framing then leads to the question, how might we best prepare our students to think like designers?

A unique strength and opportunity for Smith is the existence of several majors and programs (e.g., engineering, landscape studies, architecture) where design already plays a prominent pedagogical role. In addition, we have robust offerings in the studio and performing arts whose faculty have a shared sensibility around the pedagogical value of engaging students in creative collaboration, and strong programs in anthropology, sociology, and psychology where students learn deep methodological approaches for understanding and situating human experiences and needs. An additional opportunity presents itself in the strong identity that Smith students and alumnae have around the notions of activism, social justice, and serving as agents of change in their local and global communities.

In 2013, a group of faculty from a broad range of disciplines asked, how might we take advantage of these strengths in order to expand the educational opportunities for students to begin to think and work like designers as they tackle increasingly complex problems in a collaborative, human-centered way? These conversations paved the way for a multiyear pilot project known as the Design Thinking Initiative.[5]

Motivation and Desired Outcomes

What exactly do we mean by "design thinking"? For several years at Smith prior to our launching the initiative, a group of roughly a dozen faculty met regularly to explore this question with no concrete agenda other than developing a shared understanding and language. What we came to realize was that our definition of design thinking had to embrace *both* the problem-solving perspective that disciplines such as engineering, architecture, and landscape studies use *and* the question-provoking perspective of the arts and humanities, with the social sciences providing powerful methodologies and additional ways of understanding human behavior at various scales. For all of us, a defining characteristic of design and design thinking is that it is generative and involves the process of creating something that does not yet exist. While it is often tempting to adopt definitions that have worked in other contexts, one transferable lesson that we have learned in our experiment is the importance of being true to one's own institutional context and values when it comes to curricular innovation and change. In our case, that meant creating room for multiple points of entry into the exploration and adoption of methods, mindsets, and stages in the process of human-centered design.

The Association of American Colleges and Universities defines liberal education as "an approach to learning that empowers individuals and prepares them to deal with complexity, diversity, and change.... [It] helps students develop a sense of social responsibility, as well as strong and transferable intellectual and practical skills such as communication, analytical and problem-solving skills, and a demonstrated ability to apply knowledge and skills in real-world settings."[6] Smith's version of design thinking conceives of design in service to broader social issues of participation, intervention, and leadership. We frame design thinking as a process that can (and should!) be used to question gender, power, and ability as dynamics that shape who gets to participate in creating the world we live in. In this sense, social responsibility lies at the core of our definition of design thinking and how we introduce students to it: in the context of real-world problems in the many communities in which our students live, work, and learn. With humans at the center, design thinking encourages participants to see the past and present in new ways in order to imagine the future in new ways, toggling between big-picture thinking and a detailed view.[7]

Although our original goal with the initiative was not to directly design for the development of twenty-first-century liberal education skills per se, the processes and phases involved in design thinking and the associated mindsets, skill sets, methods, and transformational outcomes map beautifully to these skills (see the introduction to this volume).[8] More specifically, the intellectual skills of critical (convergent) and creative (divergent) thinking associated with problem framing, ideation, and problem solving are central to design thinking as a process. Furthermore, the capacities of resilience, creativity, curiosity, comfort with ambiguity, and flexibility of thinking are all cultivated in a design-based approach to iterative problem solving that is rooted in empathetic observations of human behavior. Design work is rarely done in isolation, and the collaborative nature of the endeavor requires the social skills of negotiation, cross-cultural competency, emotional intelligence, outstanding communication, and deep moral and ethical reasoning in guiding how one engages with the unmet needs of a community. In short, design thinking embodies liberal education engaged with and in action within a community.

When we embarked on this experiment, the aspirational goals of the initiative were to

- Connect campus community members who are interested in doing design as well as learning about design.
- Promote design-related educational experiences, courses, and events at Smith.
- Provide physical and virtual studio spaces and prototyping facilities for experiential collaborative design work in any domain.
- Teach concrete design thinking tools and approaches for creative problem solving that can be applied in any context.
- Facilitate groups on campus that might wish to come together to co-create.
- Encourage a culture of academic risk taking, experimentation, and co-creation as a way of thinking and learning.
- Advocate for the integration of mind and body, the virtual and the physical, through the process of making.
- Foster active and playful engagement with ideas and things.[9]

Our initial desired outcomes were rooted in seeing evidence of broad-based institutional buy-in, including

- The creation of a dedicated physical space for this type of work.
- At least one credit-bearing course being offered in design thinking—and preferably more.
- Multiconstituent (i.e., student, faculty, and staff) involvement with the initiative.

- Involvement of students and faculty across the traditional disciplinary silos of the liberal arts (humanities, social sciences, and STEM fields).
- Faculty adoption of elements of design thinking methods, mindsets, and processes in a variety of courses throughout the college.
- New experiments in co-teaching or collaborative engagement between classes from different disciplines.
- Signs that our work might be influencing more than just the curriculum but also other aspects of campus life and, more broadly, how we do what we do at the college.

When we obtained our initial funding, it was critical to hire a full-time dedicated staff codirector to serve as a strategic partner to the faculty director and advisory board and to serve as the day-to-day, on-the-ground implementer. In addition to the staff codirector, we hired a full-time prototyping studio coordinator, a half-time administrative assistant, and a group of student design partners. The faculty director received a course release for her work, and our advisory board of faculty and staff met monthly with the directors to provide feedback and assist with strategic decision making. This has become especially important in recent years as we have explored how we might move away from foundation support and into a more sustainable financial structure for the college.

Innovation Details

Our original vision was to repurpose an existing space on campus that could serve as a classroom and studio space for our work. It was imperative to us that the space not feel too pristine and that it be viewed as always open to modification and experimentation as its uses and our needs developed. In close collaboration with the college's associate vice president for facilities management and the director of sustainability and campus planning, we identified an old two-story house known as Capen Annex, which was home to several student organizations that were moving to new locations. Our renovations resulted in an open, light-filled downstairs classroom space with movable and adjustable furniture, floor-to-ceiling whiteboards, a low- fidelity prototyping cart, and basic audiovisual capability; a prototyping studio with medium-fidelity capabilities (e.g., laser cutter, 3D printer, hand tools, vinyl cutter, sewing machine); two small shared office spaces; and a small meeting room. Our inclusion of the prototyping studio was meant to facilitate making as a form of thinking, and our goal was to have student projects begin here in their early stages and then move on to higher-fidelity making facilities on campus if needed. One outcome of our work has been the creation of a maker's map of the campus to make more visible the many facilities and resources available to students for making in its many forms.

Because the space itself feels quite different than most other spaces on our campus that are used for teaching, learning, and collaboration, we frequently begin our classes and workshops with the metaphor of a doorway, inviting participants to leave their preconceived notions outside and enter into the space and our work with an open mind. This metaphorical door and Capen Annex itself then become symbolic of a liminal space—a space of transition—between an old way of thinking and working and a new emergent one that has yet to take shape for many of our collaborators.

Curricular Innovations

Through their work with the Design Thinking Initiative, students learn to engage in the practice of generative, creative thinking, but they do so while simultaneously holding a critical lens on this practice. This philosophy is most evident in our four-credit, semester-long course, [Critical] Design Thinking Studio, in which students learn and practice human-centered design thinking methodologies in response to real-world design challenges, while they are simultaneously reading and discussing critical works from sociology and other relevant fields that examine the potential negative consequences of design in our world.

In addition to stand-alone courses, we have experimented with other approaches to engaging students in the practice of design thinking. For example, during a particularly fraught year on campus related to questions of diversity, inclusion, and equity, we held a day-long Belonging Challenge, asking how we might increase a sense of belonging for students on Smith's campus. A group of eleven students who participated in the challenge wanted to continue their work, and they enrolled in a special studies project with us, which culminated in a participatory art installation at the campus center called *Smith ReAct*. Additionally, to meet the needs of an increasingly diverse student body, we collaborate across units to provide students with design tools as a means to advance equity and inclusion work (e.g., helping to develop a Leadership for Equity-Centered Design curriculum for one of Smith's identity-based leadership development student cohorts in our Wurtele Center for Leadership).

Another core component of our work has been collaborating with faculty to introduce design thinking methods and mindsets into existing courses in the curriculum though our Curriculum Enhancement Grant (CEG) Program. All told, we have supported more than forty faculty and staff on the redesign of thirty-five different courses, impacting an estimated 650 students. Our CEGs are accompanied by priority access to our staff for consulting on implementation, to the design thinking classroom space and supported prototyping studio, and to a monthly teaching circle, which supports a community of practice among faculty and staff who are currently implementing curricular innovations.

In addition to the CEG program, we offer periodic workshops for faculty, such as a two-day workshop on "making as a form of thinking" where faculty from a variety of disciplines are introduced to the concept of a prototype and then are asked to work in design teams to build some form of prototype to demonstrate their collective evolving theories around complicated questions, such as What is wisdom?, Why are some people happy and others not?, Why is there political polarization? and What is a city? Day two of this workshop is an in-depth discussion on how prototyping could be used to support deep learning in participants' courses and on strategies for avoiding a superficial reduction to activity. In all of our work with faculty, our strategy has been to encourage experimentation and to meet any skepticism or cynicism with a genuine curiosity, asking faculty to articulate their fears and concerns and to help us improve our thinking to avoid any imagined lethal mutations of design thinking.

Institutional Synergy

Because design thinking was not well understood on our campus before the initiative, one of our operating principles has been to keep an ear to the ground to identify as many possible synergies as we see, and we reach out to collaborate whenever possible. This approach has had the unexpected effect of developing a strong network of staff on campus with whom we now have ongoing collaborations. For example, in a yearlong House Sustainability Challenge, we collaborated with the Office of Sustainability, the Office of Student Engagement, and the Conway Innovation and Entrepreneurship Center on a design challenge for students to propose, prototype, and pilot residence-based innovations for energy conservation. The winning design (do-it-yourself drying racks) was then implemented across campus.

In collaboration with the Innovation and Entrepreneurship Center, we support students in the annual Draper Business Plan competition in creating prototypes of their ideas. We have collaborated with the Lazarus Center for Career Development to introduce design thinking methods, such as prototyping, to career exploration, and similar concepts have been used by the dean for academic development in approaching faculty career transitions as opportunities for intentional holistic career (re)design. We have worked with the college's Writing Committee on an ongoing redesign of the writing intensive requirement, college librarians on reimagining the library experience as our main library undergoes a major renovation, the Humanities and the Arts Strategic Planning Group, and the board of trustees on designing Smith's future.

We are often approached with curiosity by staff units on campus that are interested in learning more about what we do. In those situations, we typically offer an experiential, small taste of design thinking and then engage the group in thinking about how human-centered design might be applied to solving the unit's unmet needs.

Outcomes and Assessment

Two of our most important initial outcomes were to involve not only students but also faculty and staff in the initiative and to have equivalent involvement across the disciplinary divisions of the humanities, social sciences, and STEM fields. Based on our tracking of unique individuals impacted in some way by our work, we are achieving these goals.

In their own words (via anonymous written surveys), participants identify enhanced creativity, flexibility in thinking, new perspective taking, resilience, and the power of making as important outcomes:

> I came away from the experiences with a better understanding of the big picture—that power and oppression are literally weaved into the way we design our worlds.

> As a humanist, thinking about human centered design isn't hard.... But what DT@Smith might be doing is putting different mixes of people in the room to solve problems than there typically might be.

> After taking Design Thinking classes, I started thinking about problems more creatively and working to find different solutions when something wasn't working. I also got much better at teamwork.

> I think differently about "failure"—understanding now that it's an essential and beneficial part of the process.

> It served as a creative outlet and helped me understand my [major] coursework using a different lens.

> I appreciated that this ... gave me the chance to put it all into action. It helped to solidify my passion and made me more confident in my ability in this world.

> Design Thinking made me reevaluate my skills and abilities and understand how much more capable I am than I previously thought.

Unexpected Benefits and Challenges

One of the biggest unexpected benefits from our work has been the extent to which staff across the college have embraced design thinking with curiosity and enthusiasm, thus enabling us to make inroads into empowering people at all levels of the institution to identify and address unmet needs. One challenge that comes with a high degree of staff interest is the need to develop a more robust process for capacity building rather than having the design thinking staff act as internal consultants to various units that have identified challenges they wish to address. A new Institutional Change Partners pilot aims to address this challenge.

On the student front, our main challenge is to broaden impact while maintaining quality and depth. Our stand-alone courses are limited in enrollment due to our physical space as well as the nature of our iterative, critique-based studio approach, and thus our most substantive impact has a smaller footprint than we would like. While our CEG recipients indirectly impact large numbers of students, recent data show (not surprisingly) that these students often have a shallower experience with design thinking than do students who enroll in our stand-alone courses. Finally, while our focus on experimentation has allowed us to be nimble and respond to emerging opportunities for collaboration, we are at a point when it would be helpful for students if we identified clearer pathways through our offerings, allowing for greater depth and integration over time.

Concluding Thoughts, Next Steps

The Design Thinking Initiative at Smith is at an interesting inflection point as we slowly transition from foundation funding and as we create a larger umbrella with leadership and innovation initiatives. The co-design of a shared vision and mission for this umbrella is currently in progress. It will enable us to leverage significant resources to enhance the twenty-first-century skills of our students as they develop agency around assuming an active role in framing and solving problems and put that agency into action in real ways but always from a place of humility, engaging in every encounter and collaboration with the awareness that they always have more to learn—from those who examined these problems before them and from those with perspectives and experiences that are different from their own.

KEY TAKEAWAYS

Organic is better than off-the-shelf. Resist the temptation to import to your campus branded versions of design thinking that have worked in other contexts. Take the time to allow your definition and approach to design thinking to be authentic to the values and culture of your institution.

Find your kindred spirits. They may not even know or care about design thinking, but they may care deeply about the mindsets that design thinking cultivates and/or the twenty-first-century skills that it helps to develop in students.

Embrace critique. Faculty cynicism and skepticism are signs that people are afraid that the things they value may be at risk. Reach out to these individuals and invite them to improve your own thinking so that you can avoid any imagined lethal mutations in your implementation.

Find a space. Work to find a space, no matter how small, that can serve as the physical manifestation of your vision for design thinking, and use it to test and constantly improve your ideas.

Meet people where they are. While your grand vision for your campus may involve a required yearlong capstone design course with real projects sponsored by industry and nonprofits, your institution may not be ready for that. Break down your vision of design thinking into more tangible methods and mindsets that faculty can experiment with in their courses in order to get to a larger, more comprehensive vision over time. Experiment!

Be strategic. Seek out people and places on your campus where you can collaborate to achieve common goals so that your work becomes integral to theirs. That said, there is a delicate balancing act to be done between staying true to your vision (e.g., the pedagogical value of design thinking is in the process, not necessarily the product) and taking advantage of collaborative resource opportunities that may feel restrictive (e.g., an emphasis on the outcome of the process when functioning under an innovation and entrepreneurship umbrella). Find ways to educate others and strive for both/and. Finding ways to be inclusive does not necessarily mean you are selling your soul.

Walk the talk yourself. Be willing to play, to experiment, to test your ideas with others, to learn from failed experiments. Don't be afraid to say yes to a collaboration simply because you can't predict the outcome in advance. Be open to having your own point of view shift. Engage others with humility.

Notes

1. Although sole authored, this chapter is narrated from the perspective of the plural "we" because it represents the emergent collective work of a group of faculty, students, and staff too large to coauthor. Key players include our former staff codirector (Zaza Kabayadondo), advisory board members past and present (Susannah Howe, Fraser Stables, Angie Hauser, Chris Aiken, Suzanne Gottschang, Reid Berton-Johnson, Eitan Mendelowitz, Jim Middlebrook, Yasmin Eisenhauer), studio coordinator (Leo Selvaggio), thought partner (Ailey Picasso-Hobin), and student design partners (Isabelle Hodge, Asmita Gautam, Laura Lilienkamp, Emily Matz, Lily Qian, and others).

2. Herbert A. Simon, *The Science of the Artificial*, 3rd ed. (Cambridge, MA: MIT Press, 1996), 123.

3. "Mission of Smith College," Smith College, n.d., https://www.smith.edu/about-smith/smith-history/mission.

4. Simon, *Science of the Artificial*.

5. For a detailed description of the genesis and original aspirations of the initiative, see Borjana Mikic et al., "Design Thinking and the Liberal Arts: A Cross-Campus Initiative at Smith College," *International Journal of Engineering Education* 32, no. 3(B) (2016):1522-1529.

6. Association of American Colleges and Universities, "What Is Liberal Education?," n.d., https://www.aacu.org/leap/what-is-liberal-education.

7. E. Ben-Ur, "Developing Powerful, Portable Design Thinking: The Innovators' Compass," in *Taking Design Thinking to School*, ed. Shelley Goldman and Zaza Kabayadondo (London: Routledge, 2017).

8. Association of American Colleges and Universities, "Essential Learning Outcomes," n.d., https://www.aacu.org/leap/essential-learning-outcomes.

9. Mikic et al., "Design Thinking and the Liberal Arts."

10 Immersive Learning in the Studio for Social Innovation at Elon University

Rebecca Pope-Ruark, William Moner, and Phillip Motley

Radical Vision

Graduates of a liberal education should be adept at working together to discover challenging problems that require creative thinking and innovative practices, and they should be willing to embrace failure as a productive practice that drives them forward toward success. We envision a future where learning experiences are designed from the ground up by students, faculty, and community members working together across disciplines on projects that serve the greater good. We imagine a team-centered and team-taught model that cuts across disciplines, emphasizes developmental reflection and evaluation over grades, promotes continuous learning based on project needs, and imagines the greater community as the classroom where solutions will be implemented. We should strive to promote student confidence to participate fully, meaningfully, and collaboratively in addressing challenging social problems.

Institutional Profile

Elon University in Elon, North Carolina, is a private, not-for-profit doctoral/professional university enrolling 7,000 students. It is a four-year, medium-size, highly residential institution with additional classification in community engagement. The university consists of a College of Arts and Sciences and five professional schools: business, communications, education, health sciences, and law.

Introduction

Imagine a group of learners, well versed in their own disciplinary skills, bringing their undivided commitment into a class setting, mixing with people from other disciplines and professionals in various fields, committing to a long-term project-based immersive experience, and eagerly addressing problems collaboratively with the local community. Imagine this group applying knowledge in a space where they can practice the tools and processes that drive innovation, such as structured collaboration, design thinking, and agile project management methodologies. Imagine a shared studio learning space where more questions than answers will be encountered, all in the service of creating something new. What will students learn without a rubric to follow or a set of guidelines that spell out the challenges ahead? What happens when they are asked to confront the possibility of failure, ambiguity, frustration, and group tension as they work to solve problems together?

To find out, we created the Design Thinking Studio in Social Innovation at Elon University. The studio is an interdisciplinary curricular program open to all students in their junior or senior year after they have learned the fundamentals of their declared major. This unique program eliminates the need to take four discrete courses, instead bundling them as a single sixteen-credit "course" in a dedicated studio space in coordination with community organizations. The program was designed to minimize some of the more rigid structures commonly built into higher education, such as required seat time, credit hours, grades, rubrics, separation of disciplines, tidy course outcomes, and rigid schedules, which all stand at odds with the type of flexibility needed for immersive, deep learning. While structures are the norm, the studio establishes a shared culture of responsibility that focuses on project outcomes emerging as a result of team initiatives and twenty-first-century skills development in the liberal tradition.

Case Narrative

Elon University offers students engagement with both liberal arts and professional programs in a residential campus setting. The university's small size affords flexibility and cooperation across disciplines while faculty remain strong in our disciplinary approaches; we also are large enough to provide students with a wide array of majors, minors, and experiential learning opportunities. In this academic setting, students gain exposure to and participate in experiential learning, but the outcomes of these experiences are often limited to course-centric graded assignments, volunteerism, or superficial exposure to issues affecting populations. Our goal for the studio was to move beyond one-off experiences to build a model that places student-led initiatives at the forefront.

Additionally and luckily for us, Elon is a place that both values innovation and pursues it with great commitment. At the time our idea for the studio was beginning to percolate, others around campus were considering immersive and/or design-based approaches in our core curriculum and entrepreneurship programs, and the administration had begun to work with a potential donor who was interested in financially supporting design thinking programming on campus. After conversations with leaders and administrators on campus, we moved forward to create a program proposal and, after approval, a pilot program.

Radical Innovation in Action: A Short Story

Our work together began with a meetup in a small coffee shop to discuss a mundane topic: how to integrate agile project management techniques more meaningfully into our teaching methods. After a few moments of discussing how each of us uses agile approaches in our courses, we collectively decided that a typical class structure is incompatible with these methodologies. But we knew we had found our "wicked problem."[1] The demand for twenty-first-century skills extends from the demand for graduates to become productive members of cross-functional teams. The structures of academia impede at best, and stifle at worst, the imaginative environments that can allow students to put their skills into action. Moreover, we had hit on a problem that has plagued educators: the perils and pitfalls of long-term, interdependent group work.

Agile is a great framework for this type of work, but we all recognized that typical courses and classrooms do not allow students to experience the dynamics that emerge when they attempt to build something new, to innovate, to stretch beyond what's comfortable, to take risks, and to learn how to fail productively. As we brainstormed, we observed several problems:

- The average college student typically takes several unrelated courses a semester; each course meets two or three times a week for a set number of minutes in the same location on campus.
- Students tend to focus on individual outcomes and grades based on tidy assignment rubrics and specific faculty expectations.
- Their group work often relies on old habits, such as divide-and-conquer approaches or a dependence on the strongest student to carry the load.
- When completing major assignments or projects, students spend little time on incorporating feedback, and they don't structure revision time into their workflow.

In short, their achievements are individualized, and their focus often results in developing skills that help them to be "good at school."

Agile methodologies, in contrast, focus everyone's attention on a common goal: a product or service developed collaboratively over an extended period of time. The team's performance is the unit of analysis; the individuals are evaluated on their contributions by others doing the work. Shorter sprints allow teams to focus on a certain feature or objective over a set period of time, typically a few weeks. Teams are composed of cross-functional professionals who bring specific skill sets to the table and share tasks equitably. Every team member's progress, accomplishments, struggles, and needs are aired publicly, allowing other teammates to jump in to help. All contributors share their works-in-progress often, allowing stakeholders and end users to provide formative feedback early in the design process. To complete the larger project outcome, teams iterate: they engage in several sprints, consider feedback, build a revised version of the product or service, and test again with the stakeholders. Each iteration is intended to improve on the previous one.

So how might we make space to deliver an authentic agile experience for students? What if our classroom-based project teams had the time and space to develop their collaboration skills across disciplines in a setting dedicated to giving them the chance to imagine, try, and fail productively along the way?

Inspired by our institution's commitment to immersive learning through high-impact practices, we created the Design Thinking Studio in Social Innovation to leverage the benefits of immersion without the overt structures of higher education. Pedagogies such as study abroad, service learning, internships, and practicums are experiential learning strategies that get students out of the typical classroom, have them engage with people who are external to the university, and are often immersive in some way. Interesting things happen when you place students in immersive experiences, and we intentionally designed the program with immersion in mind.

Innovation Details

The key innovation of our program was that in a sixteen-semester-hour experience, student cohorts would work with faculty and community leaders in cross-functional teams using the agile sprint model. Rather than register for a set of separate courses, as would be typical, studio students would register just for this single program for their semester. Then, as a cohort, the students would collaborate with program faculty and a set of partners concerned about community wellness to design interventions for identified local problems. After networking across campus, we were able to offer students course credit for one advanced studies course, their required core curriculum capstone, and our professional writing studies interdisciplinary minor. In the first semester, we negotiated for several students to earn credit in their major programs as well.

The two pilot semesters of the studio were co-developed by the three authors of this chapter and a colleague from computing sciences, and the program was co-taught by three of us. We worked with our provost, deans, and department chairs to arrange course reassignments and other logistical issues related to load and contract hours. As part of the program design, we built in research about teaching and learning, and William Moner, who was the nonteaching program co-designer, served as a student-to-faculty ombudsperson during the semester.

To get started, we were drawn to the idea of a "social lab" and found inspiration in Zaid Hassan's *Social Labs Revolution*.[2] Hassan shows that social innovation is possible when problems are understood at the level of interaction with affected populations, and viable solutions often emerge from a sustained practice of co-designing with the community. Hassan's book engages with the Aristotelian concepts of *episteme*, *techne*, and *phronesis*, structures that allow innovative spaces to emerge and also permit those spaces to be theoretical, technical, and praxis-driven. With these concepts in mind, the tool sets selected for our social innovation design studio were cast in a supporting role as the problems found in the community took center stage.

We were also inspired by a mix of strategies based on design thinking as an overarching framework, derived mainly from the formative work of IDEO (and Stanford University's d.school) and its five-step nonlinear method, which aligns nicely with agile approaches: empathize with the affected population, define the problem, ideate multiple ways to address the problem, select one and develop a prototype, and test with those who will benefit.[3] The designers then iterate until a product or service is ready for launch. To guide design sprints, we borrowed from the Google Ventures sprint model to create our new, innovative studio experience.[4] We wanted to truly see what happens when you break many of the rules of higher education in search of immersive learning.

Because the program was worth the same as four full courses, we met with students three hours per day, five days a week. Initially, this made sense; Elon has a three-week winter term, so it was a similar experience, but greatly extended over the course of a regular semester. Later, this became much harder to sustain for both faculty and students (see below).

Going into the semester, we collectively defined five key focus areas that would ground all course activities:

1. *Mindsets.* The design thinking process helps people to reframe their thinking about the world around them and about what constitutes a "good idea." The studio would provide a space for students to take intellectual risks, encounter and struggle with ambiguity, and strengthen their capacities for empathy, resilience, curiosity, and creativity.
2. *Processes and tools.* We wanted students to learn, practice, and implement the design thinking five-step process along with other techniques, including empathy interviewing and other inquiry methods, strategies for divergent and convergent thinking, Scrum to help with high-level team and project management, and the use of technologies in support of solutions.
3. *Professional communication.* To assist students in developing their communication skills, we would help them learn to write, speak, and design with rhetorical effectiveness. Students would learn how to understand contexts and audiences, choose and adapt relevant genres in different moments, design reader-friendly illustrations and information structures, and write in a variety of complex situations.
4. *Social innovation.* We approached social innovation from a more theoretical perspective, including readings and conversations about systems thinking, problem framing, asset-based approaches, and effective and respectful ways to interact and work with community leaders. This would allow students to collaborate effectively at a high level and to understand complex collaborative projects.
5. *Subject matter knowledge.* The studio's cross-functional team model encourages students to develop an understanding of how their majors, minors, and liberal arts foundation courses can be adapted, synthesized, and applied in real communities to approach complex human problems. They may not be experts in the problem area, but

their skill sets are valuable in collaboration with others. We cultivated relationships with two county collaboratives focused on community health and well-being and included ways for students to engage with community members before, during, and after their project experiences.

Because the "content" of the program is first, process and then, project, we asked all students to read only three books during our first three weeks with them: *Design Thinking: Understanding How Designers Think and Work* by Nigel Cross, *Creative Confidence: Unleashing the Creative Potential within Us All* by Tom Kelley and David Kelley, and *Social Labs Revolution* by Hassan.[5] During those early weeks, we also included shorter readings on empathy, curiosity, creativity, innovation, design, and collaboration.

The majority of the curriculum, both pre- and post-community project, was totally active. For example, in the first weeks of the semester we asked our students to get to know themselves by taking value inventories, articulating their personal goals, and introducing themselves to the group through a rapid-fire presentation. To help them get to know each other, students created "marketplace of skills" posters that visualized their skills and talents for their peers to see and discuss, and we organized regular team-building and collaboration activities. We also taught and practiced a variety of strategies for brainstorming via sticky notes and affinity mapping techniques; developed humancentric thinking abilities through empathy interviews, development of personas, and journey mapping; and practiced design iteration through paper prototyping, minimal viable product creations, and redesigning after feedback.

Following these design thinking boot-camp weeks, we transitioned into the community project work. We spent less time in our studio space and encouraged students to meet and shadow community partners, attend community meetings and workshops, develop and pitch project ideas, and continue to revise and present their best ideas. In the first pilot semester, this resulted in proposals for a local foodcentric community art project, gardening workshops for parents and students at the YMCA, and a passport that encouraged children to complete challenges around the small downtown to learn more about their community. In the second pilot semester, students focused on developing and presenting empathy-building and project management workshops for community partners, which they tested and refined multiple times.

Students also worked on developing and supporting the brand and web presence of the studio itself as part of their professional writing studies credits, and they completed capstone projects. Because students were also earning credit for their required core curriculum capstone course, they developed individual capstone projects based on some aspect of their work, which were presented at campus research forums. These included a choose-your-own adventure website to teach empathy awareness, photo essays on local wellness issues, videos promoting the liberal education benefits of the studio program, and podcasts on design and liberal arts topics.

Challenges and Outcomes

The program was successful in varying degrees at addressing the thinking, being, and doing skills and knowledge that we think are essential for students of liberal education today. Based on project outcomes, community partner responses, and assessment measures, our students learned how to be more empathetic, curious, creative, and persistent and to appreciate the journey and not just the formal outcome. The design thinking method allowed students to think creatively, produce solutions collaboratively, and work through roadblocks in a systematic way.

We learned that this type of environment requires as much attention to the emotional well-being of students and faculty as to the intellectual and creative. This program was unlike anything our students had experienced, and we were clear with both cohorts that the structure of the studio itself was a design challenge that we would be collectively iterating as we went. By enacting our goals to break the typical structures of higher education, we may have expected too much from our students, who are used to addressing predefined problems in well-articulated, short-term projects.

Even though we carefully scaffolded the projects, having students jump into a space where they had to define their own projects—and the criteria to evaluate them—was challenging. Students would vacillate between wanting us to tell them what to do and wanting the faculty to back off and let them do their own thing. Several students were so uncomfortable with some of the design processes, ambiguity, and risk associated with the open project space that they occasionally lashed out at the faculty or their peers or checked out for periods of time.

The scope of the community projects and the relationships with our partners were also challenging. Our schedules were not in sync; students had difficulty scheduling meetings with members of the organizations; and the representatives from the collectives were not decision makers for their organizations. These are common challenges in service learning courses, but because we were meeting every day and had expected to move into the community projects quickly, students felt defeated. When prompted to try something anyway, students often did not feel they had any authority to determine specific details. Sometimes, projects that seemed exciting were too small. Others were too large, making it impossible to complete them in one semester.

This type of program requires a great deal of energy and commitment from the faculty members and will only work when the teaching team has a good rapport and a high level of trust, is comfortable developing the course plans together in an integrated way, and acts as a unified front with the students. Because of the need to balance schedules and service commitments, faculty burnout and frustration became a real concern, especially for Rebecca Pope-Ruark since she spent the most face-to-face time with students in the studio space. However, regular strategy meetings with our teaching team allowed us to stay ahead of the students and deal with challenging issues as they arose.

Concluding Thoughts, Next Steps

After running the program for two consecutive spring semesters, we still believe that two interventions are vital to learning in the twenty-first century: the opportunity for immersive learning and the opportunity to apply creative thinking through a structured process. The immersive nature of our program is a radical departure from the way higher education compartmentalizes and silos learning in disciplines, classes, and bounded structures. The immersive space allows for interaction between and among students, faculty, community members, and administrators, and it provides students with time to develop ideas while learning the critical skill of collaboration and focusing on project outcomes. Within this immersive structure, students had the opportunity to more deeply engage with communities to understand empathy as an important first step and a framing concept for any intervention, product, or service they create.

As we wrote this chapter, the studio did not meet enrollment requirements to run for a third semester. We are now grappling with how to share our lessons learned in hopes of bridging our model with other schools and departments at Elon that have demonstrated a need for immersive, transdisciplinary experiences. The chance to deeply engage with one endeavor, instead of four or five at a time, enables students to focus in ways that they cannot in most other education structures. Over the next year, we will work closely with our partners all over campus to decide how to iterate the program and move forward. Options we are considering include an eight-credit model and a narrowed scope of the community problem space.

The Design Thinking Studio in Social Innovation pilot program is a good representation of what can happen when you innovate quickly in higher education. We were lucky to move from idea to pilot very rapidly. Our experience shows that not all innovations go well the first or even the second time, but if we want to succeed in reframing the narrative of the value of a liberal education for the twenty-first-century student, we need time, space, and opportunity to try, fail, and revise as many times as it takes to determine if an innovation can make the difference.

KEY TAKEAWAYS

Start small, and be relentless. Your idea for transformative learning has value and merit, but the ideal model may not be feasible—at least not yet. Nonetheless, start somewhere. Our innovation is a product of smaller initiatives that got started as class assignments, one-off projects, research agendas, curiosities, and more. If your idea requires something other than a typical course load, remember that it will take more effort on the part of faculty and administrators too.

Seek and cultivate productive faculty, administrative, and community relationships. In our case, we found that key colleagues loved our initial idea and provided the support to move it forward. Each conversation helped to clarify how this model could develop. Ensure that campus and community partners appoint a representative to be a consistent point of contact throughout a project. The most significant support came from university centers whose job it is to make community connections to nonprofits.

Know your limits, and bend them without breaking them. Each institution faces different pressures in terms of launching and supporting new programs. Find the people who will be honest about what it takes to launch your program, particularly those who ask tough questions and see the institution from unique perspectives. An associate provost grilled us on how we might handle different student scenarios, including illnesses, leaves of absence, and attendance issues, and our program was better because of our awareness of these limitations up front.

Establish a structure for students and room for creative exploration. We found that using design thinking techniques for creativity and Scrum-based project management methods for collaboration provided enough structure for students to develop their ability to communicate well. We encourage an openness to productive models from other disciplines. Our studio learned a lot from our public health students trained in community-based interventions, and we found those approaches to be surprisingly compatible with design thinking.

Students are the X factor, and recruitment is hard. The long-term success of any program requires sustained recruiting efforts, thoughtful articulations with existing curricula, promotion of the program during advising sessions, and campus-wide awareness. We found success in recruiting students in the two pilot years through a combination of luck, support from the registrar and the provost's office, receptive department chairs, and flexible deans. Our best allies, though, were a few charismatic students who convinced others to join up. Nonetheless, our program required a lot of energy to build the social capital needed to launch.

Notes

1. Horst W. J. Rittel and Melvin M. Webber, "Dilemmas in a General Theory of Planning," *Policy Sciences* 4, no. 3 (1973): 155–169.

2. Zaid Hassan, *The Social Labs Revolution: A New Approach to Solving our Most Complex Challenges* (San Francisco, CA: Berrett-Koehler, 2014).

3. IDEO U, "Design Thinking," n.d., https://www.ideou.com/pages/design-thinking; Hasso Plattner Institute of Design, Stanford University, "A Virtual Crash Course in Design Thinking," n.d., https://dschool.stanford.edu/resources-collections/a-virtual-crash-course-in-design-thinking; Rebecca Pope-Ruark, "Where Did Agile and Scrum Come From?" *Agile Faculty*, November 17, 2014, https://agilefaculty.wordpress.com/2014/11/17/first-post.

4. See Google Ventures, "The Design Sprint," n.d., https://www.gv.com/sprint.

5. Nigel Cross, *Design Thinking: Understanding How Designers Think and Work* (London: Bloomsbury, 2011); Tom Kelley and David Kelley, *Creative Confidence: Unleashing the Creative Potential within Us All* (New York: Crown, 2013); Hassan, *Social Labs Revolution*.

11 Failing Forward
Writing, Design, and Organic Curricular Change at Georgetown University

Maggie Debelius, Sherry Lee Linkon, and Matthew Pavesich

Radical Vision

Writing is an essential catalyst in a liberal arts education, a way for students to act on the world, not just to demonstrate knowledge or respond to professors' questions. We envision writing courses that are engaged, messy, public, and focused on creative problem solving, much like design. A design studio approach to writing fosters the kinds of integrative thinking, feeling, and doing that define a liberal education. This model challenges students to wrestle with wicked problems, to experiment and learn from failure, and to address audiences beyond the classroom.[1] This can enrich students' experiences and inspire an ethos of creativity, iteration, failure, and transformation among faculty.

Institutional Profile

Founded in 1789, Georgetown University is a highly selective, private Jesuit institution serving 7,500 undergraduates. The university's core curriculum requires a first-year writing course and attention to writing within the major, as well as courses in philosophy, theology, and science. Many Georgetown students complete theses or capstone projects involving independent research in their majors.

Introduction

The Georgetown University Writing Program has developed an extended experiment with first-year and advanced writing courses that use design studio practices, such as project-centered learning, design thinking strategies, engagement with real audiences, and frequent critique, including from individuals outside of the class and the university community. These strategies open the classroom and reinforce for faculty and students alike the connections between writing, the liberal arts, and civic life. Embracing experimentation, iteration, and failure has transformed our vision for the writing classroom, and it has enhanced our work with colleagues within our program and across campus.

Ours is as much a case of faculty learning as it is of student learning. Initial discussions among faculty with expertise in writing, literary and media studies, teaching and learning, filmmaking, art, and computer science generated a proposal for an innovative certificate, the Studio in Design and Communication (SDC), aimed at undergraduates in the liberal arts. When that proposal was rejected by a campus curriculum committee (largely because we proposed alternative methods for rewarding credit), we incorporated some of its strategies into writing courses at multiple levels.

In our courses, students deploy user-centered design to develop responses to wicked problems, and frequent critiques and iteration help them develop ambitious and creative projects. Students have developed proposals to change university policies, produced promotional materials for nonprofit organizations, created podcasts and video series about social issues, and designed an educational escape room in collaboration with research librarians. Such work integrates research, consultation with campus and community experts, and significant collaboration. These courses help students to see writing not simply as a discrete skill but as a way of thinking and acting that crosses disciplines, domains, and semesters, thus enacting the key elements of a liberal education.

By incorporating design studio approaches into a variety of writing settings, we have been able to reach hundreds of students, and our experiences have encouraged colleagues to experiment with these methods. As the spread of this work suggests, the initial failure of the SDC became an opportunity for a significant, distributed success.

Case Narrative

Our application of design studio methods to writing instruction developed in response to several specific changes and opportunities. First, the Georgetown University Writing Program needed to update and engage its first-year writing course more fully with contemporary writing pedagogies. Our faculty, many of whom were trained as literary scholars, were uncertain about how to incorporate rhetorical analysis or add multimodal and public-oriented writing to the academic essays and research papers with which they were most comfortable. Additionally, a new integrated writing requirement compelled departments to increase attention to writing in the disciplines. As faculty leaders in the Writing Program, we faced the challenge of inspiring and guiding our colleagues' engagement with writing pedagogy.

Our efforts were in turn inspired and encouraged by a campus-wide initiative, Designing the Futures of the University, which supported new courses and curricula that emphasize experiential, problem-based, integrative learning. Along with promoting innovation and collaboration, Designing the Futures highlights design thinking and studio methods.

The writing design studio emerged from these conditions. We needed to model innovation in first-year writing and to support writing across campus, while Designing the Futures provided opportunities for collaboration and shared faculty learning and innovation. Rather than making incremental changes in pedagogical practices in our program, local conditions encouraged us to lean into the radical difference of design-based writing pedagogy.

As we began our work on the writing design studio, two key models were coming to the fore in writing studies: threshold concepts, which articulates the core ideas that students should learn about writing, and teaching for transfer, which aims to help students prepare to adapt strategies and ideas from their first-year writing in subsequent writing situations. While these approaches suggest the value of overt attention to concepts, they also point to an important new goal: to develop students' agility as writers. This shift reflects a growing emphasis in twenty-first-century liberal education on preparing students for contexts and challenges that we cannot yet envision (see, for example, Cathy Davidson's *The New Education* and Joseph Aoun's *Robot-Proof*).[2] Students must develop flexibility and creativity along with core knowledge. They must not only write good academic essays but also be prepared to write in varied situations during college, in the workplace, and in civic life.

Two other areas in writing studies also fueled our explorations: postpedagogy and attention to design and making. In postpedagogy, which emerged from Thomas Kent's post-process work, scholars such as Byron Hawk, Paul Lynch, and others have advocated for understanding teaching as the assemblage of learning environments and a series of often unpredictable experiences rather than as the transfer of knowledge from teacher to student.[3] If teaching is more assembly than explanation, and writing is more intervention than assertion, then an emphasis on making objects, including but hardly limited to texts, provides both a way of framing projects and a link between rhetoric and design. This approach has been developed through research by Kristin L. Arola, Jennifer Sheppard, and Cheryl E. Ball; Carrie S. Leverenz; Richard Marback; James P. Purdy; and David Sheridan.[4]

We have drawn on all of these models, incorporating transfer studies' focus on agility, the liberal arts' interest in synthesis and human engagement, postpedagogy's attention to environment and experience, and design's emphasis on user/audience empathy, complexity, and materiality. Weaving these approaches together has allowed us to develop a pedagogy that emphasizes how writing makes connections within the liberal arts and between college and professional and civic life.

Innovation Details

The writing design studio emerged from work with two colleagues from Georgetown's master of arts program in communications, culture, and technology—computer scientist Evan Barba and art and media studies scholar J. R. Osborn—starting in 2014. We developed a proposal for the Studio in Design and Communication, a twelve-credit certificate centered on a sequence of four studios in which students would design innovative communications projects. We envisioned a small program, annually serving about twenty students, who would earn credits based not on course time or enrollment but on how the work they produced demonstrated their understanding of eight proficiencies: craft, reflection, observation, research, communication, contextualizing, envisioning, and persistence.

Even before we completed the SDC proposal and before the university review committee rejected it, we had begun incorporating ideas from those conversations into our courses. These included a rhetoric course in which students collaborated with peers enrolled in two "content" courses to design interventions for complex health and policy problems; first-year writing courses in which students developed strategies to address campus problems; and the English Department's capstone master's seminar, in which students developed public-facing digital projects as an alternative to writing a thesis. We also offered a one-semester version of the Studio in Design and Communication and a course on the public humanities.

Our work had important roots in conversations with Barba and Osborn and the emphasis on design thinking and studio pedagogy that was central to the Designing the Futures initiative.[5] and we have built on those inspirations in our own courses and in discussions with colleagues about teaching in various settings. Throughout this process, we have approached the writing design studio as an extended experiment, consulting frequently with each other and inviting critiques from our colleagues and students. Our ongoing experimental experience parallels the learning by doing process that students experience in our design studio courses. It has been exploratory, interactive, and iterative.

Specific Innovations

To prepare twenty-first-century students for critical engagement in civic and professional life—the core of a reimagined liberal education—

undergraduate education should involve engaged, self-directed, collaborative, problem-based inquiries. Three specific elements of the writing design studio enact this pedagogical shift, offering students opportunities to reimagine writing as a critical intervention in civic and professional life.

First, our courses focus on complex problems rather than concepts, themes, or readings. For example, some courses ask students to identify complex problems in the university or a local neighborhood. They then conduct research, develop an intervention, produce the communications necessary to implement that intervention, and test their ideas with stakeholders. These assignments sometimes ask students to work with clients, including organizational partners, and they address audiences beyond the class itself. Students often work on these projects in teams, sometimes with students from other courses. These elements add complexity, and they mirror common practices in professional work and community settings. Through these projects, students come to understand and practice writing as creative, integrative, strategic, and significant beyond the classroom.

Second, a design approach complicates the familiar "outline, draft, revise" sequence of the traditional writing course by locating the development of texts in a user-centered, problem-solving process that emphasizes experimentation, critique, and iteration. This amplifies and accelerates two common elements of writing pedagogy: faculty and peer reviews of drafts and an emphasis on revision. In the writing design studio, critiques begin with frequent informal conversations, or "desk crits," as students analyze problems and develop ideas, and the feedback continues through presentations where visiting experts and users critique existing prototypes. Iteration occurs throughout the process in response to these critiques. Unlike the peer review meetings of typical writing courses, critique panels make clear that students' writing addresses real audiences and has real consequences. They also inspire substantive revision, because this form of critique often emphasizes larger-scale concerns and makes clear the stakes of intervening in complex issues.

Third, the design studio broadens the community of the classroom. The more students understand that they are writing to people outside of their writing class, the more they recognize the stakes of their interventions. Never merely a classroom community, the writing design studio intersects with other communities in complex ways. Research in these courses often involves interviews and surveys alongside secondary research. The artifacts students create explicitly address specific audiences, particular organizations, and individuals other than their professors. In one instance, students designed packaging for a major pharmacy, which was aimed at persuading patients to complete their antibiotic prescriptions in order to slow the rise of antibiotic resistance. Another group curated an art exhibit (installed temporarily at the National Institutes of Health) aimed at raising awareness of genetic privacy in the age of commercialized ancestry products and DNA testing. Others have recommended strategies for addressing the high cost of textbooks, improving awareness of resources for victims of sexual assault, and increasing peer support programs for students experiencing anxiety.

Implementation and Iteration

Although we were frustrated that our proposal for the SDC was rejected, the insights generated through that design and failure process proved invaluable and—even better—transferable. We have drawn on ideas from that project in a dozen iterations of design studio courses. In addition to our own iterations, these ideas have been taken up by our colleagues. For example, the director of the Writing Center redesigned the course that trains tutors, and students now develop ideas for how the center could better serve the campus. Faculty have also used design studio pedagogy for multimedia and public projects in courses in English, learning and design, and urban studies.

The expansion of design studio pedagogies across campus brings challenges, especially around space. Classrooms with modular furniture, whiteboards, and lots of wall space for displaying project mock-ups work best for studio-based courses, but those types of rooms are limited on most campuses. Ideally, students would also have access to dedicated studio rooms, where they could work on and store projects outside of regular class hours, but such spaces are even more scarce. We have responded to these constraints by bringing studio materials, like large post-it pads and markers, into our classrooms. We also emphasize design techniques that students can use in any setting and encourage online collaboration. These adaptations encourage students to view design studio practices as applicable to their work in other courses and in their professional and civic lives. While space and tools matter, the engaged and energetic ethos of the design studio does more to frame the work of students and faculty than any particular classroom configuration ever could.

Outcomes and Assessment

Across our courses, we have been encouraged to see students' work improve through experimentation, iteration, and critique as they develop their projects. We continue to evaluate and refine our approach, looking at evidence of learning both in the projects that students complete and in their reflective writing. A particular concern is how to help students recognize more clearly the value of their work in these courses. While our students have produced some excellent final projects and sophisticated reflections on their rhetorical choices and potential impact, some also have commented that they wished they "had done more writing." Even granting the problematic nature of student evaluations, we are troubled that students can hit all the marks that presumably foster transferable rhetorical agility yet not understand how their research, composition, making, and social engagement (text-based and otherwise) is "writing." Clearly, we have more to do on clarifying for students our expanded vision of writing. Happily, we have adopted a learning and growth mindset as faculty. The insights provided by failure will inspire further iterations to a pedagogy we find generally productive and exciting.

Unexpected Benefits, Challenges, and Failures

In redesigning our writing courses and reexamining writing's role in the liberal arts, we are also redefining our roles as faculty leaders in writing and pedagogy, shifting the emphasis from our disciplinary expertise in writing studies to our interest in and connections with students and colleagues across campus. Instead of emphasizing the specialized knowledge of writing studies—a central theme in work around threshold concepts and teaching for transfer—we approach writing as transdisciplinary and integrative. This defines writing as an adaptable element of strategic and creative problem solving and the writing program as a site of experimentation and innovation. It also positions us as curious researchers, actively seeking to learn from and with our colleagues. In this way, our engagement with design studio pedagogy has enabled us to strengthen our collaborative relationships on campus.

Concluding Thoughts, Next Steps

Looking ahead, the Writing Program envisions developing advanced writing offerings through additional collaboration. For example, we will use a design studio approach in a course called Writing for Impact for students in Georgetown's new Capitol Applied Learning Lab—a semester-long experiential learning program that integrates internships, locally oriented coursework, and personal and professional development—by using writing and design to help students connect their classroom learning with their internships. We are also planning a collaborative Writing Program-wide design charette ambitiously tasked with reimagining our first-year writing course. Put simply, our work as teachers and as faculty leaders continues to be shaped by what we have learned over the last few years.

In our courses and with these methods, we now invite our students to pursue projects that they cannot at first imagine in general or as "writing." Similarly, just as we could not know when we began how the SDC planning process would infuse our teaching and outreach work, we cannot yet predict exactly where these approaches will take us, even as we remain committed to experimenting with them. Until, that is, we inevitably fail forward and begin to imagine whatever comes next.

KEY TAKEAWAYS

Every piece of advice we offer applies to ourselves as well as to our students. Like our students, we are writers and designers who are testing and iterating designs as we prepare our courses and collaborate with colleagues across the university.

Start with wicked problems. Design studio pedagogy combines Paulo Freire's emphasis on problems that matter to students with a bias toward action and complexity. Significant, complex, messy problems make for better learning, and these qualities are common in the problems we work on with our colleagues as well.

Establish community. Collaboration is essential for writers and designers, and students need time to get to know each other and develop trust. This has also been important as we have learned from, collaborated with, and inspired our colleagues to experiment with studio learning.

Build a network. To support students' work on real-world projects, faculty need colleagues—other faculty, staff, previous students, and professionals from the local community—to provide advice and to participate in critiques. Building a studio network has nudged us closer to the integrated, unsiloed, interdisciplinary, and multidisciplinary approach that the editors of this volume called for in the introduction. Our network has helped us improve our courses and connected us with colleagues in other departments around issues of writing and design.

Teach critique, not criticism. Studio pedagogy relies on critique, but students need to learn how to offer productive feedback and respond strategically to suggestions from outside experts. Teaching critique techniques like the "I like, I wish" response to projects has proved generative and has helped students see that these projects weren't about correctness but about learning through iteration. We also had to learn to work through the critiques on our original proposal, moving from frustration to iteration as we developed a larger and more meaningful project in which our critics became our collaborators.

Know that space matters (but you can work within constraints). While it is ideal to have a designated studio space with appropriate conditions, including space to store projects and the ability to access it outside of class time, many of us only have access to traditional classrooms for three scheduled hours per week. Portable materials and an emphasis on design strategies can make the studio less space-dependent—and foster students' ability to transfer these practices to other settings.

Embrace failure. The studio model shifts the emphasis from teaching particular content or skills to providing students with opportunities to build competence and confidence by experimenting and sometimes failing—and learning from that failure. Failure is valuable for faculty as well, and in our case it inspired a guerrilla approach to curricular change that generated variations of the studio across the curriculum. Don't give up when you encounter institutional obstacles to innovation. Good ideas will spread.

Make room for students' voices and reflections in assessment. Some of the best evidence of student learning—and our most important insights on these courses—have come from students' assessments of their own work. Even when their work does not turn out as well as they or we might wish, students' writing about what they learned in the process makes their learning visible to us and to them, and it foregrounds the personal and professional value of their work. This has been true for us as well. Reflecting on what worked and what failed throughout this process has helped us sharpen our goals and build an alternative model that we are proud of.

Notes

1. Richard Marback, "Embracing Wicked Problems: The Turn to Design in Composition Studies," *College Composition and Communication* 61, no. 2 (2009): 397–413.

2. Cathy N. Davidson, *The New Education: How to Revolutionize the University to Prepare Students for a World in Flux* (New York: Basic, 2017); Joseph E. Aoun, *Robot-Proof: Higher Education in the Age of Artificial Intelligence* (Cambridge, MA: MIT Press, 2017).

3. Byron Hawk, *A Counter-History of Composition: Toward Methodologies of Complexity* (Pittsburgh, PA: University of Pittsburgh Press, 2007); Paul Lynch, *After Pedagogy: The Experience of Teaching* (Urbana, IL: National Council of Teachers of English, 2013); Megan M. McIntyre, "Reflection, Detours, and Postpedagogical Practice," *Textshop Experiments* 2 (2016), http://textshopexperiments.org/textshop02/reflection-detours-and-postpedagogical-practice; Marc C. Santos and Mark H. Leahy, "Postpedagogy and Web Writing," *Computers and Composition* 32 (2014): 84-95; Marc C. Santos and Megan M. McIntyre, "Toward a Technical Communication Made Whole: Disequilibrium, Creativity, and Postpedagogy," *Composition Forum* 33 (2016), http://compositionforum.com/issue/33/techcomm.php.

4. Kristin L. Arola, Jennifer Sheppard, and Cheryl E. Ball, *Writer/Designer: A Guide to Making Multimodal Projects* (Boston: Bedford/St. Martin's, 2014); Carrie S. Leverenz, "Design Thinking and the Wicked Problem of Teaching Writing," *Computers and Composition* 33 (2014): 1-12; Marback, "Embracing Wicked Problems"; James P. Purdy, "What Can Design Thinking Offer Writing Students?," *College Composition and Communication* 65, no. 4 (2014): 612-641; David Sheridan, "Fabricating Consent: Three-Dimensional Objects as Rhetorical Compositions," *Computers and Composition* 24, no. 4 (2010): 249-265; David Sheridan, "A Maker Mentality toward Writing," *Digital Rhetoric Collaborative*, March 28, 2016, http://www.digitalrhetoriccollaborative.org/2016/03/28/a-maker-mentality-toward-writing.

5. The centrality of these approaches in Bass's University as a Design Problem course and in the Designing the Futures initiative is discussed in the last chapter of Davidson's *New Education*.

12 Educating Business Leaders for a Better World at George Mason University

Lisa Gring-Pemble, Anne M. Magro, and Jacquelyn Dively Brown

Radical Vision

Liberal education is key to the future of people, the planet, and prosperity as we collectively tackle society's complex problems. Regardless of discipline, students need the twenty-first-century skills that a liberal education develops in order to succeed and to benefit society. Our vision is that liberal education will be integrated into all academic programs, not just through core or general education checklists but as an integral part of every discipline. Business education increasingly shares liberal education's goals of developing students with "a sense of social responsibility, as well as strong and transferable intellectual and practical skills such as communication, analytical and problem-solving abilities, and a demonstrated capacity to apply knowledge and skills in real-world settings."[1] An integrated approach combining business with liberal education prepares students to contextualize their business knowledge in order to address complex problems in a diverse and changing world.

Institutional Profile

George Mason University, with four campuses in northern Virginia and Korea, is a public, research 1, doctoral university enrolling more than 38,000 students representing all US states and more than 130 countries. With 40 percent first-generation students, 30 percent Pell Grant recipients, and more than 50 percent nonwhite students, Mason provides access to excellence for students from traditionally underserved communities.

Introduction

As Vincent Stanley, the director of philosophy at Patagonia, suggests, "We live in a time of social and environmental crisis. . . . To put things right will require an unprecedented level of cooperation and civic engagement on the part of human beings. We will need responsive government; strong, engaged NGOs and nonprofits; and socially and environmentally responsible businesses to produce our goods and services."[2] As this chapter evinces, business schools can play a critical role in this effort. We explore how the new Business Foundations curriculum at Mason integrates liberal education with traditional business curricula to provide students with twenty-first-century skills, context, and technical business knowledge necessary for lifelong learning, professional excellence, and community engagement.

Foundations offers integrative, hands-on problem-solving experiences to students from across the university.[3] Foundations sparks students' passion, educates changemakers, and transforms students' aspirations into meaningful and lasting impact. The curriculum is unique in at least three ways. First, the curriculum approaches business from a liberal arts perspective, bringing faculty viewpoints from disciplines across the university into the business school to the benefit of our faculty and students. Second, while it is unusual for business school courses to be included in university core curricula, several Foundations courses were designated as Mason core courses in recognition of their liberal education approach. Third, Foundations is a nontechnical business curriculum targeted at first- and second-year students to help them develop a broader perspective on the impact of business and their path as leaders before they begin studying the technical aspects that typically make up the curriculum.

When students from multiple disciplines come together to discuss the role of business in the world, the exchange of ideas allows our students to consider perspectives on business that may differ from their own. The courses have been extremely popular with business and non-business students alike. We initially anticipated offering 30 sections in this curriculum and ultimately offered 45 in our first semester, the fall of 2015. Four years in, we are offering 160 sections with nonbusiness students making up 15-45 percent of enrollment in our lower-level courses.

Importantly, Foundations does not operate in a vacuum. Rather, it serves as a foundation for technical business studies and is later reinforced in core and specialization courses as well as through cocurricular activities during our students' academic journey. Ultimately, we aspire to educate business leaders for a better world via a liberal arts approach.

Case Narrative

Located outside Washington, DC, Mason provides its students with access to rich cultural experiences and sought-after internships and employers. Recognized for innovation, entrepreneurship, diversity, and accessibility, Mason is noted for strong retention and graduation rates of historically underrepresented students, who have equivalent rates to other students. Mason Business enrolls more than 570 graduate students and 4,500 undergraduate students pursuing five majors. With unprecedented undergraduate enrollment growth of more than 56 percent from the fall of 2015 to the fall of 2019, Mason Business serves more than 3,000 nonbusiness students through Foundations, minors, and cocurriculars.

At Mason, liberal education is delivered through the Mason Core, a general education program designed to support the development of the Mason graduate—an engaged citizen and well-rounded scholar who is prepared to act. The Mason Core emphasizes skills (e.g., effective communication, quantitative reasoning, digital literacy), exploration (e.g., art, literature, Western civilization, social and behavioral sciences), and integration (e.g., synthesis or capstone project). Prior to our curriculum redesign, the Mason Core included no business courses. Our challenge was to redesign our undergraduate program in order to engage with our students early and often and to provide an experiential, multidisciplinary, and problem-based curriculum designated as Mason Core.

Mason Business previously faced several challenges in its undergraduate program, including a lack of connection with and engagement from students, and employer and alumni concerns that our graduates, while technically strong, did not possess twenty-first-century skills or a sufficiently robust understanding of business contexts. We recognized that business education is, first and foremost, education and not simply training for the workplace. We challenged the false dichotomy of liberal education versus professional education by integrating both approaches to develop stronger future leaders for the organizations that shape our world. By integrating liberal arts into the business context, aligning with the university's general education requirements, and targeting first- and second-year students, Foundations resolved these major challenges.

Business schools consider the needs of external stakeholders, such as employers, community partners, and alumni, as well as the motivations of students and their parents. To maintain the currency of our curriculum and best serve our constituents, Mason Business regularly meets with external stakeholders to discuss their needs, views of the future, and experiences with our students. While prepared for their first jobs, our graduates did not necessarily feel prepared for what lay five or ten years beyond.[4] A literature review on employer expectations published in 2012 revealed a shared perspective that recent graduates lag in professional skills.[5]

At the same time, calls for more liberal arts graduates have been published in leading business journals, and books extolling the value of a liberal arts education have created buzz in the popular press.[6] We chose to flip that frame and bring the liberal arts to our business students. Thus, we redesigned our business curriculum to focus on developing twenty-first-century skills as described in the introduction to this volume by adding Foundations, integrating experiential learning opportunities, and reinforcing Foundations skills throughout later courses and programming.

Innovation Details

Like many business schools, we admitted students in their junior year or later. Students spent two years taking classes outside the School of Business, except for two required preadmission courses. Business students engaged with other disciplines as they completed the Mason Core but had no opportunities to integrate what they were learning in history or sociology into their business courses. By moving to a direct-admit approach where students can enter the business school in their first semester and by building out a first- and second-year curriculum that offered at least one business class each semester, students gained the opportunity to study business simultaneously with nonbusiness courses. While the simultaneity of courses enhances potential connection making, simultaneity alone does not ensure that students fully integrate their learning. By using the liberal arts to approach business as a topic of study, Foundations maximizes the integration of student learning across the liberal arts and professional disciplines.

Foundations is a sequence of seven courses introducing students to the social, global, professional, decision-making, and legal contexts of business. Crossing disciplinary boundaries, course topics include leadership and collaboration, global political economy, ethics, diversity, conflict management, emotional intelligence, critical thinking, creative thinking, problem framing and problem solving, information literacy, and communication and persuasion. To deliver the curriculum, we hired faculty with a range of academic backgrounds; PhDs in history, German, rhetoric, communications, and political science sit side by side with PhDs in business and JDs. Realizing that students' first class in a discipline molds their thinking about the entire school and field,[7] Foundations faculty teach small classes (twenty to sixty students) and commit to high-impact practices, such as interactive classroom activities and problem-based learning. Our classrooms contain students of all majors, allowing business students to rub elbows with economists, philosophers, global health advocates, artists, and engineers.

Across Foundations, we emphasize development of the four categories of twenty-first-century skills: intellectual (critical thinking, creative thinking, problem solving, self-directed learning, creativity, curiosity, comfort with ambiguity, flexibility/adaptability); applied (analysis and synthesis); ethical (moral reasoning and judgment); and social (collaboration). Our efforts to weave these learning outcomes into all Foundations courses underscores our commitment to integrated, unsiloed, and multidisciplinary approaches to understanding the world over the traditional separation of courses, degree structures, and departments. We recognize that the complex problems we face are bigger than one discipline or major, so we challenge students with big questions upon their arrival to campus.

Foundations courses fall into four groupings:

- Business and Society and Global Environment of Business both address the social and global contexts of business and focus on twenty-first-century skill categories.
- Developing Your Professional Skills I and II address professional contexts in order to develop skills that translate into success in college, the job market, and personal and professional life after graduation.
- Business Analytics I and II address decision-making contexts, since business leaders increasingly rely on data to inform decisions.
- Legal Environment of Business focuses on the legal context. Students develop personal and civic responsibility, negotiation skills, and the ability to question norms.

Three Innovative Exemplars

Three programs tied directly to Foundations are illustrative of our liberal education approach (Honey Bee Initiative, Escape Room Module, and Embedded Global Study). Notably, these distinctive programs/modules are problem-based, deliberative, collaborative inquiries into important professional and global issues. Each received funding from the university, Mason Business, and/or outside donors.

Honey Bee Initiative

A joint program of Mason Business and the College of Science, the Honey Bee Initiative (HBI) promotes trisector partnerships on behalf of sustainable business and is integrated into the curriculum as an illustration of social enterprise. Bees pollinate one-third of the food we eat and are the "most important pollinator worldwide."[8] However, honey bees are disappearing, and HBI is working to address this national- and food-security issue. HBI offers opportunities to engage in innovative teaching and research, community outreach, and study abroad. These activities are vital for developing twenty-first-century skills, promoting creative or entrepreneurial intelligence, and fostering lifelong learning and career success, all of which are critical to addressing "wicked" problems.[9] Working in multidisciplinary, collaborative teams to address sustainable development goals, food security, gender equity, and sustainable communities promotes intellectual (creative thinking, problem solving, questioning norms), applied (analysis and synthesis, rhetorical communication), ethical (ethical reasoning, empathy, personal and civic responsibility), and social (collaboration, social awareness, cross-cultural competency) skills. Mason students are enthusiastic about HBI. As one student observed: "I went from being afraid of bees to developing great appreciation . . . for the vital role they play in our ecosystem. I [saw] firsthand how the Honey Bee Initiative has developed a sustainable way to empower women and contribute to . . . economic growth."

Escape Room Module

A project designed collaboratively by faculty from Mason Business, the College of Humanities and Social Sciences, and the College of Visual and Performing Arts, this module in our Advanced Professional Skills course calls on students to create an escape room, which is then shared with students from its prerequisite to explore. Outcomes of the assignment are to deepen students' knowledge and application of professional skills and to promote the civic engagement outcomes of the Mason Core. This problem-based learning opportunity promotes students' individual and collaborative learning through an exploratory journey involving business issues, liberal education, and game design theory. It addresses critical thinking, problem solving, curiosity, technology skills, rhetorical communication strategies, collaboration, and teamwork while addressing core business competencies (e.g., ethics, leadership, diversity in the workplace). This experience prepares students for impactful careers by providing hands-on experience in problem solving and communication skills, and it helps bridge the gap between learning for the sake of learning versus learning focused on job readiness. In a sentiment shared by many, one student observed: "The assignment involved analysis, construction, writing, reading, time management, budget management, and so many other skills.... With a project that demands such variety ... multiple people [need to] step up.... How to manage long-term goals and the importance of contribution are definitely lessons we'll never forget."

Embedded Global Study

This course explores the global contexts of business through an investigation of political economics, international institutions, trade theories, global conflicts, and cooperation around key issues (e.g., labor, human rights, income distribution, the environment). Students complete a group project comparing and contrasting different foreign markets as possible expansion opportunities for a US company. Students can elect to participate in a global discovery trip to experience the markets they are analyzing (e.g., Italy, the United Kingdom, Spain, Morocco). Students observe firsthand the historical roles these countries played in the development of modern global business. The study abroad allows students to engage in authentic learning opportunities that address the role of business in society. Courses such as this promote curiosity, flexibility/adaptability, analysis and synthesis skills, personal and civic responsibility, and social awareness and competency. Many students expressed gratitude for the course's "diversity," which allowed "students to meet people from different backgrounds." As a result, many commented that this "liberal arts class" offered them a "practical application" of "problem solving in a global business environment."

Reinforcing Foundations: A Radical Vision in Action

Recall that our radical vision in creating Foundations has been to integrate liberal education into the Mason Business curriculum—not just through general education checklists. To realize our vision, this integration must continue beyond Foundations into our majors. Therefore, we reinforce Foundations through business core and specialization courses as well as cocurricular activities. Similarly, Foundations opens cocurricular opportunities to nonbusiness majors to complement other disciplines and fields of study. We provide several Mason Business-led programs highlighting our commitment to liberal education in line with this volume's radical vision statement (see introduction) and our resolve to fully integrate liberal education throughout the school.

We value students' personal learning goals, aspirations, and exploratory journeys. With this in mind, Mason Business has developed a variety of initiatives and centers, such as our Center for Innovation and Entrepreneurship. The CIE is an interdisciplinary hub that supports innovators and changemakers from across the university. From innovative courses and clubs to start-up trips and competitions, CIE offers participants opportunities to learn about creativity, innovation, and entrepreneurship; to experiment with concepts and tools; and to start a venture or initiative. Students explore concepts like corporate social responsibility, sustainability, and smart cities in Foundations classes, and CIE provides cocurricular experiences on campus and in the community for students to further explore ideas.

We value learning experiences that prepare students for vital careers and engagement with their communities. We support hands-on learning opportunities through our mentorship program and innovative courses with real-world application, such as Social Impact and Entrepreneurship and the George Mason Student-Managed Investment Fund. Students work through career services to pair with industry experts who share the students' passion and interests and provide invaluable insights through a structured mentoring process. Courses like Social Impact provide an experiential, business-oriented, multidisciplinary case approach to exploring the growing field of social innovation and enterprise. An embedded global study abroad trip to Colombia over spring break, partially funded through the Global Office and grants, enables our students to investigate trisector solutions to sustainable development goals by visiting and interviewing stakeholders (e.g., indigenous women, plantation owners, local mayors, university collaborators, funding agencies) in industries as diverse as coffee, cacao, trapiche, paper, and honey bees. Finally, the investment fund provides finance students with the opportunity to manage and monitor an actual portfolio and make all alteration decisions. The fund offers students a hands-on approach to market research, equity valuation, and risk analysis. These experiences require the application of twenty-first-century skills from the intellectual, applied, ethical, and social categories. Moreover, these experiences prepare students to transform their academic learning into meaningful practice aligned with their career aspirations.

A contemporary liberal education should not be based solely on disciplinary specialties without considering how those disciplines connect to, inform, and are informed by other disciplines and big questions. We are committed to innovative, integrated education in Foundations and beyond. Our focus on writing across the curriculum (WAC) is another way we reinforce interdisciplinarity, twenty-first-century skills, and addressing big questions across fields. While WAC is widespread in universities' humanities departments, WAC is not typically highlighted in business schools. Like most business schools, we previously required one writing-intensive business communications course. With the redesign, we mapped where significant writing was happening across existing courses, built dedicated professional skills courses in which we explicitly teach writing, and embedded significant written work into all Foundations courses, most of which offer feedback and revision opportunities. The university-required writing-intensive course was then shifted to the majors in order to highlight writing within the disciplines. Finally, we teamed with the English Department to pair English graduate students with business faculty and students to support our WAC efforts.

Concluding Thoughts, Next Steps

Foundations has been successful by many measures: increasing enrollment, sparking cross-disciplinary collaborations, and receiving positive stakeholder feedback. Students of all majors share enthusiasm for the courses. A biology major commented he "felt educated" on the "power I hold in society as a stakeholder of various businesses, corporations, and firms." A global health major said she "realize[d] how business concepts can be applied to a lot of other fields in the real world." A business major said he "witnessed multiple opportunities for networking, skill enhancement, and observing exactly how [to] contribute to social innovation and entrepreneurship with my skills."

Moving forward, we are building on Foundations and seeking ways to foster multidisciplinary, challenge-driven, experiential business education for a better world. We have renewed our commitment to the Principles of Responsible Management Education, a project of the UN Global Compact with more than 800 business school signatories. We also are engaged with many like-minded organizations, including the Academy of Business in Society, the Globally Responsible Leadership Initiative, the Aspen Institute Business and Society Program, the UN Sustainable Development Solutions Network, and Ashoka U. Such partnerships spark innovation, enthusiasm, and persistence in our quest to integrate liberal arts and business throughout our undergraduate and graduate curricula. We are fostering more partnerships with our school, students, alumni, and community in order to enhance contemporary and meaningful applications of business. And we are investigating ways to measure our impact and develop feedback loops with constituents and stakeholders to keep our curricular and cocurricular programs timely, relevant, and focused on the big questions.

KEY TAKEAWAYS

Create a sense of urgency for change. Following Kotter's model of leading change,[10] the first step is creating a sense of urgency around making a change. Pointing to data in the education literature and business press as well as our own data effectively convinced a critical mass of faculty and staff across the school that we needed to engage in curricula redesign. Feedback consistent with our message from recruiters, advisory boards, students, and alumni was crucial to creating urgency.

Hone your message, and build a core coalition. Craft a simple message conveying what you want to achieve, why you want it, and what positive outcomes will arise. For us it was: "Our stakeholders are telling us our students lack professional skills and can't contextualize their business knowledge. We propose to redesign the undergraduate curriculum to include a foundational curriculum grounded in the liberal arts to complement the study of technical business topics. Our graduates will be able to distinguish themselves from other graduates with the skills and knowledge they acquire through our curriculum and will be more successful in their professions." We then developed a core coalition of champions, including key internal and external stakeholders, to carry that message of change and actively embrace it.

Develop a critical mass of support. You need not get everyone on board for change, but you do need a substantial minority committed to the change and another substantial minority to support the change even if they are not champions. Then, convince as many of the remaining people as possible to stand to the side and let the change happen. Talk to people one-on-one to ensure there is something in the new curriculum they can get behind. Keep people informed, and listen to their feedback.

Identify and remove potential barriers. Think strategically about what could go wrong, anticipate opposing arguments, and build solutions into the plan. We knew we would face pressure from the rest of the university if our curriculum included so many business credits that students could not complete minors in other colleges. We worked hard, including dropping courses we believed would benefit a business student, to ensure that students could complete almost every minor available in the university without requiring additional credits to graduate.

Implement an imperfect plan. Don't let the desire to get it right stop your momentum. You probably will not make it perfect the first time. You must be willing to accept feedback, acknowledge mistakes, and make revisions. In this case, an old aphorism rings true: the perfect is the enemy of the good. You can build support for the program by acknowledging that the plan is not perfect and that you did not get everything you wanted. By so doing, you model that progress is incremental.

Generate quick wins and advertise them. People need to know that their work redesigning the curriculum and the painful process of running two curricula simultaneously while teaching out the old curriculum are paying off. Identifying and advertising quick wins is key to keeping people on board. One quick win for us was a 7 percent increase in enrollment in the year following the change. Sharing those quick wins and their impact on students, communities, and the university through multiple channels is vital to gaining and maintaining support.

Acknowledge (and reward) ongoing engagement, encourage iteration, and continue conversations. People need to know that innovation and risk taking are encouraged and rewarded. Highlighting innovative approaches allows for collegial recognition and motivates others to establish partnerships with units across the university. We offer pedagogy innovation grants, "lunch and learns" on pedagogical innovations, and research and teaching awards to celebrate and sustain excellence.

Notes

1. Association of American Colleges and Universities, "What Is Liberal Education?," n.d., https://www.aacu.org/leap/what-is-liberal-education.

2. Quoted in Yale Center for Business and the Environment, "An Entrepreneur's Guide to Certified B Corporations and Benefit Corporations," n.d., http://cbey.yale.edu/sites/default/files/CBEY_BCORP_Print.pdf.

3. Barbara J. Duch, Susan E. Groh, and Deborah E. Allen, *The Power of Problem-Based Learning: A Practical "How to" for Teaching Undergraduate Courses in Any Discipline* (Sterling, VA: Stylus, 2001).

4. Hart Research Associates, "Fulfilling the American Dream: Liberal Education and the Future of Work," July 2018, https://www.aacu.org/sites/default/files/files/LEAP/2018EmployerResearchReport.pdf.

5. "The Role of Higher Education in Career Development: Employer Perceptions," *Chronicle of Higher Education*, December 2012, https://chronicle-assets.s3.amazonaws.com/5/items/biz/pdf/Employers Survey.pdf.

6. Steve Sadove, "Employees Who Stand Out," *Forbes*, September 5, 2014, https://www.forbes.com/sites/realspin/2014/09/05/employees-who-stand-out/#4fde94fa69b0; Fareed Zakaria, *In Defense of a Liberal Education* (New York: Norton, 2016).

7. Beckie Supiano, "It Matters a Lot Who Teaches Introductory Courses: Here's Why," *Chronicle of Higher Education*, April 15, 2018, https://www.chronicle.com/article/it-matters-a-lot-who-teaches/243125.

8. United Nations, "UNEP Emerging Issues: Global Honey Bee Colony Disorders and Other Threats to Insect Pollinators," 2010, https://wedocs.unep.org/rest/bitstreams/14378/retrieve.

9. W. J. Horst and Melvin M. Webber, "Dilemmas in a General Theory of Planning," *Policy Sciences* 4, no. 2 (1973): 155-169.

10. J. P. Kotter, *Leading Change* (Boston: Harvard Business School Press, 1996).

13 Educating for Global Civic Participation and a Career
German Studies in the Twenty-First Century at Elon University

Scott Windham, Andrea A. Sinn, Kristin Lange, Derek Lackaff, Anthony Hatcher, Evan A. Gatti, and Janelle Papay Decato

Radical Vision

We advocate replacing rigid school-college distinctions with curricular pathways driven by students' goals and the world's needs. Pathways should have clear, assessable learning outcomes grounded in liberal education values, career readiness, and twenty-first-century skills, and they should feature classroom study and experiential learning. The locus of work in this model is flexible groupings of faculty, staff, and students, enabling individual choice and close mentoring. This approach improves learning and career success by letting students articulate goals and ways to achieve them but does not upend ingrained structures, such as credit hours, departments, or semesters. This vision rests on an existing reality: the commonalities among disciplines—and between experiential and classroom learning—transcend college-school divisions. These common liberal education values promote students' intellectual, civic, and career development in equal measure.

Institutional Profile

Elon University in Elon, North Carolina, is a private, not-for-profit, doctoral/professional university enrolling 7,000 students. It is a four-year, medium-size, highly residential institution with additional classification in community engagement. The university has a College of Arts and

Sciences and five professional schools: business, communications, education, health sciences, and law.

Introduction

Although justifiably proud of a liberal core curriculum required of every student, our institution has created physical and curricular divides between its College of Arts and Sciences and the professional schools, which do not reflect the teaching practices of the faculty.[1] Instead, we see a fundamental congruence of educational goals across school-college divisions—and between experiential and classroom education—that serves students' intellectual, career, and civic ethical development in equal measure. We also assert a fundamental congruence among liberal education values, twenty-first-century skills, and the abilities and habits of mind required in a career.

The German studies advisory board—a group of thirteen faculty and staff across the Colleges of Arts and Sciences, Business, Communications, and Global Education—values this congruence and has taken two steps to make it actionable. First was the creation of a flexible curriculum based on student choice and mentoring. In our newly redesigned curriculum, which has been thoroughly negotiated with departments, the administration, and academic support units, students collaborate with board members to design a curricular pathway that includes coursework from across campus along with experiential education. Students' choices are determined by their academic and career plans and the program's learning goals—communicative proficiency, critical problem solving, and intercultural competency—which are grounded in liberal values, career readiness, and twenty-first-century skills. Because students articulate connections among their learning experiences, their educational path is intentional and thoughtful, and their motivation is higher.[2]

Second was the creation of a faculty-staff board whose composition mirrors the curriculum. This intentional diversity brings new perspectives to our shared work, and the relationships that cut across campus units make possible the cross-disciplinary work promised by the German

German Studies at Elon University

studies curriculum. With these two moves, the German studies program reasserts liberal education as an intellectual movement fundamental to all campus units. This view of liberal education can enliven the disciplines, let students create deeper connections among their college experiences, and resolve the tensions surrounding liberal education that are mentioned prominently in this book.

Case Narrative

From our perspective, school-college divides are problematic. They seem to serve administrative-managerial ends rather than student outcomes; they provide insufficient incentive to do work outside the home college or school; and the reductive terminology ("professional schools," "traditional arts and sciences") evacuates the intellectual integrity of business and communications and the real-world relevance of the arts and sciences. This terminology also implies a divergence in goals, values, and educational outlook that we do not think exists.

Instead, we assert that faculty members across campus teach in a way that is simultaneously professional and liberal, practical and intellectual. Inspired by the language educator Michael Byram, who challenges the assumed incongruity between language teaching for pragmatic purposes (e.g., national security, business) and the traditional goals of *Bildung* or ethos,[3] the board has sought a curriculum that makes those linkages clear. It does so through learning goals that are rooted in the liberal tradition and twenty-first-century skills: intercultural competency, critical problem solving, and communicative proficiency (including written and oral rhetorical communication strategies). As we explain below, these learning goals are built into specific course features and tied to specific abilities in order to prepare students for future careers and for active participation in civic life.

German studies supports the trend to integrate classroom study and experiential education. The goals of our university's Global Education Center and Student Professional Development Center clearly map to the learning outcomes of academic disciplines and the university itself: problem solving, communicative and rhetorical strategies, cross-cultural perspective taking, and individual responsibility. These shared values mean that experiential units are in every sense compatible with the goals and mission of a liberal education.[4]

In short, the German studies faculty and staff see liberal education not as a collection of departments but as an intellectual impulse that animates the entire university—a way of viewing liberal education that harks back to its foundations, as the liberal disciplines were historically seen as necessary to enable a *liberalis* (free individual) to participate fully in civic life. Through curriculum design, a mechanism primarily under faculty control, we offer a way to make this view a reality.

Innovation Details

In 2005, the sole faculty member teaching German sought a traditional German studies minor in order to fill a gap in the university's degree offerings. There was no German studies board at the time. The original minor required three semesters of German language and three arts and humanities electives, an arrangement that continued under the first advisory board (formed in 2008), which consisted of two German teachers and two allies in history and art history. Over time, two problems with this curriculum emerged. First, the one-size-fits-all requirements did not match everyone's goals: some students wanted advanced language proficiency, while others wanted a heavier cultural focus. Second, the minor did not always lead to a focused intellectual agenda: students selected courses from a list without necessarily perceiving the intellectual links. To address these problems and inspired by students who combined the minor in innovative ways with their other degrees, the German studies board sought more viable educational pathways.

In order to accomplish this goal, the board was more than tripled in size in 2015—from four to thirteen—to represent a broader array of interests and perspectives. New and continuing members had similar motivations: establishing German as fundamental to a twenty-first-century university; serving their professional and scholarly interests in Germany; and keeping in regular contact with students pursuing opportunities in the German-speaking world. For all board members, Germany ranks politically, economically, culturally, and historically as one of the most important countries in the world.

Once assembled, the board members established a set of priorities, foremost of which was updating the curriculum, boosting the role of experiential learning, and bringing greater attention to the opportunities afforded by German studies. The board wrote a series of tasks associated with each goal, and small working groups committed to specific tasks and time frames.

The board began the curricular revision in 2017 by adopting a set of learning outcomes—communicative proficiency, critical problem solving, and intercultural competency—judged to be compatible with the disciplines represented in German studies. These outcomes are indebted to the liberal tradition, in line with the ways the university talks about learning, and supportive of both twenty-first-century skills and students' intellectual, career, and civic development. In the board's view, these three goals were a good framework for an actionable, assessable curriculum that would also address an extensive list of abilities essential to academia, a career, and twenty-first-century civic participation, including the questioning of culturally determined norms, quantitative and qualitative inquiry, perspective taking in the service of problem solving and ethical reasoning, empathy, interpersonal and intercultural collaboration, personal and civic responsibility, and synthesis and analysis. Each of these abilities could be incorporated into the learning goal framework and from there be propagated through the courses and experiential work students would undertake.

The next step, in 2018–2019, was to organize four curricular pathways that met the learning goals. The first pathway, German cultural studies, requires two German courses and five electives from at least two other departments and/or the Elon core curriculum. This concentration is for students who want a deeper understanding of German society and culture but do not plan to use the German language in any sustained fashion. The second, German language and culture, requires four German courses and three electives. This concentration promotes intermediate German language proficiency complemented by focused cultural study.

The third, advanced German proficiency, is an answer to students' call to fulfill the minor with German courses only. These students aim for advanced proficiency in order to work or study in the German-speaking world. The fourth, German for the careers, is for those who expect to work in a German business setting or to have German business partners. In addition to a minimum of two German language courses, students enroll in business- and career-focused electives and select experiential learning options in German-speaking contexts.

Flexibility in the pathway design is coupled with mentoring to ensure intentionality. This mentoring is described below.

German studies programs across the United States take an inter- and cross-disciplinary approach that expands students' experiences of German culture and lets them see the ways in which scholars think and conduct their work. The electives in our German studies curriculum represent the expansion of the field into what might be called dynamic and reflective disciplinary thinking: spaces where students are asked to think critically about the relationship between their study of German and the other disciplines in their pathway.

Take history and art history electives as clear examples. These courses ask students to think about the (German) past as interpretation, recognizing that history and art history, like other disciplines, have been constructed and that their categories are therefore ideological rather than self-evident. This way of framing the disciplines promotes critical thinking, problem solving, and rhetorical skills, and it encourages the individually determined arguments necessary for engagement in civil society. Students consider the ways that the civilizations known as "German" have been constructed, examining the intersections of past and present in order to emphasize the dynamic qualities of civilization. These intellectual skills, developed in a disciplinary context, can be applied across disciplinary boundaries, as students see that the ways any discipline engages with Germany are more complicated than merely knowing things associated with modern-day Germany.

Examples of electives outside the arts and sciences are a 400-level global finance course, whose objectives include decision making and problem solving in international contexts; a 300-level international trade course that emphasizes the role of globalization on countries' domestic and foreign affairs; and a 300-level international communications course that problematizes communication across cultural, economic, political, and other boundaries.

Electives must support at least two of the three curricular goals. Crucially, they also support twenty-first-century skills that, in our view, can be incorporated into the intellectual framework established by the curricular goals, such as questioning culturally determined norms, quantitative and qualitative inquiry, perspective taking in the service of problem solving and ethical reasoning, empathy, interpersonal and intercultural collaboration, personal and civic responsibility, and synthesis and analysis.

One example of such an elective is a German film course in the Elon core curriculum. When taught by a board member with a background in Holocaust studies, the course features an assignment that asks students to imagine themselves in the bystander role so pervasive in films about Nazism. This seemingly radical perspective taking turns out to be not so radical in the end, as students and instructor come to confront their own failures to challenge authority. Through this exercise in ethical reasoning and civic responsibility, the instructor encourages students to look for points in their day-to-day lives where they are called to act upon their convictions.

Focus on Experiential Learning

In addition to crossing academic boundaries, the German studies curriculum seeks common ground between academic and experiential units. Internships and study abroad count in the curriculum, and career center workshops highlight opportunities in Germany. Such relationships are encouraged at Elon, which is exemplary in its infusion of experiential learning into the undergraduate curriculum. For example, 1,500 students study off campus every year, and from 2017 to 2019, 350 students from forty different majors studied in a German-speaking country. Semester offerings in Germany are appropriate for a range of language abilities and disciplines—which is essential for a German studies program where every student majors in another discipline.

Beyond the semester programs, German studies leverages its relationship with the Global Education Center to connect students with courses that explore German culture and language across disciplinary boundaries. A prime example is a course called Gutenberg to the Web. Taught in Germany and the Czech Republic, this course explores the impact of journalism, propaganda, and mass media on Western civilization from Gutenberg's printing press through the rise of the internet. The course is taught by journalism faculty (including an author of this chapter) in the School of Communications, who view it as fundamentally a liberal education course situated within a thematic framework that incorporates religion, art, film, literature, history, and architecture. Teams of students conduct research on Nazi and Communist propaganda, the Cold War, film expressionism, the Reformation, the 1936 and 1972 Olympics, and the Holocaust, keeping detailed reflections via intentional blogging.

The emphasis on experiential learning challenges students to develop new concepts and make connections among their coursework, professional development, and civic and personal growth. American educational theorist David A. Kolb's experiential learning model underpins the initiative to bring meaning to what might otherwise seem to be disconnected experiences:[5] Global Education Center staff begin every advising session by exploring a student's goals before investigating study abroad programs that afford opportunities to meet those goals. This mentoring has led to students' participating in new experiences they might not otherwise have considered.

Focus on Mentoring

In addition to the advising provided by Global Education Center staff, mentoring is a cornerstone of the German studies curriculum. The radical flexibility that distinguishes this curriculum from other pathway-driven approaches also requires mentoring interventions to ensure an intentional, meaningful journey through the curriculum.[6] Upon declaring the minor, students meet with a member of the board to select a pathway, plan their courses and experiential opportunities, and articulate the reasons for those decisions based on professional, academic, and personal goals. The university registrar is able to build this required meeting into students' degree audits.

Once it is fully in place, this mentoring arrangement will require strong collaboration and communication between board members and students' primary academic advisors. A communication model has been designed for this purpose by the university's advising center, and because German studies minors typically major in one of the departments represented on the board, connections between board members and advisors already exist or should be easy to establish.

Recent graduates who minored in German studies illustrate the value of this flexible yet intentional curricular approach. Though the curriculum described above was not yet in place, these students sought close mentoring and engaged in careful reflection, in essence carrying out the thrust of the revised curriculum. One biochemistry major chose a path that would let her pursue advanced linguistic proficiency, do summer laboratory research at a German university funded by an external grant, and study abroad, including science coursework. Multiple international business majors chose paths granting strong linguistic and intercultural competencies, internships in German companies, and business coursework in Germany. A communications major sought a path that prepared her linguistically, culturally, and professionally for graduate school in communications in Germany, including an undergraduate communications thesis on rhetorical strategies in German advertisements and a postcollege internship at a media design company in Germany. These students and others like them inspired the German studies board to redesign the degree requirements to reflect the diverse goals of students.

Implementation and Iteration: Successes and Failures

Since the establishment of German studies in 2005–2006, there have been three iterations of the curriculum and three iterations of the board, each taking the program closer to the vision outlined above. From 2015 to 2018, corresponding to the expansion of the board from four to thirteen and the decision to revamp the curriculum, the number of declared minors increased from thirty to fifty, and German studies successfully recruited five new independent majors. Because the university offers no German studies major in the catalog, students majoring in German studies must use the university's independent major mechanism, which requires a lengthy application and a three-member faculty advisory committee. The larger board provided the advising capacity and the campus visibility to recruit majors and advise them across four years.

In addition, students began to express interest in the pathways even before their appearance in the academic catalog—perhaps no surprise, since the pathways were developed in response to students' desires. Students have also expressed appreciation for German studies' integrative approach: an accounting major was routinely asked in job interviews to describe the role of German studies and study abroad in her career plans, and Gutenberg to the Web students have publicly reflected on their enhanced critical thinking skills. One student wrote that "we have to consider the media we ingest on the web and make sure that we aren't falling prey" to abuses of media, as studied during the course.

Finally, as higher education demographics shift, we anticipate that German studies' emphasis on flexibility and career readiness will resonate with students under pressure to earn career-ready degrees in timelines of four years or less.[7]

These successes notwithstanding, problems remain. The false assumption that German studies lacks value makes it difficult to sell the program to greater numbers of students. Even for those who are passionate about German studies, the bureaucracy of the independent major is an impediment. A catalog major is not yet in sight due to the tendency of universities to think in fixed ways about curricula, evidenced by the relatively slow pace of German studies' curricular reform—fourteen years between the initial curriculum and the newest iteration. The few curricula on our campus that cut across college-school boundaries tend to group courses into categories, exactly the model that the board hopes to avoid.

Concluding Thoughts, Next Steps

Reimagining liberal education may be as clear-cut as reasserting the truth: it supports civic participation as well as career preparation. Faculty and staff can act on this assertion using mechanisms under their control, specifically curricula and advising, which also means that the model proposed here could be adapted to other programs. For instance, English departments, which sometimes suffer from the same false perceptions that plague German studies, might reassert their role as indispensable contributors to the dynamic study of rhetoric, interpretation, and narrative across all dimensions. This could be done in a way that unites literary, linguistic, and cultural studies, creating powerful connections to departments of professional writing or communications.[8]

German studies was initially conceived—both at the national level and at our university—as a way to preserve German in a climate where traditional German literary studies were in decline. Opening the door to German studies created dynamic opportunities. The disciplines enliven German studies through new perspectives, professional networks, and intellectual and career opportunities for our students. Our experience, therefore, provides a way to talk about liberal education in a climate where its value is not automatically assumed by students, parents, trustees, legislatures, and other stakeholders.

Crucially, our new curriculum is designed so that it can eventually support a major. When that day comes, we expect the major to feature strong mentoring and radical flexibility—perhaps even doing away with lists of preapproved electives—and to offer more extensive experiential opportunities.

With that in mind, an open question is the sustainability of the mentoring model. In the current minor, the relationship between mentor and student is relatively short term, like a pathfinder. In a future major, the mentorship would be longer and more profound. Whether board members could sustain multiyear commitments to multiple students, in addition to the advising loads in their departments, is a question we have not resolved. In the short term, as the newest iteration of the minor is implemented, the mentoring component requires that board members stay in touch with each other about students through shared documentation and discussion at regular board meetings. Despite the logistical hurdles, we are convinced that this design will result in better learning and a greater potential for career success.

KEY TAKEAWAYS

Couple radical flexibility with timely mentoring. Students should be allowed to design their own educational paths, but they need expert guidance.

Assemble a diverse group of faculty and staff. Choose people who are committed to your program. An open call for volunteers can be effective.

Work within existing university structures where you can. In our case, these included established processes for interdisciplinary minors and majors. The board also did not challenge hotly defended structures, like courses or semesters, and did not write complex catalog language. The requirements are listed very simply, and the pathways are printed in the catalog as narrative guidelines for board members and students.

Build on existing institutional strengths. In our context, these included strong experiential programs and dynamic Schools of Business and Communications.

Seek partners whose innovative spirit matches your own. For example, any art history course can count for the German studies minor, provided students make appropriate arrangements. This agreement is possible because the art history faculty has an innovative, flexible, collaborative approach to course design.

Define your program in terms of student outcomes as well as content. This enables collaborative opportunities and curricular options.

Involve stakeholders early in the development process. As the board was writing the new curriculum, the coordinator met informally with the head of the university curriculum committee and later with the dean.

These steps are required at nearly any university. The trick may be to frame them as formative (seeking advice) rather than summative (seeking approval or rejection of a proposal).

Notes

1. For a related analysis, see Sheldon Rothblatt, "Old Wine in New Bottles, or New Wine in Old Bottles? The Humanities and Liberal Education in Today's Universities," in *A New Deal for the Humanities: Liberal Arts and the Future of Public Higher Education*, ed. Gordon Hunter and Mohamed G. Feisal (New Brunswick, NJ: Rutgers University Press, 2016), 31-50.

2. For student choice and motivation, see Marilla Svinicki, "Why Is Teaching for Motivation So Confusing?," *National Teaching and Learning Forum* 27, no. 6 (October 2018): 11-12.

3. Michael Byram, "Linguistic and Cultural Education for *Bildung* and Citizenship," *Modern Language Journal* 94, no. 2 (2010): 317-321.

4. This vision is supported by employers. See, for example, "It Takes More than a Major: Employer Priorities for College Learning and Student Success," *Liberal Education* 99, no. 2 (2013): 22-29.

5. David A. Kolb, *Experiential Learning: Experience as the Source of Learning and Development* (Englewood Cliffs, NJ: Prentice Hall, 1984).

6. The powerful effects of mentoring have been described in Peter Felten et al., *The Undergraduate Experience: Focusing Institutions on What Matters Most* (San Francisco, CA: Jossey-Bass, 2016); and Charity Johansson and Peter Felten, *Transforming Students: Fulfilling the Promise of Higher Education* (Baltimore, MD: Johns Hopkins University Press, 2014).

7. Older learners, for example, tend to choose education that is immediately relevant to their career path. Raymond J. Wlodkowski, *Enhancing Adult Motivation to Learn: A Comprehensive Guide for Teaching All Adults* (San Francisco, CA: Jossey-Bass, 2008).

8. Jessie L. Moore et al., "Seeking Growth through Independence: A Professional Writing and Rhetoric Program in Transition at Elon University," in *Writing Majors: Eighteen Program Profiles*, ed. Greg Giberson, Jim Nugent, and Lori Ostergaard (Boulder: University Press of Colorado, 2015), 228-240.

14 Pursuing Major Passions
Innovative Minors That Blend Professional Skills and Liberal Education Values for Civic Pursuits at Susquehanna University

John Bodinger de Uriarte and Betsy Verhoeven

Radical Vision

We advocate an approach that allows students to understand how real-world things call into being (interpellate) people and their characteristics. This focus begins with practical professional and civic scenarios and grounds them in particular disciplines' habits of mind, which are combined with a focus on materiality. While our students do learn applied skills, such as writing work documents or crafting museum exhibits, along the way we ask our students to think of things as theory, which allows them to cultivate the habits of mind that are hallmarks of liberal education and crucial to democratic and workplace practice.

Institutional Profile

Susquehanna University in Selinsgrove, Pennsylvania, is a private, not-for-profit undergraduate university enrolling 2,351 students as of the fall of 2017. It is a four-year, small, highly residential institution.

Introduction

We reject a national discourse that pits professional preparation against liberal education and practical skills against theoretical knowledge. Supported by an Andrew W. Mellon Foundation grant, we designed two minors—museum studies and professional and civic writing—that seek to revive enrollment in traditional liberal arts major programs. The grant was framed to support innovative minors that "allowed students to pursue their major passions." Our resulting programs are incubators for innovative assignments that can attract new students and can later spread into majors, connecting disciplinary ways of being with professional applications. The minors require few resources. They can be combined with majors, infusing them with new life. Their status as separate but related programs makes them less threatening and quicker to implement than overhauls of major curricula.[1]

The practical assignments embedded in both minors—putting together an exhibit or writing a professional or civic document—are surrounded by analyses that engage students in understanding how things embody theory, asking: what is the theoretical work of representational objects? Both the practical production of these assignments and the analyses surrounding them require students to cultivate a comfort with open-endedness and ambiguity. These characteristics might not immediately seem important to civic and professional contexts, but we show below that they are crucial results of the habits of mind our disciplines cultivate.

Case Narrative

Increasingly, students report feeling that they need to know their career path in middle school; tracking is regaining popularity in high schools; and parents show obvious concern that students in traditional liberal arts majors won't have the practical skills needed to land a "real job." The results: declining enrollments. We recognize that these changes result from fears about finding gainful employment, being able to start families, and paying off school loans. Tuition-driven institutions must consider how to attract students and maintain a reputation for solid outcomes. In line with this volume's theme, we recognize the importance of not simply teaching to our own interests, stressing interdisciplinarity instead. Simultaneously, we remain firmly committed to the core promises of a liberal education, including developing skills like careful critical thinking and the ability to approach the world with an array of provocative questions and developed curiosities, skills that are not obviously marketable characteristics.

Rhetoric pedagogy has provided several key principles. John Gage's "Why Write?" advocates teaching writing as a means of thinking critically, inflected to intellectual and civic realms, in contrast with some traditional approaches focusing on grammatical correctness and stylistic fluency.[2] Rhetoric's recent return to classical notions of textual analysis in the service of textual production includes open-ended, collaborative approaches to assignment generation and grading.[3] In addition, civic rhetoric and the teaching for transfer literature encourage us to adopt genres from outside of the classroom (e.g., museum text panels, the pieces that guide participants through an exhibit, or professional and civic writing genres, which students choose in that minor), guided by their own interests.[4]

Interpellation theory influenced the directors of both new programs. For the professional and civic writing director, this included constitutive rhetoric as elaborated by Maurice Charland in 1987.[5] The rhetorical genre movement, which explores the ways genre conventions encourage the cultivation of particular attributes—see Medway on architecture students' sketchbooks, for instance[6]—is an extension of constitutive rhetoric. For the museum studies director, this was most sharply considered in how exhibits and objects "hail" certain subjects and confirm them. Exhibit objects and written genres both interpellate subjects (audiences), encouraging them to take on certain characteristics: to be self-reflective, patriotic, or critical of authority, to name just a few.

Of course, Bruno Latour is central to considerations of things as theory. Latour requires us to consider things as agents. As Gries describes his project, "things acquire power to shape reality as they become entangled in complex relations with other actants. An actant is Latour's neologism for acknowledging the ability of all things—human and non-human—to intervene, to create change."[7] Latour's project, in our view, demands that we connect the interpretive skills of liberal education to the civic skills that allow us to comment on and advocate for policy decisions. As Santos and Johnson remark, "Latour has critiqued the separation of academics from politics, arguing that this separation has led us to a crisis of global proportions."[8] We argue that our interpretive reflection exercises embedded within the minors help connect theory to practice in political and workplace venues, achieving the goal he strives for. But we have also found interpellation theory to be a more accessible tool for accomplishing this work in our minors, as we describe below.

Innovation Details

Our fledgling programs, built with limited resources and without additional staffing, pulled together already-existing courses with a few new courses. Professional and Civic Writing was a new course. Museum studies recognized an existing course, Museums and Anthropology, as a central requirement and designed two new requirements: an internship and an individual exhibition project. Courses from our respective majors fleshed out each minor: Environmental Rhetoric and Visual Anthropology were courses the directors had previously designed for their major departments. Finally, courses were pulled from existing programs outside of the hosting departments. The professional and civic writing minor draws from communications, diversity studies, and international studies, while museum studies draws from history, art history, and our cross-cultural Global Opportunities program. Further, our university curriculum embeds core requirements within major and minor courses, which helps us run the courses regularly even with a smaller number of students in each program.

For us, at first, the practical outcomes for our students—the twenty-first-century skills—were secondary. Instead, we were designing programs that drew from our own scholarly interests (although along the way we both realized we had helpful practical experience from our pre-academia lives). One challenge for liberal education faculty like us: figuring out how to make "applied" assignments theoretically and intellectually rich.

Unearthing specific habits of mind that our fields shared helped us address this challenge. These habits of mind have in common a concern with how sense gets made. We found two that our disciplines shared: an awareness of the constructedness of representation and an interest in the interpellation of citizen-subjects.[9] Cultivating these habits of mind in our students guides the construction of our assignments and the design of our minors' curricula, allowing us to offer practical, applied skills while attending to the bigger questions that transcend disciplines and career trajectories.

We drew "habits of mind" from John Gage's "Why Write?" As part of his larger argument that writing is primarily thinking, Gage espouses "the belief that writing is not simply a 'skill' to be mastered and then applied neutrally to knowledge, but the ongoing reflection of students' developing understanding of ideas."[10] He favorably describes Aristotle's approach to writing as one that recognizes "writing itself as a means of discovering knowledge." Gage asserts that we should teach "writing as the exercise of independent thought and the ability to reason."[11] The writing across the curriculum (WAC) movement, embraced long ago by our institution, has encouraged us to understand our own disciplines within the broader liberal education context. While Gage explains the ways writing can encourage the broader liberal arts capacities, like exercising better critical judgment, WAC nudges us to consider the ways that particular disciplines encourage specific ways of exercising better critical judgment and discovering or creating new knowledge.

As Linda Adler-Kassner and John Majewski point out, the liberal education ways of thinking vary from discipline to discipline.[12] To illustrate, they cite the "aha moment" for one faculty member who overcame a hurdle in teaching disciplinary writing by recognizing that "my discipline is not the universe."[13] In their study of disciplinary threshold concepts and habits of mind, they offer "slow reading" in literature and "interpret[ing] . . . contested narratives" in history as examples of what we would call "thinking like a ___" (insert your own discipline here).[14]

These are the sort of questions that help us define that key term in liberal education: critical thinking. What does critical thinking mean for our disciplines? And how can we start with those ways of thinking, of doing—verbs, in short—as opposed to resting with the nouns of knowledge (as in: what knowledge does a curator or a professional writer need)? Moving from nouns of knowledge to skills of doing helped us create better student experiences and projects, while at the same time it helped us understand, from our disciplinary vantage points, what it means to think like a liberally educated person.

Still, there was tension between our motivations: on the one hand, our own scholarly interests, and on the other, our students' need for practical assignments. How to reconcile this tension?

Enter things and theory. Adding "things" like museum objects and written genres, inflected as twenty-first-century skills, helped us help students think like anthropologists or rhetoricians in ways that we believe are useful beyond the academy—in professional and civic worlds. Things are theory, and we soon began to consider what kind of writing our students would do if they became museum professionals or professional writers. For museum studies, one key thing is the object of study that becomes the heart of an exhibit. For a rhetorician, the key thing is the document, the written artifact that they will study and learn to write. In the professional and civic writing program, such genres include grant proposals, website text, posters, newsletter articles, and social media campaigns.[15]

Things as theory means to us, in part, that we understand things by applying theory. But things generate theory too. Both of these ways of understanding the relationship between things and theory are worth saying because things are often viewed as separate from theory, just as liberal arts are often viewed as opposite to real-world usefulness. Thing theory (including here the work of Latour and Bennett) shows us that things are agential; they are not simply inert objects to be explained but are the evidence or material manifestation of complicated networks of potential meanings.[16] Their ability to invoke this sort of intersectional position is what allows them to act as theory: they demand interpretive intervention and provoke unexpected engagement.

This challenges popular habits of mind, which then may be replaced with richer disciplinary habits of mind. For example, the overwhelming majority of our students see things in museums as inert and explained through an authoritative institutional voice. Pushing them to recognize the actual work going on in objects encourages them to develop different habits of mind in the face of "reading" exhibitionary practices. It would be tempting to call the things that could make up the course's museum exhibits "museum objects," but it would be more accurate to say that they are "potential museum objects" or even "quotidian objects imagined as museum objects." It is the act of attention that transforms an object into a museum object. It is a similar act of attention that takes workplace documents and reveals their role as elements of specific subject formations. In both instances, that authoritative institutional voice (whether a museum exhibit or unquestioned writing rules) becomes less authoritative. With both exhibitions and professional writing genres, one becomes a better reader through the careful building of those disciplinary habits of mind.

The first habit of mind we mentioned—awareness of the constructedness of representation—becomes evident to students as they begin to be aware of that authoritative institutional voice. The interdisciplinary approach of both minors helps students see how different interpretive perspectives are necessary to be a more careful thinker and assessor of questions and opportunities. The goal is that students become unwilling (and hopefully even unable) to approach a question from only one direction.

One example: an art history major was taken aback and energized by a museum case study where the majority of the exhibition elements and texts were completely invented, not created through trying to explain or contextualize "significant objects." These materials were just seductive enough to pull him well into the gallery narratives until he realized that the exhibition itself was a site-specific and multifaceted art piece that also actively played with the "authority of the museum."[17] And that such "playing" was an element of all museum exhibitionary practices. The slow process of recognizing a curator's interaction with objects—and the way that such interaction in turn constructs a representation—requires students to become more comfortable with ambiguity: they recognize that the same object in different contexts constructs different meanings.

Likewise, students in the professional and civic writing minor learn the ways that their attention can cause a genre's characteristics to morph, requiring them to be open to the ambiguity and uncertainty of rulelessness, overcoming their years of rules-based training in how to write "properly."

The projects in both minors require open-endedness: not driving the narrative from the beginning or jumping the gun on what the interpretation will be. The director of museum studies observes that there is no single authoritative narrative waiting to be discovered and deployed. Student teams have to live with the process of surfacing the interconnections within a theme or story. The title for a final exhibition project, "Mooting: Oddities in the Open," serves as an illustration. It began with anagramming an incomplete set of brass letters that once spelled out INFORMATION (from the facilities storage area): MOOT was one possibility. As students started to review its meaning, it became clear that these brass objects offered multiple handles for the project: a set of letters (mostly) preserved without a clear goal or future use, a sorting and re-sorting to gauge possibilities for use, a somewhat happy accident that combined chance, research, openness, and aesthetics. In a sense, MOOT was "hailed" from its brass constituents. While mooting as unearthing worked as a unifying concept to pull together disparate objects, it didn't enjoy an initial universal buy-in, so it also served as an example of negotiation within a museum group working to bring an exhibition together.

The project also provided an extended opportunity for thinking about things as theory, for recognizing that museum objects are representational objects.[18] The sorts of things of everyday life used in the class serve as "evocative objects [that] bring philosophy down to earth."[19] Such objects ground the theoretical in the everyday and reveal themselves as both agents and elements of entangled networks of meaning and multiple reference making.[20] Like the letters of MOOT, objects reveal their "unfixedness" to confound or confirm the practices of representation. Additionally, the objects in the museum studies signature course hail their respective and mixed subjects; they thus help to form subjectivities in the shifting we-you position of the exhibition visitors.

The attention to the thingness of museum objects and written genres helps develop the second habit of mind we found that our disciplines shared: an understanding, grounded by interpellation theory, that both exhibit objects and writing genres are formed through hailing. Even mundane objects and genres are encased in, directed by, and understood through potentially powerful stories. One important offshoot of this attention to hailing comes from recognizing that not only objects are hailed by human attention. People are hailed into being, and often the potentially powerful stories constructed by museum exhibits and by genre innovation illustrate how some people are hailed and others are left out of the narrative completely.

Stories are often the means by which power is consolidated and exercised. For instance, both minors highlight the way things (exhibit objects and writing genres) represent people with varied roles inside and outside of the university. In museum studies, the "Mooting" exhibit began with a call to represent the university through the lenses of students, faculty, and staff, and it ended up putting side by side objects from dorm rooms and faculty offices—and even a turkey tail provided by an avid huntsman and facilities staff member. In professional and civic writing, on-campus genres like flyers and incident reports brought together students and administrators as collaborators and as protagonists. One student in the Environmental Rhetoric class, for instance, performed and analyzed an on-campus installment of the international Free the Nipple movement, bringing together campus safety personnel, university lawyers, supportive faculty, and student demonstrators in an effort to show how gender norms are often environment-unfriendly. In the student's first pass, the only human agents were "men and women" or "students," but as she came to recognize that there were other stakeholders—for instance, the campus safety team wanted to make sure women in the movement were not harmed by bystanders, and the university legal counsel discouraged administrators from blocking the assembly—her narrative came to be populated with more and more previously unseen agents. Of course, this required her to cultivate open-endedness to make possible the teamwork, inclusivity, and strong communication so necessary in contemporary professional contexts.

There is a further civic benefit of projects like these: identifying the subtle ways these power dynamics occur can lead to an understanding of how they are reinforced and, occasionally, to a sense of responsibility for shifting them. For example, in the very early stages of the "Mooting" exhibit, students came across the way classes presume that knowledge production belongs to certain people. Students often live the experience of being the recipients of that knowledge production, with faculty representing the expertise of the field. For a project to ask *them* to be doing the production of knowledge was already an interrogation of power dynamics. But beyond that, as students were empowered to create knowledge in the form of an exhibit, the assignments hinted at another way power is produced and reinforced: traditionally. A traditional approach to an exhibit about university spaces would presume that the exhibition objects would come from faculty offices. The assignments for the exhibit required a shift in thought and theory, which was brought about via consideration of university spaces that belong to students and staff as well.

To offer a parallel example from professional and civic writing: one student who volunteers as an EMT modified the genre of informational articles that circulate via social media, updating these to explain how EMTs can better serve transgender people. Just as the Free the Nipple example began with a simplified story hailing only female students, in the "Mooting" exhibit an earlier version could easily have placed faculty as the "protagonists" of university life. Finally, in the EMT example, the student included transgender people, who previously had not appeared at all as "characters" (by which we mean, significant agents) in the story the medical profession had written about who its clients are.

Concluding Thoughts, Next Steps

Cultivating these habits of mind—an awareness of the constructedness of representation and an interest in the interpellation of citizen-subjects—guides the design of our minors. Simultaneously, our assignments help develop comfort with open-endedness and ambiguity, attitudes useful in civic discourse. As longtime proponents of liberal education, we firmly believe that attending to these bigger questions makes students more practically adaptable in their professional, personal, and civic lives. The specific objects and genres we teach soon give way to others. Better to focus on the disciplinary habits of mind that will help alumni adapt over time.

Figuring out how to grow the minors and assess them is a big challenge, especially given the newness of the programs. This work is complicated by the fact that both directors, as is normal in a small liberal arts university, wear multiple hats, managing a number of administrative responsibilities.

KEY TAKEAWAYS

Ask yourself: what is the intersection between the habits of mind for your field and the usefulness of those habits of mind for work and civic engagement? For us, these were open-endedness, representation, and interpellation. Understanding your disciplinary habits of mind will help your students develop the intellectual and ethical skills that ground and guide the exercising of applied and social skills.

Shared resources help small programs. Include classes that count for multiple majors and minors or for core requirements. Build bigger audiences for visiting speakers by finding shared goals and ways of thinking.

Notes

1. Program descriptions and the curricular requirements for each minor are at https://www.susqu.edu/academics/majors-and-minors.

2. John Gage, "Why Write?," in *The Teaching of Writing: National Society for the Study of Education Yearbook*, ed. David Bartholomae and Anthony Petrosky (Chicago, IL: University of Chicago Press, 1986), 8-29.

3. Cheryl Ball, "Adapting Editorial Peer Review of Webtexts for Classroom Use," *Writing and Pedagogy* 5, no. 2 (2014): 301-316.

4. Ashley Holmes, *Public Pedagogy in Composition Studies* (Carbondale: Southern Illinois University Press, 2016); Jessie Moore and Randall Bass, eds.,

Understanding Writing Transfer: Implications for Transformative Student Learning in Higher Education (Sterling, VA: Stylus, 2017).

5. Maurice Charland, "Constitutive Rhetoric: The Case of the Peuple Quebecois," *Quarterly Journal of Speech* 73, no. 2 (1987): 133-150.

6. Peter Medway, "Fuzzy Genres and Community Identities: The Case of Architecture Students' Sketchbooks," in *The Rhetoric and Ideology of Genre: Strategies for Stability and Change*, ed. Richard Coe, Lorelei Lingard, and Tatiana Teslenko (Cresskill, NJ: Hampton, 2002), 123-153.

7. Laurie Gries, "Dingrhetoriks," in *Thinking with Bruno Latour in Rhetoric and Composition*, ed. Paul Lynch and Nathanial Rivers (Carbondale: Southern Illinois University Press, 2015), 294-309, 298.

8. Marc Santos and Meredith Zoetewey Johnson, "From Constituting to Instituting: Kant, Latour, and Twitter," in Lynch and Rivers, *Thinking with Bruno Latour*, 59-77, 59.

9. Here we follow Althusser in considering the act of hailing—in text and through objects—as an exercise in recognizing formative subjectivities. See Samuel R. Delaney, *Times Square Red, Times Square Blue* (New York: New York University Press, 1999); and Louis Althusser, "Ideology and Ideological State Apparatuses," in his *Lenin and Philosophy* (New York: Monthly Review Press, 1971), 121-176.

10. Gage, "Why Write?," 8.

11. Gage, "Why Write?," 12.

12. Linda Adler-Kassner and John Majewski, "Extending the Invitation: Threshold Concepts, Professional Development, and Outreach," in *Naming What We Know: Threshold Concepts of Writing Studies*, ed. Linda Adler-Kassner and Elizabeth Wardle (Logan: Utah State University Press, 2015), 186-202.

13. Adler-Kassner and Majewski, "Extending the Invitation," 190.

14. Adler-Kassner and Majewski, "Extending the Invitation," 191, 188.

15. Although attention to writing skills is a common link across the two programs, even in museum studies, the genres of writing are important. The interrelated panels and other texts in any given exhibit are particular professional writing genres—twenty-first-century skills—that students in the minor should learn.

16. Bruno Latour, *Politics of Nature: How to Bring the Sciences into Democracy* (Cambridge, MA: Harvard University Press, 2004); Jane Bennett, *Vibrant Matter: A Political Ecology of Things* (Durham, NC: Duke University Press, 2010).

17. Lawrence Weschler, *Mr. Wilson's Cabinet of Wonder* (New York: Vintage, 1996).

18. Sandra H. Dudley, "The Buzz of Displacement: Liminality among Burmese Court Objects in Oxford, London and Yangon," in *The Inbetweenness of Things: Materializing Mediation and Movement between Worlds*, ed. Paul Basu (New York: Bloomsbury Academic, 2018), 38-56.

19. Sherry Turkle, *Evocative Objects: Things We Think With* (Cambridge, MA: MIT Press, 2011), 8.

20. Anna Lowenhaupt Tsing, *The Mushroom at the End of the World: On the Possibility of Life in Capitalist Ruins* (Princeton, NJ: Princeton University Press, 2017); see also Tim Ingold, *Lines* (New York: Routledge, 2016).

Part Two
Visions for the Future
of Liberal Education

The chapters in this part of the book anticipate the opportunities and challenges that liberal education may face in the very near future. We have invited several prominent voices at the forefront of the advancement of teaching and learning practices to offer their perspectives on how liberal education can remain vital to the development of student capacities to flourish in an era of uncertainty.

These capacities, according to these authors, can be achieved with a careful reimagining of the values that drive liberal education. The contributors grapple with the intersection of curricular, extracurricular, and co-curricular methods that recenter the student experience and reinvigorate the spirit of the liberal arts to develop in students the freedom to take part in an active and engaged civic life. From deep engagement through high-impact practices and reflective civic involvement (Finley), to the development of new dispositions in light of an increasingly dehumanizing and automated age (Bass), to calls for students to find renewed purpose through play (Sullivan), through "scholartistry" (Shanks and Svabo), through risk taking and eschewing the pervasive ranking systems of higher education institutions (Gunnarsdóttir and Twombly), to simply slowing down to engage deeply in the task at hand (Chick and Felten), these visions of liberal education cry out for a return to the roots of what it means to be a free human, confident and competent in the ways of being, doing, and knowing that have sustained liberal education throughout centuries.

15 The Future Has Gone Soft on Skills
Why Campuses Should Be Working Harder to Cement Personal and Social Development with Learning

Ashley Finley

The conversation around twenty-first-century skills is getting old. Literally. Two decades into the twenty-first-century, every institution—whether community college, land-grant university, private liberal arts college, or the state school in the middle of nowhere—in one way or another is asking what a liberal education means *now*. That immutable *now*, emergent over the past twenty years, is the acknowledgment and growing appreciation that students are different, that the environment for learning is different (in good and not so good ways), and that the needs of employers continue to change.

We have known for some time that employers largely value broad skills over narrow job training.[1] That workforce advantage means employees are nimble enough to problem solve through technological changes, job redesign, or restructuring. It also means that college graduates can use a diverse skill set to navigate an increasingly complex, globally dependent job market and successfully maneuver through an average of nearly twelve career changes, half of which will occur when employees are between the ages of eighteen and twenty-four.[2] These abilities encompass a set of intellectual and practical skills, such as written and oral communication skills, critical thinking, quantitative reasoning, and information literacy, in addition to the ability to integrate and apply these proficiencies in various conditions or settings.

But something else is beginning to define workforce needs.

A person's efficacy in the workplace or in the world does not depend on intellectual, practical, and integrative skills alone. How individuals manage others and themselves in complex environments also matters. The attributes of these capacities often get discussed in terms of employees' interpersonal skills, such as the ability to work in teams or "with diverse groups,"[3] or in terms of their individual capacities, like motivation, curiosity, or risk taking. If employers value graduates who can function effectively both *inter*personally and *intra*personally, it is increasingly up to colleges and universities to provide those abilities. But the manner in which they are provided and to whom demands examination.

The Problem with the Term "Soft"

The Association of American Colleges and Universities (AAC&U) defines a liberal education as "an approach to learning that empowers individuals and prepares them to deal with complexity, diversity, and change," which is achieved through the development of "a sense of social responsibility, as well as . . . intellectual and practical skills . . . and a demonstrated ability to apply knowledge and skills in real-world settings."[4]

Implicit in this definition is the assumption of students' development of "soft skills," that is, a set of affective capacities or qualities of individuals that enable them to be productive, assured, introspective, and even empathetic. To be explicit about these skills is to recognize, as employers are beginning to do, that employees are even more effective when they persevere through failures, when they act with confidence, and when they reflect on their performance. Notably, these are similar to the capacities that faculty members often describe, sometimes wistfully, when talking about the "unmeasurable" skills that also contribute to student success.

Indeed, among the skills respondents ranked most desirable in the AAC&U's 2018 employer survey were the ability "to work independently (prioritize, manage time)" and to be "self-motivated, take initiative, and be proactive with ideas or initiatives."[5] A study by Georgetown University's Center on Education and the Workforce has recognized the job market value of self-esteem and resilience.[6]

It has become commonplace to refer to these skills as "soft," perhaps because they are "inherent" or "personal" or because their subjectivity eludes the usual assessment methods of quizzes and tests. Whatever the reason, labeling any set of skills, particularly those that are increasingly so important, as "soft" is problematic. "Soft" skills have historically been equated with the feminization of certain jobs and associated skills in the labor market. Female-dominated jobs, such as nurses, flight attendants, or primary school teachers, have been defined by their reliance on managing situations, managing one's emotions,[7] and working well with others. What is "soft" about these jobs is that women tend to do them. The term "soft skills" serves to reinforce gender stereotypes about what women supposedly do best and so effortlessly that it renders the work they are *actually* doing as virtually invisible.[8] The element of being unseen contributes to these skills being undervalued. The consequence of these abilities being invisible and undervalued is a correlation with the systematic devaluation of the jobs in the American labor market that rely on these types of skills and the very real economic (i.e., wage) consequences on the people, primarily women, who hold these jobs.[9] Relatedly, references to the social sciences as "soft" and the natural sciences as "hard" are demarcations that implicitly attack the rigor of fields like sociology and psychology and underscore the growing feminization of these disciplines.

Thus, the emphasis on soft skills in today's workforce invites an exquisite tension: championing the importance of students' personal and social development while simultaneously labeling such abilities in a way that ultimately undermines their value. This tension also extends to how we recognize (or miss) the development of soft skills (i.e., personal and social development) within some of the most innovative, high-impact learning experiences happening across college campuses.

Just as the forces of a rapidly diversifying twenty-first-century economy have influenced the growing importance of soft skills, so too have they shaped the learning environments in which students will encounter these skills. A commitment to students' personal and social development will require colleges and universities to grapple with the influences that have uniquely shaped higher education in this century. Those forces are driven by diversification, anxiety, stress, and the imperative to define what student success means and how to achieve it.

The Development of Soft Skills in a Changing Educational Environment

We have gained a much clearer picture of just how diverse students are in the twenty-first century. Today's students are both younger *and* older. The influx of students of traditional age into colleges and universities is due to increased numbers of students from historically underserved groups.[10] The greatest area of consistent growth between 2000 and 2016 was among Hispanic students, whose enrollment in postsecondary institutions more than doubled.[11] Other underserved racial groups (African American, Asian and Pacific Islander, and American Indian and Alaska Native) boosted their enrollment by an average of 43 percent from 2000 to 2010.[12] Institutions of higher education are also increasingly being shaped by an influx of students over the age of twenty-four, as more adult students seek a postsecondary credential.[13]

Additionally, one-third of college students will transfer at least once, making movement across institutions much more common.[14] Though the proportion of first-generation college students has declined over time, the size of this population is still noteworthy at about one-third of all college students.[15] Altogether, the diversity of the student population in higher education demands that all institutions take notice. Not because diversity is a problem, but because it is a reckoning. Higher education's reflection of larger national demographic shifts does not simply require a greater awareness of those students traditionally underserved by higher education. It also requires understanding that those students' backgrounds, viewpoints, and cultural legacies and competence have been equally underserved.[16] This means that the expression of the outcomes of a liberal education in general, and personal and social development in particular, must be encouraged to manifest in new ways.

Today's college students are also reporting greater levels of anxiety and stress than ever before. Data from the American College Health Association indicate that 52 percent of undergraduates reported feeling "things were hopeless" at some point in the previous twelve months, 86 percent reported feeling "overwhelmed by all they had to do," and 61 percent felt "overwhelming anxiety."[17] The National Survey of College Counseling Centers reported a 44 percent increase in counseling services in 2014 from the previous year.[18] By and large, counselors are responding to students' anxiety, which has far outpaced both depression and stress from relationships as the leading reason for visits to counseling centers since 2012.[19]

There is little doubt that increasing diversity and attention to students' mental health have affected the current environment of students' learning on college campuses. At the same time, growing attention has also been given to the positive benefits of the amount and quality of certain engaged learning experiences, often referred to as high-impact practices. Though many of the most common high-impact practices, such as learning communities, service learning, first-year seminars, and capstones, have existed for decades, the use of the term "high-impact practices" is a twenty-first-century coining. The inclusiveness of this single term to refer to a breadth of practices acknowledges the efficacy of these experiences in the aggregate, particularly for underserved students.[20] Though much has been written about the value of these experiences in achieving the intellectual and applied skills of a liberal education, relatively little systematic connection has been made between these practices and students' personal and social development.[21] That could be because student development has traditionally been seen as the purview of student affairs professionals. But the growing recognition of the need for intra- and interpersonal capabilities (e.g., empathy, resilience, confidence, belonging) and the campus imperatives to expand high-impact practices provide an opening to link the two in a way that effectively takes the discussion of whole student development from the cocurriculum to the classroom and beyond. High-impact practices may not just be the key to building students' cognitive skills; they may also be every bit as effective in building students' personal and social capacities.

The Link between Soft Skills and High-Impact Practices

A caveat to the efficacy of high-impact practices has always been that they be done "well."[22] This means recognizing the characteristics of the experiences themselves that contribute to the intentionality with which they transform students' learning and development. These characteristics are often thought of as the "quality" dimensions of high-impact practices.[23] Among the qualities posited are three core elements that highlight the inherent connection between high-impact practices and students' personal and social development: reflection, high levels of interaction, and high levels of feedback.[24] Reflection is vital for students to recognize instances of their learning in real time and the pathway of their learning over time. Doing this well, however, demands treating reflection as a skill to be developed over time through a series of reflection prompts, as opposed to a single reflection paper. The sequence of prompts should invite students to peel back layers of the experience.[25] Rather than asking "What did you do and how did you feel about it?" Carol Rodgers advocates for a four-part sequence that begins with students learning to be mindful in the moment of the experience itself.[26] Only then can they move to step two (describe the experience) and step three (analyze the experience from multiple viewpoints). It is not until the *fourth* step that students are asked to consider their own individual positionality and responses to the experience.

Reflection is also about personal discovery. Just as reflection provides a means for students to evaluate the path of their learning across experiences, it also helps students to understand who they are vis-à-vis their learning. Reflection enables students to consider their strengths and abilities, their limitations, and their own sense of purpose. Reflective discussions can occur as easily between students and faculty as they can between students and career services professionals. Evidence suggests that students will benefit most by having multiple conversations with a constellation of higher education professionals.[27] Ideally, students' engagement in high-impact practices will invite these reflections and discussions. Even better would be that reflection and discussion happen early and often, so that by the time a student begins looking toward a career path, they have had the opportunity to fully consider what they have learned in the classroom and what they have learned about themselves.

High-impact practices should also contain high levels of interaction with faculty, peers, community members, and campus staff. The more diverse these interactions, the better. Exposing students to different viewpoints forces them to reconcile their own perspectives with the views of others with whom they disagree. This quality component of high-impact practices will serve students well when, upon graduation, they are asked to work with colleagues in other parts of the world, of different faiths or sexual and political orientations, or of different racial or ethnic backgrounds.

Finally, high-impact practices should provide students with structured and consistent feedback. Feedback in any setting is a mechanism for, at minimum, telling students what they got right or wrong. In high-impact practices, consistent feedback builds resilience, motivating students to improve by illuminating the path forward. It also strengthens self-esteem and confidence by underscoring not just what was right but what was brilliant.

In important ways, each of these quality dimensions—reflection, interaction, and feedback—is relevant for the success of a generation of students entering college campuses from traditionally underserved backgrounds, whether they are first generation, low income, nonwhite, or some combination of all of these. High levels of reflection, interaction, and feedback can be the difference between a student leaving college and staying. With reflection comes the chance to recognize a student's voice and cultural wealth. With interaction comes the chance to build a community of their own and foster a sense of belonging. With feedback comes the chance to be seen as exceptional and college ready, even when a wider network of support may be lacking or nonexistent. We know that high-impact practices can be particularly effective for improving retention and graduation rates of underserved students,[28] but we currently possess little understanding of exactly why. By explicitly linking the quality components of high-impact practices with students' personal and social development, we are getting closer to comprehending the full potential of these experiences.

Community Engagement as a High-Impact Thread to Soft Skills

Lists of the most common high-impact practices often contain references to service-learning courses and study abroad programs. These are the places in the curriculum and the cocurriculum where civic and community engagement usually live. But to confine civic or community engagement to a few programs is to miss the mark. Today's world is more globally connected than ever. Local issues are global issues. Domestic markets are internationally influenced. Communication skills do not stop at state or even continental borders. Students themselves are also more connected—to each other, to physical and virtual worlds, and to new modalities of expression. The extent of interconnectivity between environments and relationships makes civic and community engagement not just one specific high-impact practice but a potentially catalyzing component of *every* high-impact practice. Community engagement can be woven into first-year seminars, learning communities, capstone projects, or undergraduate research, providing applicability, timeliness, and perhaps even a boost to outcomes.[29]

Though community engagement can be viewed as resource intensive, conceptualizing these activities as a robust, connected set of practices can be helpful. Community-engaged activities are often concurrent but siloed across multiple areas of campus life. For example, a single campus might have forms of community engagement that span service learning and study abroad programs; clinical rotations, practicums, or field placements; internships; and pockets of community-based research. Cocurricular community engagement is also siloed with students participating in volunteer initiatives, alternative spring break programs, and various club or campus ministry service projects. Each form of community engagement, curricular and cocurricular, is a potentially powerful mechanism through which students can explore their personal and social development. These experiences would be even more powerful if they were thought of in the aggregate, rather than piecemeal.

At the core of any community-engaged experience is a rich opportunity for reflection, interaction, and feedback. This could be in the form of students' understanding another culture (whether local or global) or interacting with a community member, organizational partner, or business entity. An intentionally structured and organized community-engaged experience is also a powerful mechanism for students to explore who they are and to apply that learning in a real-world context. Additionally, through guided reflection, interaction, and feedback, students can be invited to explore their own sources of bias and misinformation. Such experiences help students to tether the problem-solving and critical-thinking skills gained in the classroom to actual "wicked" problems that by definition lack clear solutions, such as climate change, systems of social inequality, or democratic participation.[30] But community engagement is not a silver bullet for fully equipping students with personal and social development skills, nor is any other high-impact practice. What is needed is a more expansive view of how personal and social development skills are fostered across campus. This might include high-impact practices, like community engagement, but the scope of the practices should go even further. If colleges and universities are going to get serious about students' personal and social development, they must also align institutional missions, college-wide learning outcomes, faculty work, and assessment with these promising educational practices.

Taking on the Hard Part of Soft Skills: Definition, Implementation, Assessment

Although faculty members largely recognize the cross-disciplinary relevance of abilities such as written and oral communication skills, critical thinking, and information literacy, far more ambiguity exists when it comes to adding personal and social development to a list of general education or institutional outcomes. Nevertheless, national frameworks have begun to provide guidance for such articulations. For example, the

Lumina Foundation's beta Credentials Framework identifies personal skills, such as autonomy, responsibility, self-awareness, and reflectiveness, as essential components of students' overall skill set.[31] The AAC&U has identified developing students' sense of "agency" as a guiding principle of its General Education Maps and Markers framework. Entire state university systems have also begun to recognize particular "noncognitive" skills, such as academic mindset and belonging.[32]

Additionally, institutions have found pathways into discussions of personal and social development through connections to institutional core purposes or missions. Georgetown University, like many Jesuit universities, promotes self-care (*cura personalis*) as a defining principle of its mission. This mission-centered orientation provided leverage for launching the successful Engelhard Project, in which faculty infuse modules related to student well-being and personal development into traditional academic courses. Additionally, large-scale institutional commitments to well-being have fostered university-wide commitments to wellness and healthy-living programs and initiatives at George Mason University and the Healthy Campus initiative at Simon Fraser University. Finally, a handful of colleges and universities have explicitly identified well-being outcomes, such as "personal development" and "spiritual, physical, and mental health," among institutional or general education outcomes.[33]

Another challenge in fostering personal and social development is the imposition of adding one more thing for faculty to do. Giving students opportunities for reflection, interaction, and feedback, not to mention all three, can feel like a substantial time commitment. Faculty alone should not be responsible for helping students to connect the dots between the development of their cognitive skills and certain affective or civic skills. The job is too great and classroom time too constrained. While as educators and academic advisors, faculty play a significant role in shaping students' personal and social development, an opportunity exists to explore a larger network of support for students' development of these skills. Mentoring programs, available on most campuses, are one type of resource. Whether peer, academic, or career, mentors provide support from which all students, and particularly those from increasingly diverse and underserved backgrounds, can benefit.[34] Holistic or team-based advising programs, such as Dominican University of California's integrative coaching program, Agnes Scott College's Summit program where each student chooses a "personal board of advisors," and LaGuardia Community College's advising teams are a few examples of this type of mentoring.[35]

Finally, even if students' personal and social development skills can be articulated, championed, and reinforced, they still need to be assessed. This can be a challenge for any institutional learning outcome, but assessment can seem particularly nebulous when considering constructs like hope, flourishing, resilience, self-efficacy, growth mindset, and belonging. Though such skills are sometimes assumed to be unmeasurable, a number of reliable and valid instruments exist and have been widely deployed.[36]

The connection of students' personal and social development to the classroom, however, suggests some linkage of assessment with students' demonstrated ability, perhaps through reflection papers, journals, or other efforts. This type of assessment complements standardized instruments that, while valid and reliable, are based on students' self-reported feelings and behaviors. Direct assessment offers the opportunity to expand the evidence base by explicitly linking these skills with classroom learning through assignments and faculty feedback. The AAC&U VALUE rubrics, released in 2009, provide a resource for the direct assessment of some of these proficiencies, particularly as they relate to teamwork and civic skills, such as civic engagement, ethical reasoning, and intercultural knowledge and competence.[37] Though VALUE rubrics for personal and social development outcomes do not yet exist, the rubric template provides a model for how such assessments might be constructed. Two such campus-based examples are Tidewater Community College's rubric for "personal development" and Chattanooga State Community College's rubric to evaluate "work ethic."[38] Both possess a structure and layout similar to the VALUE rubrics.

Looking Forward: Changing the Narrative for
Student Learning and Success

Based on what we know two decades into the twenty-first century, here are some hopeful predictions for the changing narrative in higher education. Colleges and universities will increasingly highlight the ways in which a college degree is a certification of students' ability and confidence not just to get a job but to nimbly move between career paths. Campus narratives will emphasize the ways in which students are prepared to join, manage, and lead within a diverse global workforce. Higher education as a whole will be viewed as the training ground for equipping students with the self-esteem to get things done, the perseverance to stare down crises, and the risk taking to innovate, precisely because they have had a sandbox in which to practice confronting failure and persisting.

Supporting students' personal and social development will more fluidly and authentically connect the curriculum and cocurriculum. The inertia that keeps these two halves of the campus separate will disappear under the weight of resource realignment and the desire for a holistic student experience. Even as faculty "own the curriculum," faculty and student affairs professionals will develop greater understanding of the ways in which they mutually share responsibility for students' learning. In part, this will be through the understanding that contributions to high-impact practices are a collective, not a singular, endeavor. Additionally, campuses will find new innovations and recognition for advising and mentoring programs, possibly as part of those high-impact practices. As the campus community works together in service of students' cognitive, personal, and social development, new understandings of equity will be forged by honoring how students' affective strengths are fundamental to their success.

Ultimately, the coming decades will recognize that who students are and how they feel—about the world, about each other, and about themselves—is every bit as important as what they know and can do. The first step is to stop calling any of this "soft." It is going to be hard. It is going to be rigorous. It is going to be consequential. And what we know of liberal education in the twenty-first century will be better because of it.

Notes

1. Hart Research Associates, *It Takes More than a Major: Employer Priorities for College Learning and Student Success* (Washington, DC: Association of American Colleges and Universities, 2013), https://www.aacu.org/leap/presidentstrust/compact/2013SurveySummary; Hart Research Associates, *Falling Short? College Learning and Career Success* (Washington, DC: Association of American Colleges and Universities, 2015), https://www.aacu.org/leap/public-opinion-research/2015-survey-falling-short.

2. Bureau of Labor Statistics, "Number of Jobs, Labor Market Experience, and Earnings Growth: Results from a National Longitudinal Survey," August 22, 2019, https://www.bls.gov/news.release/pdf/nlsoy.pdf.

3. Hart Research Associates, "Fulfilling the American Dream: Liberal Education and the Future of Work," July 2018, https://www.aacu.org/sites/default/files/files/LEAP/2018EmployerResearchReport.pdf.

4. Association of American Colleges and Universities, "What Is Liberal Education?," n.d., https://www.aacu.org/leap/what-is-a-liberal-education.

5. Hart Research Associates, "Fulfilling the American Dream."

6. Anthony P. Carnevale, Nicole Smith, and Jeff Strohl, *Recovery: Job Growth and Education Requirements through 2020* (Washington, DC: Georgetown University, Center on Education and the Workforce, 2013), http://cew.georgetown.edu/recovery2020.

7. See, for example, Arlie Russell Hochschild, *The Managed Heart: Commercialization of Human Feeling*, 3rd ed. (Berkeley: University of California Press, 2012).

8. See, for example, Sharon C. Bolton, "Conceptual Confusions: Emotion Work as Skilled Work," in *The Skills That Matter*, ed. Chris Warhurst, Irena Grugulis, and Ewart Keep (Basingstoke, England: Palgrave Macmillan, 2004), 19–37.

9. See, for example, Paula England, *Comparable Worth: Theories and Evidence* (New York: De Gruyter, 1992).

10. National Center for Education Statistics, "2019 Fast Facts," https://nces.ed.gov/fastfacts/display.asp?id=372.

11. National Center for Education Statistics, "The Condition of Education," https://nces.ed.gov/programs/coe/indicator_cha.asp, accessed February 8, 2019.

12. National Center for Education Statistics, "Condition of Education." The enrollment gains recorded between 2000 and 2010 have diminished in recent years, however. All racial groups, except for Hispanic students, enrolled in colleges and universities at lower rates from 2010 to 2016.

13. National Center for Education Statistics, "2017 Fast Facts"; Grace Chen, "Changing Student Demographics: Rising Number of Professional Students," *Community College Review*, May 1, 2019, https://www.communitycollegereview.com/blog/changing-student-demographics-rising-number-of-professional-students.

14. Doug Lederman, "The Bermuda Triangle of Credit Transfer," *Inside Higher Ed*, September 14, 2017, https://www.insidehighered.com/news/2017/09/14/reports-highlight-woes-faced-one-third-all-college-students-who-transfer.

15. Emily Forrest Cataldi, Christopher T. Bennett, and Xianglei Chen, "First-Generation Students: College Access, Persistence, and Postbachelor's Outcomes," National Center for Education Statistics, US Department of Education, February 2018, https://nces.ed.gov/pubs2018/2018421.pdf.

16. See, for example, Tara J. Yosso, "Whose Culture Has Capital? A Critical Race Theory Discussion of Community Cultural Wealth," *Race, Ethnicity, and Education* 8, no. 1 (2005): 69–91; Laura I. Rendón, Amaury Nora, and Vijay Kanagala, *Ventajas/Assets, Conocimientos/Knowledge: Leveraging Latin@ Strengths to Foster Student Success* (San Antonio: Center for Research and Policy in Education, University of Texas, 2014), 5.

17. American College Health Association. *American College Health Association-National College Health Assessment II: Reference Group Executive Summary Fall 2017* (Hanover, MD: American College Health Association, 2018), 13–14. https://www.acha.org/documents/ncha/NCHA-II_FALL_2017_REFERENCE_GROUP_EXECUTIVE_SUMMARY.pdf.

18. American Psychological Association, "Campus Mental Health," n.d., http://www.apa.org/advocacy/higher-education/mental-health/index.aspx.

19. David R. Reetz et al., *The Association for University and College Counseling Center Directors Annual Survey* (Indianapolis, IN: Association for University and College Counseling Center Directors, 2017), https://www.aucccd.org/assets/documents/aucccd%202016%20monograph%20-%20public.pdf.

20. George Kuh, *High-Impact Practices: What They Are, Who Has Access to Them, and Why They Matter* (Washington, DC: Association of American Colleges and Universities, 2008); Ashley Finley and Tia McNair, *Assessing Underserved Students' Engagement in High-Impact Practices* (Washington, DC:

Association of American Colleges and Universities, 2013), https://leap connections.aacu.org/system/files/assessinghipsmcnairfinley_0.pdf.

21. See, for example, Ashley Finley and Tia McNair, "The Intersection of Life and Learning: What Cultural Wealth and Liberal Education Mean for Whole Student Development," in *Intersectionality in Action: A Guide for Faculty and Campus Leaders for Creating Inclusive Classrooms and Institutions*, ed. Brooke Barnett and Peter Felten (Sterling, VA: Stylus, 2016), 125–135.

22. Kuh, *High-Impact Practices*, 20; George Kuh and Ken O'Donnell, *Ensuring Quality and Taking High-Impact Practices to Scale* (Washington, DC: Association of American Colleges and Universities, 2013), 10.

23. Kuh, *High-Impact Practices*; Kuh and O'Donnell, *Ensuring Quality*.

24. Alma R. Clayton-Pedersen and Ashley Finley, "Afterword: What's Next? Identifying When High-Impact Practices Are Done Well," in *Five High-Impact Practices: Research on Outcomes, Completion, and Quality*, ed. Jayne E. Brownell and Lynn E. Swaner (Washington, DC: Association of American Colleges and Universities, 2011), 53–57.

25. Carol Rodgers, "Seeing Student Learning: Teacher Change and the Role of Reflection," *Harvard Educational Review* 72, no. 2 (2002): 230–253.

26. Rodgers, "Seeing Student Learning."

27. Leo M. Lambert, Jason Husser, and Peter Felten, "Mentors Play Critical Role in Quality of College Experience, New Poll Suggests," *The Conversation*, August 22, 2018, https://theconversation.com/mentors-play-critical-role-in-quality-of-college-experience-new-poll-suggests-101861.

28. Kuh, *High-Impact Practices*; Kuh and O'Donnell, *Ensuring Quality*.

29. Ashley Finley and George Kuh, "The Case for Connecting First-Year Seminars and Learning Communities," in *Building Synergy for High-Impact Educational Initiatives: First-Year Seminars and Learning Communities*, ed. Lauren Chism Schmidt and Janine Graziano (Columbia: University of South Carolina, National Resource Center for the First-Year Experience and Students in Transition, 2016), 3–18.

30. Paul Hanstedt, *Creating Wicked Students: Designing Courses for a Complex World* (Sterling, VA: Stylus, 2018).

31. Lumina Foundation, *Connecting Credentials: A Beta Credentials Framework* (Indianapolis, IN: Lumina Foundation, 2015), 6, http://connectingcredentials.org/wp-content/uploads/2015/05/ConnectingCredentials-4-29-30.pdf.

32. See, for example, the College System of Tennessee, "Academic Mindset," n.d., https://www.tbr.edu/student-success/academic-mindset; and the University

of Texas System's focus on belonging: "Affinity Groups," n.d., https://www.utsystem.edu/offices/academic-affairs/affinity-groups.

33. See, for example, Dominican University of California, University of Northern Colorado, Tulsa Community College, and Tidewater Community College.

34. Lambert, Husser, and Felten, "Mentors Play Critical Role"; see also *Great Jobs, Great Lives: The 2014 Gallup-Purdue Index Report* (Washington, DC: Gallup, 2014), https://www.luminafoundation.org/files/resources/galluppurdueindex-report-2014.pdf.

35. Dominican University of California, "Integrative Coaches," https://www.dominican.edu/academics/advising/integrative-coaches; Agnes Scott College, "Personal Board of Advisors," http://summit.agnesscott.edu/boardofadvisors.html; LaGuardia Community College, "Academic Advising: Advising Teams," https://www.laguardia.edu/advising.

36. See, for example, the University of Pennsylvania's Positive Psychology Center for a comprehensive list of resources: "Questionnaires for Researchers," n.d., https://ppc.sas.upenn.edu/resources/questionnaires-researchers. See also Corey L. M. Keyes, "Promoting and Protecting Mental Health as Flourishing: A Complementary Strategy for Improving Mental Health," *American Psychologist* 62, no. 2 (2007): 95-108; Carol D. Ryff and Burton Singer, "Interpersonal Flourishing: A Positive Health Agenda for the Millennium," *Personality and Social Psychology Review* 4, no. 1 (2000): 30-44.

37. Association of American Colleges and Universities, "VALUE," n.d., https://www.aacu.org/value.

38. Association of American Colleges and Universities, "Additional Campus Rubrics," n.d., https://www.aacu.org/additional-campus-rubrics.

16   Can We Liberate Liberal Education?

Randy Bass

> To engage in learning always entails the risk that learning might have an impact on you, that learning might change you. This means that education only begins when the learner is willing to take a risk.
> —Gert Biesta, *Beyond Learning*

The world has changed, and liberal education won. Through a combination of forces, the world has largely come to a consensus that the skills and abilities most relevant to the future of human work, and indeed human survival, are highly aligned with the kinds of learning and capacities that are cultivated in a liberal education: critical thinking, creativity, complex systems thinking, design, imagination, empathy, acting in conditions of uncertainty, and many more. The outcomes that have traditionally been associated with liberal education seem well poised for the future. What is in question and under threat is the status of liberal education *institutions* and whether liberal arts as disciplinary fields and practices are going to be the central homes and drivers for the future of these outcomes. If liberal education institutions are going to leverage this situation—the ascendancy of liberal education outcomes—then they will have to think and act very differently than they do now.

This challenge requires both imagination and humility. It asks those of us in liberal education institutions to listen to this new consensus and see it as neither a pure threat nor a simple affirmation. It asks educators to try and imagine what it could look like to lift certain outcomes of liberal education out of their professionalized disciplinary formations and to see them in new kinds of purposeful engagements with the world. It asks us to consider remaking some of our core practices in light of new modes of human creativity, productivity, community, and meaning making, which have partially emerged outside of higher education. It asks us to consider—in the spirit of liberal education—the blind spots and biases in our practices that perpetuate some of the binaries (e.g., between theory and practice) that the rest of the world has blurred and complicated.

Four Propositions

If our traditional higher education institutions are going to continue to play a formative and defining role in the cultivation of the outcomes that have been associated with liberal education, then I suggest that we come to grips with four propositions:

1. As we look to the future, and as machines get better at being machines, the primary purpose of higher education must be helping humans get better at being human.
2. If we are to reorient around human capacity, then we need to balance our orientation by disciplines with at least an equal orientation by dispositions.
3. The critical context for cultivating dispositions is applied learning, which has to become the core of liberal education for it to survive and flourish.
4. If we are to manage this shift, liberal education must liberate itself from its resistance to transformation. Liberal education institutions must become flexible, adaptable, and reflective in the same ways we hope for our graduates.

The purpose of this chapter then is to ask: What would it look like for liberal education to live up to its own intrinsic principles such that it might liberate not just individuals, but the institutions where we educate them? Rebecca Chopp has argued that "to make the case for the

Can We Liberate Liberal Education? 223

liberal arts, we need to assert a more proactive claim about our special relevance for linking knowledge, community, and freedom in the future. Although the critics' conclusions may be reductionist, we are not recused from the task of making the case for the liberal arts as a leader of change for education."[1] How might liberal education embody this leadership and take ownership of the demands of our age around creativity and adaptation in order to refit our institutions, educationally, for the future?

Proposition 1: The Primary Purpose of Higher Education Must Be Helping Humans Get Better at Being Human

The environment, polarization, inequality, and the advance of artificial intelligence and machine learning—one need only look to the existential threats that loom in the coming years to contextualize the assertion that liberal education must focus on helping humans get better at being human. Educating a generation to grapple with these wicked challenges globally and in everyday life compels us to consider the full range of human abilities, from systems thinking about wicked problems, to expansive approaches to innovation, to empathetic capacities to think beyond one's own horizon. This also includes the skills and capacities that equip humans for the narrowing range of work left to them by computers and automation, which Levy and Murnane framed several years ago as solving unstructured problems, working with new information (including complex communication), and carrying out nonroutine manual tasks.[2] Although much of what goes on in our institutions of higher education is preparing students for this future, by and large we are not evolving fast enough, doing it intentionally enough or well enough, nor providing it equitably and comprehensively.

Every institution of higher education has an implicit (if not explicit) set of beliefs about two questions regarding students and their education: Who belongs here? How hard should the institution work to help them succeed? In many ways the history of US higher education is the unfolding expansion and evolution of the answers to those two questions, which can also be put into a two-by-two matrix. The first axis is

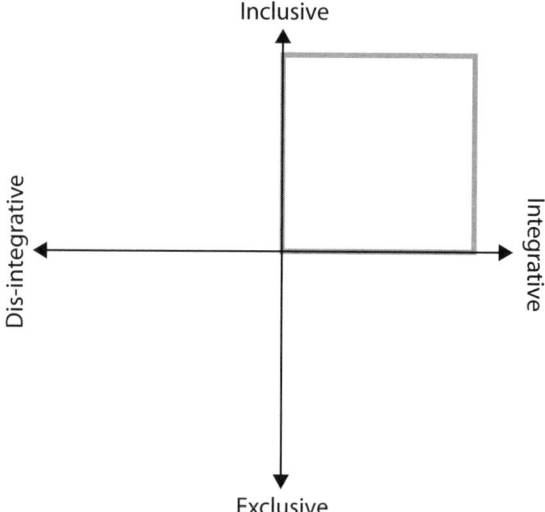

Higher education is now driven to design for the upper-right quadrant of this two-by-two matrix, valuing integrative learning and inclusion.

about belonging or inclusion and all that has been associated with the movement for "inclusive excellence" launched by the Association of American Colleges and Universities about twenty years ago, which is "designed to help colleges and universities integrate diversity, equity, and educational quality efforts into their missions and institutional operations."[3] We can think of this as the inclusive-exclusive axis.

The other axis is about what it means to support student success and to what end. This axis is defined by the central tension of our era in higher education: between an "integrative" and a "disintegrative" vision of education.[4] What is at stake in this axis is perhaps the difference between "learning" and "education"—whether one thinks that it is sufficient to conceive of higher education as merely a collection of granular or discrete learning experiences, narrowly aimed at particular outcomes, or whether one thinks of higher education as a sum of diverse learning experiences aimed at developing different aspects of the whole person, which is greater than the parts.

Higher education, and liberal education specifically, must be focused in the upper right quadrant of this two-by-two matrix—where inclusion and integration define the values—because our contemporary context demands that we must now maximize our institutions for both inclusion (equity both in access and in outcomes of experience) and integration (striving for the kinds of holistic learning outcomes that are fitted to the demands of the age). This quadrant is new territory. Higher education as a sector may have valued one or the other, but recent decades have put nearly all higher education institutions in a position where both inclusion and integration are now a priority.

The implications of this quadrant are both direct and complex. The direct implication is that we need to create the most holistic education for the most diverse range of students. That is difficult enough. But the more profound and complex implication is to believe in education as a context for the restless interrogation of questions about what it means to be human and what is the most human (integrative) approach to education. Who belongs and how the institution reshapes itself to new learners (and not the other way around) are important because liberal education has long been deeply rooted in humanistic ideals, as well as the privilege of a particular class. If we are to imagine a future for liberal education that speaks to the future of humanity, then it has to implement a version of liberal education beyond privilege and exclusion.

"The problem with humanism," says Gert Biesta, "is that it posits a *norm of humanness*, a norm of what it means to be human, and in doing so excludes those who do not live up to or are unable to live up to this norm." Biesta wants to see "the question of the humanity of the human being as a radically *open* question, a question that can only be answered by engaging in education rather than as a question that needs to be answered *before* we can engage in education."[5] The inclusion pole of this two-by-two matrix stresses the need for a radically open approach to the humanity of the human being; similarly, the integrative pole of the matrix represents an emergent definition of the traits and capacities that define education for a volatile and complex world. Both inclusion and integration become animating questions, not just mandates. This is what it means for higher education to take as its project helping humans get better at being human.

What then is the best way to organize an education that is designed for this integrative and inclusive context? This is where we come to the centrality of what I call, collectively, "dispositional learning."

Proposition 2: If We Are to Reorient around Human Capacity, Then We Need to Balance Our Orientation by Disciplines with at Least an Equal Orientation by Dispositions

In 2012, David Scobey suggested that higher education was experiencing a "Copernican moment": on the verge of shifting to a new, more holistic, and civically minded educational paradigm.[6] If such a change is truly Copernican, then something paradigmatic—something comparable to an earth-centered to sun-centered shift—is afoot. I propose that this change is well under way, and it involves a reconceptualization of the curriculum from revolving around disciplines to revolving around dispositions.

Dispositional learning—which I define briefly as the dimensions of learning associated with the traits that make us most human—distinguishes human capacities from those of machines and forms the underlying basis of all competence. In the concept of dispositional learning, I bring together in one category a large body of work that has burgeoned over the last twenty or thirty years in the learning sciences to include growth mindsets, self-efficacy, self-regulated learning, metacognitive abilities, and traits such as grit, empathy, resilience, and humility. This body of work on dispositions has had a formative role in shaping learning and the human capacities and skills that are widely regarded as on the ascent due to the rise of automation and artificial intelligence. This convergence around dispositional learning brings new salience to the long traditions that put the cultivation of a humanistic essence at the heart of the liberal arts. However, the contexts in which these intrinsically human qualities are cultivated are changing.

In many ways, the rise of dispositional learning is reconnecting something fundamental in higher education that got disconnected somewhere between 100 and 200 years ago. For many centuries the liberal arts were solely for foundational study and were aimed at moral character formation. One could go on to advanced study only in theology, law, or medicine. It was not until the nineteenth century and the rise of the research university with its sole project of "knowledge creation" that the liberal arts developed ambitions to professionalize with master's and doctoral studies. By the end of the nineteenth century, moral character formation had all but been banished from college and university classrooms. Professors were no longer responsible for such formation, but only for the foundations of knowledge creation and the development of the mind. Residential colleges and other institutional services started to carry the burden of moral character formation through an increasingly professionalized staff and elaborated student affairs, residential, and extra- and cocurricular life, which developed around the perimeter of the academic core.[7]

With the rise and spread of dispositional learning in higher education, we are witnessing a reconnection of broader human formation with the kind of intellectual development associated with the project of knowledge creation. Certainly a powerful dispositional concept like Carol Dweck's work on "growth mindset" is an example of such a bridge,[8] as would be similar dispositions, such as resilience, or even our increasingly broadened understanding of critical thinking to include social dimensions of learning and intrapersonal dimensions, such as belonging and self-efficacy.

Worldwide, there is burgeoning interest in lists of skills, abilities, mindsets, and broad capacities that often go under the name of "twenty-first-century skills." A focus on dispositions is inclusive of this perspective but also allows us to move beyond "twenty-first-century outcomes" aimed solely at workforce effectiveness and career resilience. All of these lists and formulations share the goal of preparing graduates for being effective in the world, typically for success in the workplace, but often with an eye to diverse teams and global settings, changing skill sets, and long-term career resilience. Typically, these lists look something like this: critical thinking, creativity, collaboration, communication, information literacy, media literacy, technological literacy, flexibility, leadership, initiative, productivity, social skills.[9]

Give or take, you'll find most of these dispositions, literacies, and skills on many lists, forming a metalanguage for understanding the needs of "today's learners." What if such lists were just the beginning? What if this new metalanguage were a prototype for a reconceptualization of the curriculum and its place in the overall educational journey that was intended to prepare students not only for careers but to be effective at coping with and repairing the kinds of wicked problems and existential threats facing our world?

Let's expand that list to include an even wider range of capacities: cognitive flexibility, comfort with ambiguity, comfort with discomfort, judgment in uncertainty, action with integrity, integrative thinking, conscientiousness, playfulness, entrepreneurial thinking and action, reflective learning, metacognition and self-monitoring, adaptability, systems thinking, synthetic thinking, consensus building, engaged leadership, managing polarities, cultural agility and humility, self-advocacy, self-care, perspective taking, sensitivity to opportunity, and critical hope.[10] Although not all of these are purely dispositional, as some directly imply skills and abilities, all are deeply dependent on abilities and capacities that are integrative and intrinsically human. What is critical about them is that they are all deeply integrative of knowledge and skills belonging to disciplines, but they are also the skills and abilities for exercising judgment and acting in the world shaped by sensitivity to context, others, and the self. Reorienting our sense of the educational journey around such concepts has at least five distinct advantages:

- They are learner-focused and student-centered, emphasizing competence, personal development, and agency.
- They span cognitive, metacognitive, and socioemotional dimensions and thus address the whole person and the broad scope of human effectiveness.
- They span the curricular and the cocurricular and have the potential to build a more integrative ecosystem.

- They span the disciplines and therefore have the potential to foster interdisciplinary and integrative designs and break down silos.
- Perhaps most important, and flowing from the above, they have the potential to provide a language that liberates the outcomes of liberal learning from the disciplinary structures, departmentally defined requirements, and contested and often privileged institutional settings that are too often hindrances to innovation and to extending the benefits of liberal education to new populations of learners in new settings.

This is not to deny the importance of the disciplines (and interdisciplinary inquiry) as critical systems and practices for liberal education. Nor is it to claim that we should not continue to organize our research enterprises around disciplines and interdisciplinary domains of study. I am merely arguing that an inevitable consequence of positioning liberal education for the demands of the future is a shift to seeing the disciplines as instrumental—not fundamental—to liberal educational practices designed for learning how to learn, how to navigate change, and how to be effective in the world. As Charles Muscatine, the founder of Strawberry Creek College at the University of California, Berkeley, puts it:

> Imagining the problems of life in the twenty-first century, the problems of coping with a future more complex and dangerous than any of us has ever faced, we would not come up with anything as abstract, as narrow, as insular, in short as "subject oriented" as an academic major. We would, instead, be thinking of intellectual powers, of experience, the ability to cope, to come to right judgments.[11]

All liberal education institutions and most of their stakeholders would claim to value some significant portion of the list above, even if they use different language. But valuing outcomes is not enough; you have to design for them. This brings us to the matter of applied learning.

Proposition 3: The Critical Context for Cultivating Dispositions Is Applied Learning, Which Has to Become the Core of Liberal Education for It to Survive and Flourish

In discussing how to develop people to be effective in a world that is "radically contingent, hyper-connected, and constantly changing," John Seely Brown suggests that "the real job of universities is to cultivate, not to teach."[12] Indeed, one axiom about dispositions is that they cannot be acquired through direct instruction, but they can be cultivated. That is, you cannot lecture someone about adaptability, sensitivity to opportunity, or humility, but you can create environments and experiences where those capacities are more likely to be cultivated. Broadly, and at the risk of underdetermining something I mean quite robustly, I am calling these learning environments "applied learning."

Joseph Aoun in *Robot-Proof: Higher Education in the Age of Artificial Intelligence* posits his own compact list of "cognitive capacities," which I included in my longer list above: "Critical Thinking, Systems Thinking, Entrepreneurship and Cultural Agility."[13] He groups these under the banner of "humanics," because he believes they are the traits that most distinguish us as humans and that will most "robot-proof" our students in the future. As the president of Northeastern University, a school with a long-established program in co-op education, he naturally associates these capacities with those developed in experiential learning workplace settings:

> We have seen that when learners put their knowledge into practice in real-life situations, they develop a better understanding of themselves, their strengths and weaknesses, and their drives and possibilities. They also sharpen their cognitive capacities, leading to the robot-proof qualities of creativity and mental flexibility—both aspects of far transfer. By contrast, no computer has yet displayed creativity, entrepreneurialism, or cultural agility. And although machines are continually improving in their ability to map knowledge onto recognizable problems—in other words, improving in

their near transfer abilities—they cannot perform far transfer well, at least not in the infinite contexts of real life.[14]

Aoun's argument is that if experiential learning is critical to the future of human work, then we can no longer think of experience as extrinsic or peripheral to core academic learning. Aoun's words are very rich: "when learners put their knowledge into practice in real-life situations, they develop a better understanding of themselves, their strengths and weaknesses, and their drives and possibilities." So rich that the term "experiential learning" seems like a very limited way to understand this process of practice and self-understanding. I prefer "applied learning" over "experiential learning" because of its triple-layered implications: first, applied learning is a characteristic of a domain's knowledge itself (i.e., the application of ideas, theories, and methods of a domain to the world); second, applied learning is the opportunity for individuals to apply their learning to authentic situations; and third, applied learning invokes a larger sense of purpose, the way that one learns from certain experiences what it can mean to apply oneself to a particular path or calling.

It is with all three of these meanings that applied learning becomes the crucible that integrates the personal development of individual learners (the legacy of moral character formation of the eighteenth and nineteenth centuries), professional development (the imprint of late nineteenth- and twentieth-century utilitarian education), and the more purely cognitive knowledge creation that emerged in the modern university and ultimately dominated all levels of the US higher education ecosystem in terms of classroom-based curriculum. This crucible goes by an increasing diversity of names in higher education: undergraduate research (course-embedded and cocurricular), community-based learning and service learning, credit-bearing internships and practicum experiences, entrepreneurship, social innovation, global education, project-based learning, and problem-based curricula (including notable infusions into core curricula and general education). Nearly all high-impact practices are applied learning practices, integratively and equitably executed.

Collectively, though, these emerging practices have made only modest gains in changing the academic core, let alone truly integrating the heart of the academic curriculum with the most learning-intensive dimensions of the cocurriculum. If applied learning is critical to the future of human work, and the future of being human, then it must become the new core of liberal education. This will of course require functionally liberating an educational focus on individual students' learning experience and human formation from the long-standing biases of the research enterprise, which elevate theory over application, pure research over practice.

It also requires eliminating our educational biases about where liberal education happens. Lee Shulman suggested in 2005 that "liberal education's signature pedagogy should really be the seminar," implying that this is the key setting where teachers and students practice daily the kinds of social interactions that characterize the essence of liberal learning.[15] Looking forward, we need to add applied learning (mentored, reflective, integrative) as another signature pedagogy of liberal education.

The future of a democratized liberal education depends on reframing applied learning from anomalous educational enrichments to core practices. Only in isolated pockets have higher education institutions taken seriously the idea that we might organize students' progress through their education differently in ways that would push us to the next paradigm. In part, the problem is that we have not had anything to replace the disciplines as the coordinates of the educational journey. Some have suggested reorganizing by "grand problems." Others focus on choosing a mission not a major. In the twenty-first century, the essential learning outcomes of the Association of American Colleges and Universities have been a powerful framework for starting this shift and democratizing liberal education outcomes. In the broadest sense, we can also understand this shift as what David Labaree calls the "mutual subversion of liberal and professional education," where across the tiers of higher education, professional education gets increasingly liberal in content while liberal education gets increasingly practical and vocational in purpose.[16]

Can We Liberate Liberal Education?

What this transition looks like will vary widely across institutions and the different tiers of the system, and it will take a couple of more decades to really shift the center of curricula. The most daring experiments will come out of exigency: for example, small liberal arts colleges might consolidate departments into divisions or clusters, or reorient some majors and minors into new interdisciplinary degrees, where curricular and cocurricular experiences are intrinsic to the requirements. We might see changes in areas such as the humanities in public institutions where as a matter of revitalization, if not survival, they could reconceive their centrality as being as much about cultivating the dispositions of cultural agility and humility or contributing to capacities for managing polarities as about replicating the disciplinary study of literature and culture.

Similarly, I suspect we'll start to see a next generation of general education reform that shifts, for example, from developing inquiry-based learning as an enhanced way of introducing a discipline, to any given discipline being an effective and instrumental way to introduce students to inquiry as a fundamental learning modality and practice. We might see more schools elevating design and entrepreneurial thinking to a complementary (and fundamental) learning modality, developed as a core practice for all students. Finally, as polarization and inequality continue to rise in the United States, more institutions will take more seriously the imperative for intergroup dialogue skills, empathy, and, more broadly, moral imagination as other essential learning modalities that do not merely arise through abstract reading, classroom discussion, and writing, but have to be taught as a matter of practice through experiential and applied learning. Moral character formation through practice will be increasingly seen as essential to both workplace preparation and social preservation.

In US higher education, standards and signals flow from the top— from the most selective and influential schools—but innovation and creative expansion typically flow first from the broad base. If the changes I am predicting take place, they will occur through a convergence coming from two directions: small but high-profile incremental changes in the most elite schools as they angle for differentiation in a mature and competitive marketplace, and bolder versions of these changes driven by necessity among schools that either are struggling for sheer survival or aiming to serve increasingly diverse populations with increasingly market-responsive and integrative approaches, often with dwindling public funding.

Yet, to state the obvious, most liberal education institutions are not built to optimize their curricula in order to develop these traits in students. That will require a new way of thinking and doing.

Proposition 4: If We Are to Live Up to This Challenge, Liberal Education Must Liberate Itself from Its Resistance to Transformation

Liberal education is widely understood to be emancipatory, preparing individuals not only to deal with complexity and change, but to do so by liberating them from their own narrow assumptions and blind spots. Yet despite its emancipatory power to equip individuals for change, liberal education is often defended on campuses as a bulwark against institutional change. The very framework that its advocates argue is the best way to prepare learners for a lifetime of resilience and adaptability is too often defended on campuses as the path of preservation against innovation and institutional adaptability. This irony is particularly pointed in a moment when liberal education must reinvent itself not only to survive in its institutional forms, but to reposition itself to prepare future generations of students to navigate and heal the world. What might it look like to apply to our own institutional change practices the same values (and ambitions) we propose for our students' growth and development? Is it reasonable to expect that if we want to produce graduates who are agile, adaptive, self-reflective, and resilient, then liberal education institutions must embody those very traits?

In the same way that Daniel Kahneman explores "thinking, fast and slow,"[17] liberal education institutions need a combination of slow change and fast change processes, whose dynamic is guided by the higher aspirations and greater purposes of our institutions. The slow change processes are those that make liberal education—and colleges and universi-

Can We Liberate Liberal Education?

ties broadly—the kinds of institutions they are. At its best, this change modality is rooted in evidence-based practices, sustained institutional values, the scholarship of teaching and learning, and the social and communal sharing of knowledge that characterizes both critical inquiry and shared governance.

In the face of the challenges and shifts I've been discussing, slow change processes are no longer enough. They need to be complemented by fast change processes that adapt the practices of agile design to accelerate the pace of innovation so as to respond to the volatile and uncertain conditions of our world. This change modality asks institutions to adopt innovation, even imagination, as an official institutional stance, along with an entrepreneurial mindset for expanding, bending, and reshaping the ways they manifest their core practices.

Adopting a combination—even a dialectic—of fast and slow change processes is essential to move forward, not because we know they are the way to achieve a certain outcome but precisely because we really have no idea what this next paradigm will look like. This is what Ann Pendleton-Jullian and John Seely Brown mean by designing for "emergence":

> If we want to have agency, we need to understand emergence. We need to think in terms of emergence and we need to design for emergence. Understanding emergence lets us see the world in a new way, and designing for emergence lets us put that new vision to work in the world with agency at many scales, from the small and catalytic, to the ecosystemic.[18]

The preservation and transformation of liberal education cannot be a conservative act. The future liberal education needs to exercise all of the same modalities that our students need: inquiry, design, agility, humility. Moreover, as we work to maximize the values of inclusion and integration, we need change processes, underpinned by mindsets, that are comfortable with seeing both whom we serve and how we serve them as radically open questions, where explorations of the limits and possibilities are deeply embedded in the act of education.

This moment asks us to take risks. The question we should be asking ourselves is which risks are worth taking, not whether we should change. I invoke Gert Biesta's words in the epigraph to this chapter: "To engage in learning always entails the risk that learning might have an impact on you, that learning might change you. This means that education only begins when the learner is willing to take a risk." He goes on to say: "To negate or deny the risk involved in engaging in education is to miss a crucial dimension of education. To suggest that education can be and should be risk free, that learners don't run any risk by engaging in education, or that learning outcomes can be known and specified in advance, is a misrepresentation of what education is about."[19]

The same is definitively true of institutions. And to play with Biesta's words, perhaps "education only begins when *educators* are willing to take a risk." We must find ways to integrate imaginative, speculative, empathetic, and conscientious practices into our ways of doing business. If we are to write a positive future for liberal education, its outcomes, and its institutional practices, we must demand from ourselves the coherence— one might even say the integrity—that aligns the modalities of student learning and development with our institutions' learning and capacity for change.

Notes

1. Rebecca Chopp, "Remaking, Renewing, Reimagining: The Liberal Arts College Takes Advantage of Change," in *Remaking College: Innovation and the Liberal Arts*, ed. Rebecca Chopp, Susan Frost, and Daniel H. Weiss (Baltimore, MD: Johns Hopkins University Press, 2013).

2. Frank Levy and Richard Murnane, *Dancing with Robots: Human Skills for Computerized Work* (Cambridge, MA: Thirdway Publishing, MIT, 2013).

3. Association of American Colleges and Universities, "Making Excellence Inclusive," n.d., https://www.aacu.org/making-excellence-inclusive.

4. I wrote about this previously in Randy Bass, "The Impact of Technology on the Future of Human Learning," *Change* 50, nos. 3-4 (2018): 34-39. An even earlier version appeared in Randy Bass and Bret Eynon, *Open and Integrative: Designing Liberal Education for the New Digital Ecosystem* (Washington, DC: Association of American Colleges and Universities, 2016).

5. Gert J. J. Biesta, *Beyond Learning: Democratic Education for a Human Future* (Boulder, CO: Paradigm, 2006), 6 (emphases in original).

6. David M. Scobey, "A Copernican Moment: On the Revolutions in Higher Education," in *Transforming Undergraduate Education: Theory That Compels and Practices That Succeed*, ed. Donald W. Harward (Lanham, MD: Rowman and Littlefield, 2012).

7. Chad Wellmon, *Organizing Enlightenment Information Overload and the Invention of the Modern Research University* (Baltimore, MD: Johns Hopkins University Press, 2015); Andrew Delbanco, *College: What It Was, What It Is, and What It Should Be* (Princeton, NJ: Princeton University Press, 2012).

8. See, for example, Carol Dweck, *Mindset: the New Psychology of Success* (New York: Ballantine, 2007).

9. Applied Educational Systems, "What Are 21st Century Skills?," n.d., https://www.aeseducation.com/career-readiness/what-are-21st-century-skills.

10. I've compiled this list from numerous sources, including Joseph E. Aoun's *Robot-Proof: Higher Education in the Age of Artificial Intelligence* (Cambridge, MA: MIT Press, 2017); Bennington College, as listed in Charles Muscatine, *Fixing College Education: A New Curriculum for the Twenty-First Century* (Charlottesville: University of Virginia Press, 2009); the Carnegie Foundation for the Advancement of Teaching's studies of the profession, http://archive.carnegiefoundation.org/previous-work/professional-graduate-education.html; and George Kuh, *High-Impact Educational Practices: What They Are, Who Has Access to Them, and Why They Matter* (Washington, DC: Association of American Colleges and Universities, 2008). See also the "engagement competencies" at the University of Arizona (http://ose.arizona.edu/100-engagement/competencies); the Taxonomy Project, EASEL, at Harvard (https://easel.gse.harvard.edu/taxonomy-project); the Mastery Transcript Consortium (https://mastery.org/); and the Self-Authored Integrated Learning initiative at Northeastern (https://sail.northeastern.edu/).

11. Muscatine, *Fixing College Education*, 37.

12. John Seely Brown and Ann M. Pendleton-Jullian, interview on *Future Trends in Higher Education*, hosted by Bryan Alexander, 2019.

13. Aoun, *Robot-Proof*, chap. 3.

14. Aoun, *Robot-Proof*, 87.

15. Lee S. Shulman, "Pedagogies of Uncertainty," *Liberal Education* 91, no. 2 (2005), https://www.aacu.org/publications-research/periodicals/pedagogies-uncertainty.

16. David Labaree, *A Perfect Mess: The Unlikely Ascendancy of American Higher Education* (Chicago, IL: University of Chicago Press, 2017), chap. 3.

17. Daniel Kahneman, *Thinking, Fast and Slow* (New York: Farrar, Straus and Giroux, 2011).

18. Ann M. Pendleton-Jullian and John Seely Brown, *Design Unbound: Designing for Emergence in a White Water World* (Cambridge, MA: MIT Press, 2018), 1:65.

19. Biesta, *Beyond Learning*, 25.

17 Aligning Liberal Education for an Age of Inequality

William M. Sullivan

Resilience is a highly sought-after personal quality. There is good evidence that it underlies and supports adult well-being and success. It is also something that can be learned. But resilience often turns out to be the consequence of finding a larger purpose for living, one that leads beyond the individual self toward concern for others and the world.[1]

Finding and developing such a sense of orientation and meaning is the great promise of liberal education. This is a crucial "value added" of liberal learning. When college is promoted only as an investment for the sake of future career success, liberal education must object that career utility does not do justice to the value higher education provides. Rather, learning is to be brought to bear on the conduct of living. In this sense, liberal education is not in itself a distinct intellectual field or discipline. It entails immersion in the arts and sciences but for the purpose of achieving a practical rather than a purely theoretical synthesis of ideas and methods.[2]

Liberal educators seek to equip their students to put their learning to use by applying knowledge within a reflective yet engaged stance toward both making sense of the world and contributing to it. Liberal learning succeeds when it enables students to do these things. But this depends on engaging students in the ferment of ideas, encouraging learners to seek connections between experiences and concepts. Today, there is considerable evidence that higher education's success at this core mission has become more difficult to achieve.

Public trust in higher education institutions is wavering even as worries about inadequate preparation for the workforce crowd out all other educational goals. Among students, there is also a worrisome bifurcation of attitudes toward college and academic learning. On the one hand, there is the intensely anxious and competitive stance of a high-achieving minority. The position of these achievers stands in marked contrast to that of a larger number of their peers who appear at once little involved in academic culture and detached from aspirations toward adult goals and responsibilities. This disquieting divergence resonates with the macrocosm of a US society grown more polarized in political and social values, more divided in cultural attitudes, and—the underlying driving force of these trends—increasingly separated by highly unequal economic and social positions. This presents a challenge for educators seeking to foster more thoughtful and informed graduates of higher education who are equipped to address the threat that inequality presents to America's democratic future.

In this chapter I offer a simple, basic argument: liberal education can make an important contribution to escaping the socially entropic threat that inequality poses by giving students the resilience that a broader sense of meaning and purpose provides. But achieving this depends on making it possible for students to reliably develop the capacity and motivation for intellectual engagement. That, in turn, demands a widespread revitalization of liberal learning and in particular a realignment of its core practices of teaching and learning to better support this goal. The knowledge exists to support and guide this reconfiguration. Imaginative pedagogies have been shown effective in shifting student attitudes away from anxiety and sullenness and toward the intrinsic rewards of a striving to understand self and world. This is the kind of college experience the public can trust to prepare resilient students able and willing to confront the consequences of inequality.

My first task, therefore, is to show how the growth of socioeconomic inequality underlies many serious problems confronting today's students.

Aligning Liberal Education for an Age of Inequality

This entails exploring some findings from the health sciences, behavioral economics, and other social sciences that provide a deeper understanding of the powerful ways that social forces shape individual and group attitudes and motivations—both negatively and positively. An explanation of the social infrastructure of learning and motivation, finally, reveals how and why active pedagogical strategies are able to engage students in intellectual inquiry despite adverse conditions.

Student Achievers and Drifters: Today's Generational Bifurcation

Here, I consider two widely discussed analyses of a troubling division among US undergraduates. Like much else in this age of economic and social inequality, it appears that collegiate Americans are increasingly split into a minority of high-achieving academic "winners" and a much larger number of students whose experience and outlook are characterized by "drift." The latter students' thinking abilities and orientation to the world are only weakly affected by four years of undergraduate study.

Richard Arum and Josipa Roksa have produced much-discussed sociological studies of undergraduate learning across a large range of institutions with different student bodies and varied academic standards.[3] They describe a student generation in which many emerge from college much as they entered it, largely adrift, neither driven to achieve nor adequately prepared for making their way in either a career or life. Arum and Roksa's unsettling conclusions resonate with other research that has discovered American adolescents too often fail in developing that sense of meaning and purpose that underlies adult well-being. For example, in an often-cited 2008 study, psychologist William Damon found that about a quarter of young Americans are "disengaged," while about 20 percent have achieved a sense of purpose for how to use their abilities in a socially positive way; the remainder are unsteady, either "dabbling" in various stances or "dreaming" of a meaningful life but unable to find the motivation to pursue their dreams.[4]

In *Excellent Sheep: The Miseducation of the American Elite and the Way to a Meaningful Life*, William Deresiewicz has indicted the typical moral outcome of graduation from the nation's most selective institutions.[5] His criticism has clearly struck a chord, arousing considerable controversy. Deresiewicz argues that institutions such as the Ivy League universities provide a much sought-after education that in practice avoids issues of purpose and meaning by keeping the most ambitious and capable students busy running hard for competitive distinction. This relentless competition leaves such students little time or interest to pose questions of purpose or direction beyond the next rung of "success." The resulting mindset is described by Deresiewicz as "technocratic" rather than intelligent. By this he means that the programs most students pursue in college are heavy on analysis and problem-solving techniques but push to the margins questions of the meaning or value of these abilities and skills. These matters are left to the less well-subscribed fields, such as the humanities and social sciences, which, though sometimes regarded as a welcome relief from the relentless pressure to outperform others analytically, are not to be taken too seriously by aspiring elites.

Largely missing from the different academic scenes portrayed both by Arum and Roksa and by Deresiewicz is explicit attention on the part of educators to teaching the skills and motivation for integrating and evaluating analytical knowledge and methods.

The Underlying Reality: Growing Inequality and Its Effects

Underlying the inadequate responses by liberal education dissected by its critics is the stark reality of increased social distance between groups. Social inequality not only creates wider chasms of distance, but also affects how members of higher and lower economic strata see themselves and each other. As inequality grows in a society, this magnification of social distance—as our experience with racial and ethnic separation demonstrates—significantly weakens relations of trust and sympathy. This, in turn, makes a sense of common identity and shared aims difficult to build, let alone sustain. It undermines social cooperation in the face of common problems, even serious threats to the general well-being, such as climate change and the growth of inequality itself. All of this makes the acceptance and integration of newcomers into US society more fraught with fear and uncertainty.

How has this happened? Following World War II, US society enjoyed several decades of remarkable economic success, during which economic equality declined significantly from what it had been earlier in the twentieth century. Economists now refer to this period as the "great compression" of incomes. After about 1980 these trends began a U-turn. Since that time, wage increases, along with economic mobility, has stalled for all Americans except for the upper fifth of the income distribution. This is the economic stratum that includes professionals and managers, all college educated. Since the 1980s, the economy as a whole has expanded by several multiples. However, literally all of that growth has gone to the upper 20 percent, proportionately more to the upper 10 percent, with the biggest chunk captured by the top 1 percent.[6] What was once described as a pyramid, with a broad base and a gradual narrowing of incomes toward the apex, has become more of an hourglass, with a smaller top, a drastically narrowed middle, and a large mass of lower-income people with parlous future prospects at the bottom.

It is important for educators to recognize that these are the conditions in which today's student generation has grown up. It is not surprising that aspirants to the more selective colleges, who are disproportionately children of the upper 20 percent and especially the upper 10 percent, have become increasingly academically competitive. Nor, perhaps, is it unexpected that those less well positioned should tend toward withdrawal from a competition they find daunting or distasteful. But it is hard to argue that this represents a good distribution of the nation's human resources, much less the recipe for a balanced and cohesive society.

The most dramatic discovery about the effects of inequality has occurred not in economics or sociology but in the fields of epidemiology and public health. There, researchers have discovered strong and consistent relationships between socioeconomic status and a variety of serious health threats. Biologists have long known that chronic stress is related to increased rates of morbidity and early death. But less clearly understood is the striking correlation between social status or rank and health outcomes due to the skewed distribution of chronic stress, with those at the top suffering significantly less than those less well positioned.

This was first discovered in an analysis of health among British civil servants, which tracked health outcomes from the 1960s into the 1990s. To the researchers' surprise, they found that shorter life expectancy, obesity, diabetes, drug and alcohol addiction, anxiety, depression, and a host of other stress-related problems were increasingly prevalent as one descended from the higher to the lower ranks of the civil service.

Spurred by these findings, researchers in the twenty-first century have uncovered similar patterns in epidemiological surveys of larger national populations. Perhaps most surprising has been the discovery that the key factor is not absolute levels of inequality nor absolute levels of poverty or surfeit beyond a basic minimum, but inequality. This same relationship turns out to hold for states, regions, and nations as a whole. Inequality, in other words, can be lethal. And it is especially lethal for those living in high-inequality societies (such as the United States and the United Kingdom) as opposed to low-inequality nations (such as Scandinavian countries, Japan, and the Netherlands). Within unequal societies, it is most lethal for those in lower economic positions.[7]

How Inequality Gets under the Skin: Implications for Students and Educators

These are the facts about the social consequences of living in highly unequal societies. But what actually causes those on the lower rungs of the economic ladder to suffer so disproportionately? How does inequality, as Wilkinson and Pickett put it, get "under the skin" to ravage whole social groups and classes? Drawing on a variety of studies as well as their own work, Wilkinson and Pickett put forward an explanation. They call it "social evaluative threat," meaning that stress hormone levels are raised by the perception of one's low status and lack of respect from others.[8] When individuals persistently feel negatively evaluated by others—or shamed and stigmatized in the traditional moral vocabulary—they become highly sensitive to how others regard them. This is a recognizable feature in many adolescent lives, as is the frequent response of trying to shore up one's pride by efforts at self-promotion.

The data on the steady increase in anxiety and depression, as psychologists measure these, among young people appear to bear out Wilkinson and Pickett's hypothesis. Reasonably comparable data are available about child and student mental health since the 1950s, which has allowed researchers to trace a continuous upward trend, beginning in the 1980s, in reports of anxiety and depression, as the experience of social evaluative threat has increased. By the 1990s, for example, the average college student was more anxious than all but 15 percent of students in the 1950s. Even more striking, the average child in the 1990s was more anxious than those whom school counselors referred to psychiatrists in the 1950s. And by 2006, more than 60 percent of college students taking routine psychological tests exhibited higher tendencies toward narcissism than students whose scores in the 1980s led to their diagnoses as narcissistic personalities. These statistics provide evidence for Wilkinson and Pickett's claim that a widespread rise in perception of social evaluative threat takes a heavy toll among young people as inequality progresses.[9] So students grow both psychically fragile and touchy while demanding attention and praise. Little wonder that there is so much concern about raising resilient children.

But psychological difficulties are not the only result of living under conditions of significant inequality. Considerable evidence suggests that it also profoundly affects how individuals are likely to think about their lives and their choices. Contrary to "commonsense" notions that individual character (or genetic makeup) largely determines a person's reactions to life's challenges, it turns out that inequality, especially group perception that an individual occupies a high or low status position relative to others, has independent force in shaping an individual's basic strategies for engaging with life. These findings indicate that inequality of status is the major causal factor. Status is wider than economic position, including racial, ethnic, and gender differences and their complex interplay in modern societies. In US society, it is evident that economic position and economic competition are overwhelmingly important, though not all-determining, in shaping the contemporary social and cultural landscape.

Groups living in stable and relatively equal social situations tend to approach life with what researchers call a "slow" strategy. Such people plan for and invest in the future (since they imagine it as relatively secure), marry and have children relatively late, and believe in following and enforcing rules of fairness. In sharp contrast, in unequal societies, especially among groups whose conditions of life are uncertain and often changing, the common approach to life is to "live fast, die young." That is, groups that feel disrespected and seen as having low or declining worth tend to live for the here and now, ignoring the future consequences of decisions and valuing only what can improve the current situation in the short term. This "fast" strategy therefore encourages current consumption rather than saving, marrying and having children young (they can't count on the future working out), and taking more risks and worrying less about rules.

Using the epidemiological data amassed by Wilkinson and Pickett, other researchers have showed that the mere fact of inequality is a strong predictor of risk taking, which in turn is strongly correlated with health problems and social pathologies.[10] In the larger context of constricting opportunity, the emotional defense of the self, especially relentless efforts to raise self-esteem and avoid humiliation, becomes a more consuming task, especially for adolescents. In other words, the macro environment is making finding a job, let alone stable career possibilities—the essential platform for other life opportunities and the commitments involved in thinking "slow"—significantly harder to come by. These are the forces driving one of the most conspicuous phenomena of our unequal society: the increasing investments of families in the economically fortunate top fifth in enhancing the competitive advantage of their children.

The Process in Microcosm: High School as Intellectual and Moral Formation in Inequality

What is it, then, that keeps this demanding, churning, but ultimately socially entropic cultural pattern so powerfully in place? Social science is able to provide some important illumination through an analysis of these processes in the microcosm of the American high school. Virtually all of today's undergraduates have already been through years of educational formation—academic, social, and moral—in high school. They have learned by participating repeatedly, as a distinct and closed social group, in a set of practices that rehearse an understanding of what life and learning are about. This amounts to an intensive immersion into a morally dubious culture of status competition. This culture, concludes sociologist Murray Milner after a national research effort, replicates at the intimate level of personal psychology and peer relationships the main features of contemporary America's individualistic culture of competition.[11]

Public high schools, in Milner's portrait, echo the occupational shifts in the larger economy that I noted above as underlying today's growing inequality. Respect and status adhere in two social roles above all: occupational prestige in a competitive labor market and "lifestyle," particularly as manifested in material possessions and displays of status through various markers of distinction and exclusivity.[12]

High school, then, immerses students in a peer status system that dominates adolescent life at least as much as the larger socioeconomic status system preoccupies adults. The high school version centers above all on being perceived as "cool." However, coolness contains inner contradictions, and these mirror similar paradoxes of America's individualist culture. Coolness is the quality that allows an individual to stand out, to be admired, or even to be resented but never ignored. Yet achieving cool status requires conformity to group norms and fashions in order to receive acceptance and recognition as, for instance, getting more "likes" than other peers on social media. To stay cool requires constant effort to gain competitive advantage by strategizing how to gain or keep winning positive attention from one's similarly competing peers.[13]

Paradoxically, the individual striving to be cool reinforces acquiescence to the common pursuit of narrow, perpetually insecure, self-focused goals. This takes a lot: natural endowments, social skills, plenty of consumer goods as material props, and good luck. Only a few students succeed in achieving admittance to the ranks of the school's cool kids. The deciding norms vary with race, ethnicity, and above all social class. However, while the ranks of the cool, like the economically successful, now include more women and a broader representation from racial and ethnic groups other than whites, the big winners of the coolness race—and often, college admission—share demographic as well as cultural traits. Cool kids are the mostly upper-middle-class students who can be at once popular, academically successful, athletic, known as good partiers, and able to do and have the latest things. Most everyone else—the "alternatives" as they are known—struggles to define dignity for themselves as the "freaks" and "geeks" of Milner's book title.

Milner points out that this closed status system is also a breeding ground of jealousy, resentment, and cynicism toward the formal ideals presented by adult authorities. "Alternatives" frequently disparage the norms and tastes the cool kids subscribe to, a divergence that continues into adult life, adding to the distrust between these social groups. And just as in the larger world of adult status, the cool kids' lifestyle—their stressful focus on hard work and hard play—is all-consuming. Typically, this keeps the ambitious kids' and elites' attention focused on their status competitors (and later, on their children's competitive success), so that the realities and travails, as well as the anger and resentment, of those below them in the status order are typically unseen or despised.

It is not hard to see in this picture a microcosm of a culture of runaway status competition focused on economic achievement and lifestyle display, the source of many of today's social divisions and political conflicts. Such a society is weak in social solidarity. Its absorption in competitive individualism undermines the civic solidarity on which democracy depends. Lacking common purpose, such a society is likely to lack the collective resiliency needed to face the looming shocks of demographic and economic change or environmental crisis.

Simulation Pedagogy as Educational Judo

In this US environment, what means do educators have at their disposal that have been shown to be effective in overcoming the toxic effects of inequality? A significant battery of means, it turns out. Liberal education

Aligning Liberal Education for an Age of Inequality

holds out the promise of enabling today's undergraduates to become the more resilient and committed adults their anxious parents wish them to be. But this can happen only if today's students can be effectively brought into a community of learning concerned with liberal education's goals. How can such an educational aim get a hearing in the self- and credential-focused environment determined by the inequality of our times? How, in other words, can an educational journey toward developing intellectual passions and serious concerns with the direction and meaning of life get under way? Perhaps by tapping the same motives that keep many students so focused on succeeding in peer competition. This surprising answer is the inspiration for a remarkably effective liberal arts pedagogy that employs role-immersion games to bring students actively into simulated historical dramas.

The educational method behind the games, known as Reacting to the Past, is explained by its originator, historian Mark Carnes of Barnard College, in *Minds on Fire: How Role-Immersion Games Transform College*.[14] Carnes argues that what today's students need are forms of teaching that can recognize and then redirect the students' present absorption in peer status concerns—which he describes in ways not unlike Milner's account of status competition in high school culture—toward higher aims. Carnes claims that well-conducted role-immersion games can do just that. By utilizing students' penchant for "subversive play" like a form of pedagogical judo, these games can direct that energy toward common learning and opening to new ideas. The subversive play element is the secret to students' engagement in learning. Carnes contends that role-immersion games like Reacting to the Past succeed because they enable students to draw on their love of subversive play and their need to be recognized and valued as skillful players in their own social worlds—to be cool—in order to transform themselves through their performances as characters in intricate dramatic narratives with uncertain endings, which excite serious thought.

Learning by active participation in simulations is a pedagogical strategy that is relatively new to liberal arts education, though it has long been used in professional fields and other institutional sectors outside the academy. Students learn through structured social participation that involves intense team interaction. Faculty direct the activities and coach the learners, but the outcomes of the simulations are determined by the play of the students themselves. In Reacting to the Past, each game places students in an actual clash of ideas that proved to be a historic turning point, with students taking the roles of key players in the historical debates and conflicts. When the pedagogy succeeds, the effect is role immersion as students enter deeply into the thought-worlds and motivations of the characters they are assigned to play. The result, Carnes argues, is that students' consciousness is changed.

Immersion and Detachment as Poles in Educating for Reflective Judgment

Reacting to the Past games are sometimes used as part of otherwise conventional courses at any level in a number of disciplines, including history, political science, philosophy, literature, and the sciences. But three of the games, which take three weeks each, can be used to form an introductory liberal arts course of a unique kind. For each game, the class is focused on a game book, which includes extensive readings in primary and secondary sources related to the historical incident. During the first two weeks, the instructor leads the students in discussing and writing analysis papers on the readings and the themes they introduce. Considerable attention is given to understanding the major actors, their outlooks, their actions, and their likely motives. Then in the third week, students are assigned individual roles and are typically divided into teams whose characters embody opposing viewpoints. Intentionally, the game pits groups of students competitively against each other. In these sessions, the students become historical characters, and the instructor becomes the game master, who functions as a referee, a poser of questions, and a coach and advisor. Notably, the game may fail to end in the same way the actual historical debates did; the game's outcome is uncertain.

In the heat of play, the games demand spontaneous invention, which stretches students' imaginations and sympathies. The themes and topics can range widely: the French Revolution, Socrates on trial in ancient

Athens, a conflict among Confucian scholars at a crucial moment in Ming China, or scientific controversies, such as the conflict between Galileo and the philosophical and religious establishment of his time. The competitive structure of the games reflects the actual historical oppositions being enacted. This requires students to enter seriously into the outlooks, situations, and purposes of their characters.

The results of this pedagogical approach, so far, are impressive. Compared to students in first-year seminars at one liberal arts institution, students from first-year Reacting to the Past courses outperformed their peers not only on measures of motivation and involvement but in critical writing as well. The most surprising finding, repeated at several institutions, has been that while students are highly enthusiastic about their learning experience, they rarely elect to recommend it to other students—because they judge that the games made them work harder than in their other courses![15]

Reacting to the Past advocates have put forward this form of simulation pedagogy as a new option for liberal education. However, it is not proclaimed to be a total replacement for more didactic approaches. Working by empathetic identification, much like drama or literature, it contrasts with the critical detachment that is the academic norm. And like drama, the games draw students beyond themselves to consider and take seriously other, even conflicting identities and points of view very different from their own. Players find themselves in the exciting situation of exploring new ways to be in the world. They are led by the excitement of subversive play and group competition to expand their intellectual repertoires, and by doing so they discover intellectual exploration as a value in its own right, a kind of higher-order desire that game participants often report as outlasting their earlier aim at winning the game itself. Effective teaching through simulation turns on this point. After the excitement has died down, participants learn how to reflect on themselves and how they have been changed by their learning, how they have come to enjoy and find meaning in the learning itself: the core goal of liberal education.

Through struggles with the complexity of conflicting outlooks, students become more confident that they could live amid such tensions without retreating from efforts to expand their moral imaginations. Their experiences with the historical simulations enhance their ability and often their willingness to contrast and compare different perspectives: the kind of thinking associated with mature adulthood. Students report that they came to value empathetic engagement with others' views as a way of learning. But the structure of the games also requires the stepping back of critical detachment and the further exploration of ideas, which the issues involved are felt to demand. Simulation pedagogies, then, offer a promising escape route from the crushing weight of status competition toward more proactive and expansive student growth.[16]

Conclusion: Realigning the Social Infrastructure of Liberal Learning

The advances in learning theory and cognitive evolution provide intellectual tools for analyzing the strengths and failures of the current social infrastructure of liberal education. The key educational challenge is clear. The problems of disengagement, divided student attitudes, faculty fatigue, and psychic and physical ill health on campus have a common root, as explained by the epidemiology of inequality.

The key developmental project is the search for and assessment and further development of promising pedagogies that can overcome those entropic tendencies. In other words, we should seek to align that infrastructure in ways that can serve students better by providing entry into liberal learning. This will require nothing less than a movement to promote an educational agenda built on our knowledge about the social infrastructure of learning and motivation. We must be committed to fulfilling the civic ideals that are the heritage of liberal learning and the democratic aspirations that define the US enterprise.

Notes

1. William Damon, *The Path to Purpose: How Young People Find Their Calling in Life* (New York: Free Press, 2008); Angela Duckworth, *Grit: The Power of Passion and Perseverance* (New York: Scribner, 2018).

2. Anne Colby et al., *Rethinking Undergraduate Business Education: Liberal Learning for the Profession* (San Francisco, CA: Jossey-Bass Wiley, 2011).

3. Richard Arum and Josipa Roksa, *Aspiring Adults Adrift: Tentative Transitions of College Graduates* (Chicago, IL: University of Chicago Press, 2014).

4. Damon, *Path to Purpose*, 59-67.

5. William Deresiewicz, *Excellent Sheep: The Miseducation of the American Elite and the Way to a Meaningful Life* (New York: Free Press, 2014).

6. Lane Kenworthy, *Social Democratic America* (New York: Oxford University Press, 2014).

7. Richard Wilkinson and Kate Pickett, *The Spirit Level: Why Greater Equality Makes Societies Stronger* (London: Bloomsbury, 2010).

8. Wilkinson and Pickett, *Spirit Level*, 41-42.

9. Wilkinson and Pickett, *Spirit Level*, 36-40.

10. Keith Payne, *The Broken Ladder: How Inequality Affects the Way We Think, Live, and Die* (New York: Viking, 2017), 66-78.

11. Murray Milner Jr., *Freaks, Geeks, and Cool Kids: Teenagers in an Era of Consumerism, Standardized Tests, and Social Media*, 2nd ed. (New York: Routledge, 2016).

12. Milner, *Freaks*, 174-180.

13. Milner, *Freaks*, 44-60.

14. Mark C. Carnes, *Minds on Fire: How Role-Immersion Games Transform College* (Cambridge MA: Harvard University Press, 2014).

15. Carnes, *Minds on Fire*.

16. Carnes, *Minds on Fire*, 120.

18 Slow

Liberal Learning for and in a Fast-Paced World

Nancy L. Chick and Peter Felten

Liberal arts education often is critiqued as out of touch with the rapid-fire pace of contemporary work and life. Students need to be able to ride the rapids, navigate uncertainty with agility, and innovate continually. Liberal education is not practically focused on job skills, nor is it affordable for the vast majority of students; instead, as a college president described this vein of criticism: "liberal education is a hopelessly romantic endeavor designed to give privileged students cultivated tastes for an outdated, elite life."[1] That's the last thing students need today. The purpose of any higher education institution, according to this common critique, is to graduate as many students as possible as quickly and as cheaply as possible, so that they can get jobs. To serve this purpose, undergraduate education must be practical and efficient. Full speed ahead.

In this chapter, we invite readers to consider a counterintuitive response to this view. Rather than speed up, we suggest slowing down. Inspired by the notion of "slow"—which originated in the slow food movement and has been explored more recently in a range of activities and professions, including a book called *The Slow Professor*[2]—we suggest that measured attention to learning and learners is the most practical, efficient, and ethical approach to challenge the frantic pace, superficial engagement, and standardization of education that are so prevalent today. Indeed, for our students to thrive both professionally and personally after graduation, they need to learn to pay close attention, to think deliberately, and to communicate with care. Another college president has called this kind of education "robot-proof" precisely because it challenges students to develop the distinctly human skills—the abilities to create, invent, and discover—that will allow them to flourish in a rapidly changing and profoundly digital world.[3]

The future requires slow.

Students—all of them—need slow. Indeed, the students who are running fastest to make it into higher education, including those who are first in their family to attend college, may benefit the most from a slow liberal education that cultivates essential yet often unfamiliar habits and capacities to reflect on big questions of meaning and purpose.

Fortunately, the deep traditions of liberal education are rooted in deliberate and critical habits of reading, thinking, and being. All students need this kind of robot-proof education. The future of liberal education is slow.

Learning, Fast and Slow

In his book *Deep Work*, the computer scientist Cal Newport skewers the chronic busyness that pervades higher education and our culture more broadly. If we don't have a clear sense of what it means to do work that has a purpose, Newport contends, we default to an industrial era definition of being productive and successful: "doing lots of stuff in a visible manner."[4]

This emphasis on rapid and public activity is woven into the fabric of today's undergraduate education. To graduate, students must accumulate a specified number of credit hours—a proxy for time spent in class, not for learning. Ambitious students sign up for double or triple majors, requiring an even bigger stack of credits. As students earn those credits, effective instructors divide class periods into smaller chunks of time and activity, providing clear and prompt feedback to help students learn as much as possible in the shortest possible time. This focus on activity and time is not necessarily misguided, but we risk making classes into yet another space where students are rewarded for "doing lots of stuff in a visible manner" without a clear and deep educational purpose. Even as students count credits and as institutions assess outputs, politicians and policy makers stress the importance of reducing the time to graduation. While some of this attention is grounded in concerns about equity, much of it is about the pace of a student's progress toward a degree. As the governor of Tennessee remarked, "Higher ed needs more speed boats."[5] In an uncertain world, more and faster are better.

The process of learning, however, does not follow market-based expectations about productivity. Learning tends not to occur in a linear progression, yet undergraduate courses typically move forward at a preestablished pace through the term—and the curriculum marches along to a similar cadence: *We've got to cover the Great Depression today, or we won't get through the war on Friday.* If the vast majority of students in a major haven't mastered a core disciplinary concept or skill by their junior year, we assume it's probably because they are lazy or distracted (not like we were when we were undergraduates!), rather than because our pedagogies, assignments, and curricula are not challenging and supporting them to deeply learn.

This full-speed-ahead approach to pedagogy and curricular coverage fails to cultivate meaningful learning for at least two reasons. First, rapid-fire activities primarily develop short-term memory. More "durable learning" requires time to develop.[6] To deeply learn, students need to think about and try out what they are learning in varied ways over time, and then they need to use reflection or metacognition to apply it in new contexts.[7] In other words, progressing rapidly and sequentially through learning objectives is a sure path to a superficial, forgettable education. Ciccone illustrates this distinction when looking at his students' initial analysis of comedy: "Their responses indicated that when it came to understanding complex phenomena, many seemed naturally inclined to a type of spontaneous, unreflective interpretation of experience. They want to believe that things are as they appear, so their first understanding is sufficient: Something is either funny or it's not."[8] The ubiquitous pedagogical advice to extend our "wait time" longer than a few seconds in order to make space for students' responses takes on greater significance in this context.[9] Our colleagues advocating for contemplative pedagogy know this as well.[10] Meaningful learning is slow learning. Students need time and practice to think, be curious, make mistakes, and rethink. Secondary education rarely prepares students for this kind of deep learning. Liberal educators have an opportunity and an obligation to slow students down so that their learning will be durable and purposeful.

Second, deep learning requires cultivating "certain ways of thinking and knowing."[11] If faculty teach and assess in ways that promote a transactional approach to thinking and knowing, students are not likely to develop the knowledge-making skills and mindsets that are essential to meaningful learning.[12] As the Stanford psychologist and historian Sam Wineburg has noted, "the problem with students is not that they don't know enough about history. The problem is that they don't know what history is in the first place."[13] To come to know history, or any other discipline, students need to wrestle with foundational facts and skills as well as the "troublesome knowledge" and epistemological and ontological questions at the heart of their field of study.[14] They need to practice and cultivate habits of mind that require time and practice and repetition and routine and reflection. Crossing a threshold to deeper understanding rarely occurs through a neat and tidy sequence of steps forward; instead, students typically experience deep learning as struggle; as "wobble" and "swerve"; as pause, backtrack, "retreat"; in "fits and starts"; and as a path "of recursiveness and of oscillation" toward the threshold of learning that matters.[15]

To create environments that acknowledge this reality of human learning, liberal education faculty, curricula, and institutions need to reimagine our approaches to and uses of time. *We need to slow down.*

Our use of the word "slow" is deliberate. We are walking in the footsteps of the slow food movement and the various movements that followed (not Kahneman's influential but altogether different claims in *Thinking, Fast and Slow*), which don't focus on simply doing what we already do more slowly, but rather focus on rethinking how we use our time and attention.[16] Slow approaches aim for meaningful outcomes by creating space and opportunity for "hanging out, messing around, and geeking out."[17]

We believe that integrating the principles of slow into liberal education will deepen not only students' learning of disciplinary content and intellectual skills, but also the affective experiences of learning and teaching (theirs and ours). It will foreground the meaning, joy, and warmth of our teaching; honor the humanity of our students and ourselves as learners; and resist the isolation, cynicism, and homogenization of the academy.[18]

Slow Reading

There are myriad ways to cultivate slow in liberal education. Indeed, the principles and practices of slow could be applied to any of the frameworks used for the liberal arts. The LEAP campaign of the Association of American Colleges and Universities, for instance, emphasizes the importance of a range of capacities and outcomes that invite—and perhaps require—slow learning, such as intercultural knowledge and competence and ethical reasoning and action. A curriculum that races through these is nonsensical and surely inadequate to the needs of our students and our world. Rather than using this chapter to touch lightly on the myriad possibilities of slow liberal arts, we take our own advice and here delve deeply into one skill that's used in all disciplines and professions: reading.

The Modern Language Association (MLA) points to reading as one of the three skills (along with speaking and writing) "at the heart of education"; they are "key qualifications for full participation in social, political, economic, and cultural life."[19] The MLA contends that "those who learn to *read slowly and carefully* . . . will also acquire the nimbleness and visual perceptions associated with working in an electronic environment," in part by developing "the patience, knowledge, and craft required to move beyond our insular selves."[20]

While we expect the MLA to make such assertions, psychologists Kidd and Castano offer a similar conclusion in their *Science* article titled "Reading Literary Fiction Improves Theory of Mind."[21] Theory of mind (ToM) is a term that describes "the capacity to identify and understand others' subjective states," which they claim "is one of the most stunning products of human evolution. It allows successful navigation of complex social relationships and helps to support the empathetic responses that maintain them."[22] It's worth pausing at length to consider what Kidd and Castano uncovered in their experiment:

> Literary fiction, which we consider to be *both writerly and polyphonic*, uniquely engages the *psychological processes needed to gain access* to characters' subjective experiences. Just as in real life, the worlds of literary fiction are replete with complicated individuals whose inner lives are *rarely easily discerned but warrant exploration*. . . . Readers of literary fiction must *draw on more flexible interpretive resources to infer the feelings and thoughts of characters*. That is, they must *engage ToM processes*. Contrary to literary fiction, popular fiction, which is more readerly, tends to portray the world and characters as internally consistent and predictable. . . . Therefore, it may reaffirm readers' expectations and so not promote ToM.[23]

Kidd and Castano emphasize "literary fiction" as the necessary variable, similar to the MLA's focus on "literary texts." However, while we love a good work of literature, we want to draw attention away from the actual texts and to the very specific reading processes and practices described by both the MLA and Kidd and Castano, processes and practices at the heart of liberal education.

As illustrated in the italicized language in the passages above, meaningful reading is *slow, careful, exploratory,* and *inferential*. Literary scholars call it close reading, or "reading *as if the words belonged to a person at some distance from ourselves in thought or feeling*. Perhaps they must be seen as the words of someone else before they can be seen as words at all—or, more particularly, as words that need to be read *with close attention*."[24] Manarin describes this way of reading as "being willing to consider multiple interpretations of a text, even those that don't seem immediately obvious to us because of our assumptions."[25] Qualley describes it as "risky reading" because "one's own beliefs and assumptions are disclosed, and may themselves become the object of interpretation, critique, and even metamorphosis. It is this risk of alteration to one's views of the world that makes this kind of reading dangerous, but also valuable."[26]

Notice the mental moves in these explanations. Scholes describes imagining another's thoughts and feelings, not just a specific character in a work of fiction, as Kidd and Castano suggest, but the words themselves as necessarily coming from someone other than the reader. Manarin describes imagining another's interpretation, the meaning made by someone with different assumptions than ours. And these moments of imagining another occur *while reading*. Hayles describes this "cognitive style" as "deep attention": "concentrating on a single object *for long periods* (say, a novel by Charles Dickens or Edwidge Danticat), ignoring outside stimuli while so engaged, preferring a single information stream, and having a high tolerance for *long focus times*."[27] This way of thinking cultivated by deeply attentive reading is "superb for solving complex problems."[28]

This reading is slow in part because the reader is doing several things at once. She is reading the words on the page, parsing the denotative meaning. Some of the words, phrases, allusions, and ideas may be unfamiliar, so she's also working out what's being said more broadly. At the same time, she is inferring beyond the words on the page, an act of meaning making or interpretation that unpacks the multiple layers of meaning embedded in connotation and ambiguity and in the contexts of the writing in another place and another time by another person. She is also thinking about the contexts of others' voices embedded in the text, as in references to others' work or words. She is also considering the reliability of these others, where they're coming from, and how they know what they claim to know. She is also imagining how other readers may make different inferences and what leads to those differences. And so on.

This reading is slow.

Slow reading requires deliberate pausing. The reader must occasionally back up and reread something again, perhaps pause even longer to dwell in it, and at times sit back and follow one or more of these moves wherever it takes her. Slow reading is reflective and metacognitive, as multiple streams of thought are occurring in tandem with and about the reading. Slow reading also requires repetition and recursiveness, moving forward but then circling back to try again, each time with a different lens—a question, or a folding in of later parts of the text to see how they change or clarify something. Slow reading "treats a first reading of a text like the first draft of a paper": it's tentative and messy.[29] It involves meandering and misreading, being open to "a process of trial and error, entertaining before rejecting possibilities."[30] It involves experimentation and play, which two learning theorists call "the single most important skill to develop for the twenty-first century."[31] Pen or stylus in hand, it may involve annotation to chronicle these trains of thought, recurring questions, and moments of clarity and confusion.

Slow reading is independent of any specific kind of reading material and any specific discipline. Manarin notes that she can apply close reading to "drawings, photographs, performances, sculpture, web design, music, interior design, and more, depending on context," and she frequently applies it to student "artifacts" like "essays, journals, in-class writing, exams that aren't multiple choice, even assignments with visual components like research posters."[32] Graff argues that once this skill is learned, an educated person can and should read "any text . . . in rigorously analytic ways instead of simply enjoying them unreflectively as leisure entertainment."[33] Even the geneticist Barbara McClintock famously taught her students to "take time with your material, adopt a contemplative stance toward it. Read the poem slowly and repeatedly, observe and reflect on the plant before you. Select a single line from the poem to hold in the mind until it begins to reveal its full multilayered significations. Live your way into each plant organ until you attain 'a feeling for the organism.'"[34]

Indeed, slow reading is a foundational skill in a liberal education, one that requires intentional effort to learn and practice and one that can be transferred to many aspects of work and life. In a fast-paced world, we cannot assume our students will bring with them the capacity to do (or to value) slow reading, nor will they necessarily become more skillful slow readers simply by doing the reading we assign for our courses. Slow reading is both a skill and an orientation that must be taught and practiced, iteratively over time and across contexts, until it becomes a habit that students can use in their work and their lives after graduation.

Slow Liberal Arts

For students to learn to read slowly and carefully, we need to teach them to do so. They need to practice this approach in courses and across the curriculum so that they become fluent slow readers. And they need to be encouraged and rewarded for developing and applying this skill. This means that liberal education courses and curricula must be designed for slow reading.

We may not like what we see when we look critically at our own syllabi. Long reading lists privilege "doing lots of stuff in a visible manner" rather than meaningful engagement with texts or the development of deep reading capacities. Rapid-fire lectures and frequent active learning activities might keep students entertained, but they also encourage students to skim the surface of intellectual engagement.

Faculty need to think about if and how they teach their students to read and about the reading habits their pedagogies cultivate and their assessments reward. This thinking needs to happen alone and in community with other faculty, for if we slow down in isolation, we risk becoming something like pedagogical speed bumps—with students racing through the curriculum, pausing only once or twice to slow down when required. To reach the full potential of slow liberal education, we need to weave slow through entire curricula and institutions. All students should begin to develop these skills and orientations—slow reading, writing, calculating, creating, questioning, observing, critiquing—in their first courses, and then continue to practice slow as their studies unfold. As they approach graduation, they should be highly skilled at slow reading, perhaps completing capstone experiences that aren't about synthesizing a vast body of knowledge but rather about diving deeply into a single text or experiment or performance. The signature work students do in higher education should be immersive, critical, and slow.

Finally, if we ask our students to slow down but maintain and model our own hectic pace, we reinforce the notion that slow is a luxury, like a retreat from reality—which is precisely the image of liberal arts education we aim to counter. A slow liberal education will thus challenge faculty, whose work may also be fairly described as "doing lots of stuff in a visible manner," as much as it will challenge students. If we are going to teach slow, we need to learn to be slow ourselves. We need to cultivate slow in our work, from how we plan and conduct our courses, to how we interact with students and colleagues, to our scholarship.[35] And, of course, such changes in students and faculty will challenge our institutions to value, celebrate, and reward slow in their broader practices, habits, and systems.

Our students need and deserve a slow liberal arts. And so do we.

Notes

1. Rebcca Chopp, "Remaking, Renewing, Reimagining: The Liberal Arts College Takes Advantage of Change," in *Remaking College: Innovation and the Liberal Arts*, ed. R. Chopp, S. Frost, and D. Weiss (Baltimore, MD: Johns Hopkins University Press, 2013), 16.

2. Maggie Berg and Rebecca K. Seeber, *The Slow Professor* (Toronto, ON: University of Toronto Press, 2017).

3. Joseph Aoun, *Robot-Proof: Higher Education in the Age of Artificial Intelligence* (Cambridge, MA: MIT Press, 2017).

4. Cal Newport, *Deep Work* (New York: Grand Central, 2016), 64.

5. Romesh Ratnesar, "Higher Ed Needs More Speed Boats, Fewer Battleships," *Bloomberg Opinion*, June 4, 2018.

6. Peter C. Brown, Henry L. Roediger, and Mark A. McDaniel, *Make It Stick* (Cambridge, MA: Harvard University Press, 2014), 49.

7. Doug Rohrer and Kelli Taylor, "The Shuffling of Mathematics Problems Improves Learning," *Instructional Science* 35, no. 6 (2007): 481-498; Lauren Scharff et al., "Exploring Metacognition as Support for Learning and Transfer," *Teaching and Learning Inquiry* 5, no. 1 (2017): 1-14.

8. Anthony Ciccone, "Learning Matters," in *SoTL in Action*, ed. N. L. Chick (Sterling, VA: Stylus, 2018), 15-22.

9. Mary Budd Rowe, "Wait Time," *Journal of Teacher Education* 37, no. 1 (1986): 43-50.

10. Tobin Hart, "Opening the Contemplative Mind in the Classroom," *Journal of Transformative Education* 2, no. 1 (2004): 28-46; Daniel P. Barbezat and Mirabai Bush, *Contemplative Practice in Higher Education* (San Francisco, CA: Jossey-Bass, 2014); Alexis T. Franzese and Peter Felten, "Reflecting on Reflecting," *International Journal for the Scholarship of Teaching and Learning* 11, no. 1 (2017): article 8.

11. Tony Harland, "Deliberate Subversion of Time," in *Educating the Deliberate Professional*, ed. F. Trede and C. McEwen (New York: Springer, 2016), 175.

12. F. Marton and R. Säljö, "On Qualitative Differences in Learning: I. Outcome and Process," *British Journal of Educational Psychology* 46 (1976): 4-11; David Perkins, "What Is Understanding?," in *Teaching for Understanding*, ed. M. Wiske (San Francisco, CA: Jossey-Bass, 1998), 39-57.

13. Samuel S. Wineburg, "Probing the Depths of Students' Historical Knowledge," *Perspectives on History* 30 (1992), https://www.historians.org/publications-and-directories/perspectives-on-history/march-1992/probing-the-depths-of-students-historical-knowledge.

14. Jan H. F. Meyer and Ray Land, "Threshold Concepts and Troublesome Knowledge (2)," *Higher Education* 49, no. 3 (2005): 373-388.

15. Jill DeTemple and John Sarrouf, "Disruption, Dialogue, and Swerve," *Teaching Theology and Religion* 20, no. 3 (2017): 283-292; Dianne Fallon, "'Lucky to Live in Maine,'" *Teaching English in the Two-Year College* 33 (2006): 410-420, 415; Ray Land, Jan F. K. Meyer, and Caroline Baillie, "Threshold Concepts and Transformational Learning," in *Threshold Concepts and Transformational Learning*, ed. J. F. K. Meyer, R. Land, and C. Baillie (Boston: Sense, 2010), xi.

16. Carlo Petrini, *Slow Food*, trans. W. McCuaig (New York: Columbia University Press, 2004); Berg and Seeber, *Slow Professor*.

17. We borrow this phrase from Mizuko Ito et al., *Hanging Out, Messing Around, and Geeking Out* (Chicago, IL: John D. and Catherine T. MacArthur Foundation Series on Digital Media and Learning, 2007).

18. Parker J. Palmer, Arthur Zajonc, and Megan Scribner, *The Heart of Higher Education* (San Francisco, CA: Jossey-Bass, 2010); Berg and Seeber, *Slow Professor*.

19. Modern Language Association, *Report to the Teagle Foundation on the Undergraduate Major in Language and Literature* (2009), https://www.mla.org/content/download/3207/81182/2008_mla_whitepaper.pdf.

20. Modern Language Association, *Report to the Teagle Foundation*, 4 (emphasis added).

21. David Comer Kidd and Emanuele Castano, "Reading Literary Fiction Improves Theory of Mind," *Science* 342, no. 6156 (2013): 377-380.

22. Kidd and Castano, "Reading Literary Fiction," 377.

23. Kidd and Castano, "Reading Literary Fiction," 377 (emphasis added).

24. Robert Scholes, "The Transition to College Reading," *Pedagogy* 2, no. 2 (2002): 165-172 (emphasis added).

25. Karen Manarin, "Close Reading," in Chick, *SoTL in Action*, 100.

26. Donna J. Qualley, *Turns of Thought* (Portsmouth, NH: Boynton/Cook, 1997), 61.

27. N. Katherine Hayles, "Hyper and Deep Attention: The Generational Divide in Cognitive Modes," *Profession* (2007): 187-199 (emphases added).

28. Hayles, "Hyper and Deep Attention," 188.

29. Gary Weissman, "The Virtue of Misreadings: Interpreting 'The Man in the Well,'" *College English* 73, no. 1 (2010): 28-49.

30. Weissman, "Virtue of Misreadings," 46.

31. Doug Thomas and John Seely Brown, *A New Culture of Learning* (Seattle, WA: CreateSpace, 2011), 114.

32. Manarin, "Close Reading," 101.

33. Gerald Graff, "Why How We Read Trumps What We Read," *Profession* (2009): 66-74.

34. Palmer, Zajonc, and Scribner, *Heart of Higher Education*, 113.

35. Nancy Chick and Peter Felten, "Slow SoTL," *ISSOTL* blog, August 23, 2017, https://www.issotl.com/slow-sotl-kind-manifesto.

19 Shifting Paradigms
College Admissions as a Lever for Systemic Change in Liberal Education

Kristína Moss Gudrún Gunnarsdóttir and Meredith Twombly

In November 2018, a diverse group of stakeholders gathered in Washington, DC, for the Movement Builder Intensive, an event designed to ignite a movement to reimagine education in the United States. A statement from the visioning document of the Education Reimagined group captures the imperative motivating this gathering: "The current system was designed in a different era and structured for a different society. Our economy, society, and polity are increasingly at risk from an educational system that does not consistently prepare *all* children to succeed. . . . we see both an imperative for transformation and many promising avenues for re-envisioning the learning experience."[1]

At the closing session, the executive director was pushed on the question of what comes next. How do we transform from critical analysis to constructive action when there isn't agreement on the correct policy interventions? Her response highlighted the importance of thinking bigger, beyond incremental change: "It's time for a paradigm shift."

Our Paradigm

There is widespread consensus around the need for profound innovation in American education. It would be difficult to find an educational theorist, policy maker, or practitioner—regardless of political orientation—who doesn't actively advocate for change. Although there is consensus in favor of change, the vision for how to move forward is fractured. Prescriptions overwhelmingly focus on reforming the existing system by improving measurable outputs and increasing the efficiency of current programs. But what if this is the wrong approach? What if we've reached a point in history when a new mindset and paradigm are needed?

From a historical perspective, the US educational system is, in many ways, working exactly as intended. After all, the founders of our conventional system never intended education to be for *all* students. The system was precisely designed to sort and categorize students, justifying exclusion and segregation in education and the workforce.[2] It cultivates obedience, uniformity, and the capacity to retain and recall memorized information, skills that were essential to the eighteenth-century economy. Unfortunately, in the modern economy, these are exactly the behaviors that stifle innovation.

In the age of the internet, changing demographics, and a globalized economy where the neatly defined disciplines of the past are increasingly interdisciplinary, there is growing agreement about the new set of skills and values we must cultivate to prepare students for the future. A mere accumulation of information is no longer sufficient. Many leaders call these "twenty-first-century" skills. Ashoka calls them "changemaker" skills.[3] Regardless of how they are classified, these traits are fundamental to thriving in our modern society and workforce.

Many schools, universities, and other institutions are already exploring strategies to adapt to the shifting needs of our economy. Communities are investing in professional development for teachers, schools are adjusting their curricula and teaching practices, and universities are putting attention on innovating their pedagogy. Even multinational institutions like the World Bank are investing resources into this work by conducting a series of rigorous impact evaluation studies to better understand the potential of new models to cultivate twenty-first-century skills.[4]

All of these involved constituencies have good intentions, but unfortunately even the most thoughtful, resourced, and well-executed reforms will fall short of their potential when implemented within our existing educational paradigm. To fully realize the type of transformative change on the scale the founders of the conventional educational model dreamed of when they first started their work, we must acknowledge and actively dismantle the dominant paradigm.

To dismantle this paradigm, we must first recognize how it shapes the narrative around the role and purpose of education in the United States. Increasingly, Americans understand the "purpose" of K-12 education to be not about self-discovery, passion, or personal fulfillment, but rather about preparation for college and, specifically, success in the college admissions process. Beyond the importance we place on having a college degree as a sign of cultural capital, our economy is structured in a way that makes gainful employment and social mobility increasingly difficult without an undergraduate degree. As long as the purpose of K-12 education is tied to getting *into* college, the design of the college admissions process will dictate the cultural narrative around what "matters" in an educational experience. The requirements and evaluation criteria used by elite institutions will continue to act as a series of incentives that powerfully shape the decisions made by high school students and their families about higher education.

If college admission requirements reward students who submit high SAT and ACT scores, the perceived quality of a high school will be tied to its ability to produce those scores. Strategic students will prioritize SAT prep courses at the expense of other activities deemed to matter less because they are not valued in the college admission process. Community engagement and service work will be increasingly commodified as students compete to grow their laundry list of involvements. If merit-based scholarships are tied to grade point average, students will be incentivized to take courses where they are guaranteed a high grade and will avoid environments where more risk is involved. Families will be critical of any well-intentioned reforms that schools attempt to implement if they diverge from the time-tested blueprint of what gets a student into college.

To truly rethink liberal education and realize change at a systems level, we must recognize and harness the power of college admissions to

Shifting Paradigms

incentivize behavioral change in education. We ask, how might college admission policies act as a catalyst, rather than a barrier, to the widespread adoption of innovation in education?

The Current System Is Failing

In a report prepared for the National Bureau of Economic Research, Caroline M. Hoxby, an associate professor of economics at Harvard University, discusses the profound failure of the public K-12 system in the United States. Hoxby notes, "It is clear why Americans are so interested in structural school reform for K-12 education. On a per-pupil basis, American public education is the most expensive system in the world. The per-pupil expense for K-12 education has grown by nearly 80 percent (after adjusting for inflation) since 1970, yet student achievement has been almost flat over the period."[5] In addition to the imbalance of outcomes in international comparisons, we also see a number of other objective indicators that speak to the failure of our conventional educational model. For example, 25 percent of high school freshmen fail to graduate on time, and 7,000 students drop out of high school each day.[6]

These statistics cannot be explained away by focusing on higher-"quality" schools. In 2017, the *Chicago Tribune* published a powerful exposé on the mental health crisis in school districts considered elite, finding that "in many top-performing schools, students and experts describe an atmosphere of intense, sometimes disabling, pressure connected with test scores, college admissions and Advanced Placement course loads."[7] The article quotes a Yale psychology professor: "one in four teens between the ages of 13 and 17 meet the criteria for having an anxiety disorder. . . . when you look at the fact that in Australia, it's only 7 percent of teens with anxiety, compared to 25 percent in the U.S., it's really startling."[8]

Critics call these anomalies. They argue that systems are always flawed and that education can still succeed in preparing students for college and work despite these realities. However, even if we ignore these indicators and look solely at the experience of students in college and beyond, we still find compelling evidence that our system is broken.

Overwhelmingly, employers report that they are not finding the skills they desire and need in current college graduates. In 2017, researchers at the University of Massachusetts, Dartmouth, synthesized findings from a series of studies measuring how satisfied the business community is with the preparation of recent graduates. Their report showed that employers are "generally dissatisfied."[9] According to a survey by the Association of American Colleges and Universities (AAC&U), "Seventy-five percent of employers believe recent graduates are not well prepared in critical thinking and analytic reasoning, written and oral communication, complex problem solving, innovation and creativity, and applying knowledge and skills to real-world settings."[10] This statistic is particularly astonishing considering that these are precisely the skills that liberal education in particular seeks and claims to cultivate in its graduates. If we believe that our colleges and universities are making a good faith effort to develop these skill areas, then we must take a step back and examine the larger system and framework in which this work is occurring.

These are longitudinal realities, not anomalies. If one in four of our young people are developing diagnosable anxiety related to their educational experience, and one in four aren't even making it to their high school graduation, isn't it time to profoundly rethink this model? How might we embrace these unfortunate realities as opportunities for innovation?

Innovations and Barriers: K-12

In an attempt to better equip students to thrive in the twenty-first century, K-12 schools across the United States are incorporating problem- and project-based learning, design thinking, personalized learning, performance-based assessments, and a variety of other pedagogical approaches into their curricula. And these innovations are garnering attention.

In 2016, *Business Insider* ran a feature on the fourteen most innovative schools in the country. The diversity of the cited examples showcases the breadth of potential innovations in this space. The STAR School in Flagstaff, Arizona, where 99 percent of the students have an affiliation with the Navajo Nation, built its curriculum around elements of the Navajo culture. At the THINK Global School in New York City, students spend each semester in a different country. At P-Tech, launched by IBM, students embark on a six-year journey culminating in the receipt of both a high school diploma and an associate's degree.[11]

We're also seeing investments designed to incentivize bold innovation. In 2015, the XQ Superschool project launched a $100 million national competition to design high schools for the future. In one of XQ's white papers, founder Russlynn Ali asks, "How [can we] teach truly relevant skills? How [can we] move away from just memorization and abstract concepts and instead nurture self-directed learners who can apply what they've learned, collaborate and solve complex problems in a rapidly changing world?"[12] In 2016, the winners were announced, and school construction began.

One of the biggest challenges for school communities eager to adopt such innovations is how these changes will impact preparedness for the college admission process. In reaction to a wave of education reforms, including the adoption of nonstandardized, competency-based transcripts by a group of 100 elite private high schools, the executive director of the American Association of Collegiate Registrars and College Admissions Officers noted, "Until [mastery-based transcripts] are common currency, students would be negatively impacted when they seek to transfer to more traditional institutions."[13] Sentiments like these are common among families too. As long as college admissions use grades and standardized test scores as central criteria, students will feel pressure to perform well on them and will assign value to schools according to their ability to optimize these variables.

Innovation and Barriers: Higher Education

Increasingly, Americans share a genuine commitment to realizing innovation at institutions of higher education. Although there remains some debate around the point and purpose of going to college, there is widespread agreement that an increase in experiential opportunities enhances the overall student experience. In response, colleges and universities are investing millions of dollars in the development of new programs and centers focused on interdisciplinary studies, experiential learning, and community engagement. Since 2014, the Academy for Innovative Higher Education Leadership has asked more than 125 academic leaders to consider what innovation means and how it can make a difference.[14] Ashoka U, founded in 2008, asks this same question but with a specific focus on social innovation education. During the same time frame, South by Southwest (SXSW), known most commonly as a celebration of tech and arts innovation, has expanded its programming to include a three-day conference on education.

Alongside efforts to adopt more experiential pedagogies, there is also a growing interest in institution-wide innovation. Some colleges have taken an incremental approach by creating new centers and programs, while others have taken a systems approach by exploring dramatic shifts that impact the entire college community. In both scenarios, there is no question that the success of these programs is intimately connected to the quality and depth of students' participation. A powerful force shaping the degree to which a student might get involved in these types of programs is the mindset instilled in them by the conventional educational paradigm. We must then ask, how does our risk-averse college-prep culture shape a student's behavior? Would experiential learning opportunities be more widely and impactfully utilized if students entered college having prepared differently? Can pedagogical innovations ever flourish without shifting the paradigm?

In a 2018 *Chronicle of Higher Education* article on the growth of the experiential liberal arts, Tim Cresswell states, "The admissions process needs to take a more rounded view of the skills, talents, and varied forms of knowledge that are likely to signal an aptitude for integrated learning across a continuity of experience."[15] Simply put, if we want to see change in higher education, admissions needs to come to the table as a true partner in that process. The evaluation criteria used by an institution to determine admission must align with the characteristics of thriving students and successful graduates and should be harnessed to incentivize behaviors in high school that prepare students for *college*, not for college *admission*.

Employers Want More

There is no lack of recent research and data demonstrating the mismatch between what employers want from new college graduates and what colleges actually teach and reward. According to the AAC&U, employers seek the following skills in college graduates:

1. The ability to work well in teams, especially with people different from yourself.
2. An understanding of science and technology and how these subjects are used in real-world settings.
3. The ability to write and speak well.
4. The ability to think clearly about complex problems.
5. The ability to analyze a problem to develop workable solutions.
6. An understanding of global context in which work is now done.
7. The ability to be creative and innovative in solving problems.
8. The ability to apply knowledge and skills in new settings.
9. The ability to understand numbers and statistics.
10. A strong sense of ethics and integrity.[16]

A similar study published by the National Association of Colleges and Employers notes that participants in a Job Outlook survey listed "problem-solving and an ability to work in a team" as the most valued and desired attributes in college graduates.[17]

It is quite notable that teamwork not only is listed as a top attribute, but also that it has retained this position for more than a decade. If we focus for a moment solely on this critical skill area, we must ask not only how it is cultivated pedagogically, but also how its cultivation is incentivized. How do colleges and college admission offices signal the *value* of teamwork and collaboration, and how do we reward it when it shows up in an application? This is an essential question because what we reward is the ultimate reflection of what we value.

College Admissions as Gatekeepers to Innovation

According to Thaler, Sunstein, and Balz, "Decision makers do not make choices in a vacuum. They make them in an environment where many features, noticed and unnoticed, can influence their decisions."[18] Human behavior is profoundly shaped by incentives, some more easily noticed than others. In the field of behavioral economics, choice architecture is shown to be one of the most powerful forces influencing decision-making behavior. When we recognize the role that environment plays in the choices people make, we have a framework to understand why college admissions must be reimagined if we are to realize profound innovation in education. Choice architecture theory states:

> Many people will take whatever option requires the least effort, or the path of least resistance. . . . if, for a given choice, there is a default option . . . we can expect a large number of people to end up with that option, whether or not it is good for them. These behavioral tendencies . . . will be reinforced if the default option comes with some . . . suggestion that it represents the normal or even the recommended course of action.[19]

Let's unpack this in the context of our educational paradigm.

In many ways, there is an illusion of choice when it comes to the decisions we make about education. Although for many families choice does exist in a literal sense, the architecture of these choices and the cultural environment in which they exist have very clear and powerful incentives. We argue that the conventional educational paradigm establishes college as the default purpose of K-12 education and gainful employment as the purpose of college, as evidenced by the quality of a high school being tied to its college placement rates and the quality of a college being measured by employment statistics. Even when an institution adopts a divergent purpose—say, self-discovery or a path to meaning making and fulfillment—it still operates within a paradigm that values and supports the default: K-12 education is for getting into college.

In a 2017 article entitled "What Colleges Want in an Applicant (Everything)," the senior education writer Eric Hoover illustrates the power of the college admission process in shaping the choices that students and families make along their educational journey. Hoover comments, "What colleges look for sends a powerful message about what matters, not just to admissions officers but in life, and students often respond accordingly."[20] Once we recognize the importance of college admissions in assigning value to behavior, we have the power to use it as a lever to spark systems change in education.

Our colleagues in K-12 intimately understand the influence of college admissions on the educational experience. Often, they are the most vocal advocates for change. If college admission is really such a powerful force in shaping education, one might logically ask why it has been so slow to change. In the same article, Hoover offers some insight by referencing a conversation with the dean of admissions and financial aid at Olin College: "Generally, colleges are risk-averse. Rocking the boat with a newfangled admissions process could hurt their reputations. The challenge for many admissions offices is to make a change, but not so much change or innovation that you're risking the position you're in. . . . Asking students to do more could scare off would-be applicants."[21]

This fear of rocking the boat is real and stifling, so most colleges do not have the support or will to change. They are concerned about the very real ramifications. Many colleges live and die by their *U.S. News* ranking and their selectivity. Why? Because these are metrics used by high schoolers to assess the quality of a school. Furthermore, boards, donors, and alumni often place high value on such rankings and use them as a proxy for institutional progress and success. On both sides of the desk, institutions, families, and students are locked in a stalemate, their curiosity and desire to innovate eclipsed by a fear of acting.

Reimagining the Future

Instead of continuing to support the growth of the test-coaching industry, what if high school seniors spent the summer prior to their senior year at a "teamwork camp" where they learned to listen, empathize, collaborate, constructively discuss, and implement their ideas—all for the purpose of getting into the college of their dreams and leading purposeful and successful lives? Imagine a new normal where ambitious high school juniors and seniors skip the test-prep classes and instead spend a few hours a week in a problem-solving boot camp applying different tools, like design thinking and root-cause analysis, to understanding the complex problems facing their local and global communities.

Better yet, imagine if this kind of activity was rewarded by college admission offices based on the understanding that this work will both help students prepare for the next phase of their educational journey and set the foundation for learning critical life and career skills. If these kinds of skills and activities were rewarded through the admission process, how might we start to shift the culture of our colleges, workplaces, and society?

At Clark University, an approach to undergraduate learning described as "liberal education and effective practice" has led to innovations and embedded experiences, including Problems of Practice courses offered in all departments, in which students work in teams to investigate and respond to a complex question or problem beyond the traditional classroom. They engage in local and global communities in a substantive way, using skills from multiple disciplines that are well beyond anything that could be measured on a test.

Starting in 2017, every senior at Clark has been required to do a culminating capstone project. The Clark capstone requires a demonstration of mastery of five key learning outcomes: knowledge of the natural world and human cultures and societies, intellectual and practical skills, personal and social responsibility, ability to integrate knowledge and skills, and finally the defining skill called "capacities of effective practice," which includes creativity and imagination, self-directedness, resilience and persistence, and the abilities to collaborate with others across differences and to manage complexity and uncertainty.

Clark is proud of its curriculum and the associated outcomes but still must work hard to convince prospective applicants that it truly values creativity, collaboration, and self-directedness when the rest of the world is telling students to follow the rules and focus on the test. When Clark tells students that the admission process is test-optional, too many express doubt, seemingly unable to bring themselves to believe that their application won't suffer if they don't submit a test score. Clark's approach to the experiential liberal arts requires students who are comfortable working outside the narrow traditional model of lecture, memorization, and regurgitation. When raised in this context, integrative or interdisciplinary thinking often feels untethered and out of control. Across the US education culture, students shaped by a high-stakes admission process driven by GPAs and test scores may feel that intellectual risk taking is *too* risky, and many students carry that dangerous discomfort beyond college and into their career and life.

Practices used at Clark are being adopted by other colleges as these institutions continue to imagine how they can stay relevant in the coming decades. But even when these innovations are rolled out according to plan and receive the necessary resources, they will struggle when they find that students don't feel equipped to engage. These new boundary-shifting models continue to be undermined by a college admission system that still rates students based on high-stakes tests, GPAs, and rankings, all of which reward the same docile habits of mind and grade-grubbing tendencies of the last century of elite American education. As a result, otherwise bright students become risk-averse, competitive, and hesitant to ask for help or admit failure—qualities neither colleges nor employers want.

The Future of College Admissions

With a crisis in the business model of higher education growing increasingly apparent, there is no better time to break through this stalemate. In this case, reforming college admissions will be a win-win-win for the most important stakeholders: K-12 education, colleges, and employers. Notably, this reform will not be a win for *U.S. News and World Report* rankings, the College Board, or the myriad other companies that profit from exploiting the anxieties created by the dominant college model. Breaking through will require a true paradigm shift that includes changes to cultural assumptions and legislative policy.

This work is already under way in pockets across the country, and momentum is building. What we now need is for institutions like Olin and Clark, which do have the support to experiment and innovate their college admission process, to tell their stories. We need the Gates Foundation, Bloomberg Philanthropies, and others that support innovation in higher education to support this research, which is central to removing one of the primary obstacles to real innovation and cultural change in higher education. We need to squarely address the stranglehold that traditional college admissions and deeply embedded notions of merit have placed on innovation in education.

As we build this movement, we need more research around student success and what really predicts a student's likelihood to thrive. We need evidence from diverse institutional environments to show that tests and GPAs are not in fact the most reliable predictors of preparedness and should not be the default proxies for the quality of a student or an institution. We need more nuanced research into the variability in assessing GPA and SAT scores. For example, do we know that a student with a 4.0 is more likely to persist than one with a 3.8? Do we know that a student with a 1600 SAT score is more likely to persist than one with a 1400? We are operating under assumptions that higher scores are always better, but are they? Maybe a B+ average with exceptional demonstrated creativity leads to a stronger twenty-first-century student and graduate. We need to test our assumptions across the sector and widely report the results.

A Call to Action

The widespread adoption and integration of twenty-first-century skills development will require a culture shift, and admission policies are foundational to this. The next frontier of advancing innovation in education is to take a systems-based approach, looking at education from kindergarten through college and at how admission policies shape the way education is imagined in our culture. Leaders in higher education must commit to a comprehensive reevaluation of their admission processes by taking inspiration from insights in social science research on how to measure and evaluate twenty-first-century skills like empathy, self-awareness, resilience, collaboration, leadership, and creativity. By partnering with institutions outside of education that are experimenting with new recruitment and hiring processes, institutions of higher education can model the type of true multisector collaboration vital to success in the twenty-first century.

Higher education is an industry that loves to study itself. Within the industry, we recommend that colleges proactively engage in an open and honest inquiry into how the values, rewards, structures, and processes of their admission practices impact the culture of their classrooms, the quality of students' lives and learning, and the success and happiness of graduates. Specifically, university leadership should ask, does our admission system reward and amplify the skills and competencies that are demanded and desired in the twenty-first-century world and workplace? Or does our admission system unintentionally obstruct progress toward twenty-first-century learning goals and instead cause persistent widespread harm?

To answer these questions, each college should examine the most critical factors that lead to consideration and admission at their institution. How do these metrics promote students' success beyond the point of admission? Do they represent the most valuable skills and attributes that we seek to promote in students over the course of four years, or do they represent something else? Are they tied to our unique mission in any tangible way? Do they actually correlate with students' success?

There are few more powerful signals put out by selective universities about what they value and what matters in terms of student quality and potential than their admission criteria. To students, "admission" to the right school is the ultimate key, the code that unlocks the door and grants lifelong identity and membership. No matter what they study, what they learn, or how their experience plays out after that, their admission is experienced as the ultimate prize and leaves an indelible mark on students' notions of what makes them personally valuable and worthy. If a paradigm shift is needed in education, we must recognize that all innovation efforts on both sides of the admission process will never become more than experiments, at best, and hollow posturing, at worst, until college admission policies embrace, represent, and ultimately reward the values of the new education paradigm.

Notes

1. Education Reimagined, "A Transformational Vision for Education in the US," 2015, https://education-reimagined.org/wp-content/uploads/2019/01/Vision_Website.pdf.

2. Thurston Domina, Andrew Penner, and Emily Penner, "Categorical Inequality: Schools as Sorting Machines," *Annual Review of Sociology* 43, no. 1 (2017): 311–330, doi:10.1146/annurev-soc-060116-053354.

3. Ashoka, "Changemaking 101: The Discovery Framework," Changemakers, n.d., https://www.changemakers.com/DiscoveryFrameworkTool.

4. Harry A. Patrinos, "How a Time-Tested Education Model Can Prepare Students for a High Tech Future," World Bank Education for Global Development, December 20, 2017, https://blogs.worldbank.org/education/how-time-tested-education-model-can-prepare-students-high-tech-future.

5. Caroline M. Hoxby, "The Economics of School Reform," National Bureau of Economic Research, n.d., https://www.nber.org/reporter/spring98/hoxby_spring98.html.

6. "11 Facts about High School Dropout Rates," *DoSomething.org*, n.d., https://www.dosomething.org/us/facts/11-facts-about-high-school-dropout-rates.

7. Karen Ann Cullotta et al., "'No Worse Fate than Failure': How Pressure to Keep Up Is Overwhelming Students in Elite Districts," *Chicago Tribune*, November 13, 2017, https://www.chicagotribune.com/suburbs/anxietyhigh/ct-teen-anxiety-part-one-tl-1116-20171120-story.html.

8. Cullotta et al., "No Worse Fate than Failure."

9. Anthony M. Baird and Satyanarayana Parayitam, "Are Employers Dissatisfied with College Graduates? An Empirical Examination," *International Journal of Arts and Sciences* 10, no. 1 (2017): 151–168.

10. Ryan Craig, "Think Students Are Unhappy with Higher Education? Try Employers," *EdSurge*, May 26, 2016, https://www.edsurge.com/news/2016-05-26-think-students-are-unhappy-with-higher-education-try-employers.

11. Chris Weller, "The 14 Most Innovative Schools in America," *Business Insider*, May 28, 2016, https://www.businessinsider.com/the-most-innovative-schools-in-america-2016-4.

12. Russlynn Ali, "A Letter from Our Founder," XQ, n.d., https://xqsuperschool.org/about.

13. Scott Jaschik, "A Plan to Kill High School Transcripts . . . and Transform College Admissions," *Inside Higher Ed*, May 10, 2017, https://www.insidehighered.com/news/2017/05/10/top-private-high-schools-start-campaign-kill-traditional-transcripts-and-change.

14. Kate Ebner and Noah Pickus, "The Right Kind of Innovation," *Inside Higher Ed*, July 25, 2018, https://www.insidehighered.com/digital-learning/views/2018/07/25/yes-higher-ed-needs-innovation-it-should-be-right-kind-opinion.

15. Tim Cresswell, "The Promise of the Experiential Liberal Arts," *Chronicle of Higher Education*, September 2, 2018, https://www.chronicle.com/article/The-Promise-of-the/244419.

16. Hart Research Associates, "Top Ten Things Employers Look for in New College Graduates," Association of American Colleges and Universities, September 11, 2014, https://www.aacu.org/leap/students/employers-top-ten.

17. Kevin Gray and Andrea Koncz, "The Key Attributes Employers Seek on Students' Resumes," National Association of Colleges and Employers, November 30, 2017, http://www.naceweb.org/about-us/press/2017/the-key-attributes-employers-seek-on-students-resumes.

18. Richard H. Thaler, Cass R. Sunstein, and John P. Balz, "Choice Architecture," *SSRN*, April 2, 2010, http://dx.doi.org/10.2139/ssrn.1583509.

19. Thaler, Sunstein, and Balz, "Choice Architecture."

20. Eric Hoover, "What Colleges Want in an Applicant (Everything)," *New York Times*, November 1, 2017, https://www.nytimes.com/2017/11/01/education/edlife/what-college-admissions-wants.html.

21. Hoover, "What Colleges Want."

20 Scholartistry
Creativity and the Future of the Liberal Arts

Michael Shanks and Connie Svabo

What role should be played by programs offered by universities and colleges, as institutions of higher education and learning, in complementing primary and secondary schooling to prepare students for life and employment?

This question, the focus of this book, has featured prominently in educational policy since the development of state-sponsored schooling in the late nineteenth century. It is an old question that takes us back to the earliest of state polities in antiquity, temple bureaucracies, state scribes, and Plato's academy in the Greek polis. The issue has always been one of state, institutional, and corporate regulation of society, how people become members of a community, and the way that community is conceived in relation to its members—questions of governance; the role of the temple, for example, in the management of the state; and broader questions of social order, ethics, and right and proper behavior. What constitutes a full and rewarding life? And for whom?

In this context of the state, the constitution of power, political economics, membership, and agency (who gets to make a difference), we recall what the liberal arts are in principle. They are not "liberal" in a political sense, nor are they the "arts." The *artes liberales* are the skills and competencies (*artes*) that free members of a community (*cives liberi*) need to pursue a rich and fulfilling life. Included are any fields fitted to this end, such as arts, sciences, social sciences, and humanities.

The key topic is the reconciliation of modes of learning and knowing in a history or, more accurately, a genealogy of the body politic, the constitutional organization of members of a community, since the days of the first ancient city-states. The challenge after the constitutional innovations of the Greek polis has been to reconcile *episteme* (scientific knowledge), *sophia* (theoretical wisdom), *techne* (practical know-how and applied knowledge), and *phronesis* (sociocultural savviness)—manifold approaches ranging from formal bodies of propositional knowledge, through technical skills and creativity, to ethical dispositions with respect to knowing what constitutes the good life. We are dealing here with an elision of learning and knowing: these forms of knowledge all refer to competencies thought essential to leading, contributing to, and shaping a rich life as a full member of a political community, an active agent. That is, the artes liberales deal in the production of knowledge for society and citizenship.

Knowing and learning are, in this context, not merely technical issues of (higher) education policy and curriculum design, but constitute a vital component of world building, the production and reproduction of our lifeworlds. This asserts the affiliation of knowing and learning in agency—the capacities and competencies to act and make a difference—which share in the building of the society and communities we need and desire according to a particular constitutional arrangement or agreement.

Why should we take this broad view of the genealogy of the issues at the heart of contemporary debates about the shape and role of higher education programs? To reassert in this way the credentials, value, and scope of a liberal arts education reframes the debates about higher education by establishing a context for the issues well beyond specific matters of educational policy and curricula. The challenge to rethink the role of the liberal arts and their pertinence to twenty-first-century schooling is as much about political economics as it is about curriculum design and pedagogical style.

For example, consider the declining enrollments in the humanities. The bigger context we are sketching suggests that this has as much to do with perceptions of a complex labor market in considerable flux because of a crisis of confidence in uncertain futures as it is about a need to adjust humanities curricula. Students may well adore classes in history and literature as they exist now, but they don't enroll because they think vocational programs with a tight and obvious link to the job market are what will help them build a career.[1]

Consider also the continuing exclusivity of the two cultures of the sciences and arts/humanities (techies versus fuzzies, as they get called at Stanford). The bifurcation is a key in preventing the establishment of interdisciplinary programs that many deem so important to the future of higher education. Yet the long history of the liberal arts, as well as studies in the history of disciplines and of knowledge, shows how intimate the sciences, arts, and humanities have always been when related to the diverse roles people may play in building their communities and lifeworlds.[2] Raising questions of the role of the liberal arts in facing twenty-first-century challenges is to raise questions of constitutional arrangements and personal and collective agency, our capacities to create our own lifeworlds.

Scholartistry Defined

Given this reframing, a strong argument for a revitalized liberal arts education is that it can facilitate learning to integrate and synthesize, to read across disparate bodies of knowledge and disciplines, and in so doing, creatively make meaning and act with context-sensitive flexibility. It is with the aim of foregrounding this creative, integrative, and flexible agency that we introduce the concept of scholartistry.

We define scholartistry as a hybrid of rigorous empirical disposition (as in the attentive scholar) and creative agency (as in the persona of the artist). Scholartistry subsumes transdisciplinary, creative research practice by combining scholarly and artistic ways of thinking, acting, and engaging with the world. Scholartistry integrates the critical/analytical with the creative/imaginative in hybrid scholarship-arts knowledge creation.[3] In this context, artistry is not about the fine arts but about aesthetics; invoking the etymology of the word "aesthetics" as *aistheta*,

Scholartistry 285

meaning "of or for perception by the senses," scholartistry integrates logic and aesthetics in sensitive knowing.

We introduce scholartistry to highlight aesthetic and artistic ways of working and suggest that these are desirable in research and education. Art and aesthetic experience are a fruitful way of developing capacity for sensitive knowing. Dewey, for example, points out: "works of art are means by which we enter, through imagination and the emotions they evoke, into other forms of relationship and participation than our own."[4] Elliot Eisner builds on Dewey in arguing for the value of artistry in education: artistry can serve as an important cognitive countermodel to mechanized and hyperrationalized visions of education, which give priority to the prespecification of intended outcomes through standards and are governed by desires for educational measurement. According to Eisner, developing familiarity with artistry helps cultivate dispositions, which are of general educational value.[5] Artistry contributes cognitive and perceptual flexibility, the ability to imagine, and familiarity with self-directed activity. These are crucial world-building capacities, empowering individuals to deal with complexity, diversity, and change.

Scholartistry has three dynamic aspects:

- *Creativity in action.* Scholartistry involves an open, exploratory, autotelic dynamic. It may not be directed toward specific goals or ends other than reproducing and refreshing lifeworlds—the world building that is also part of the concept of agency.
- *Integrative experience.* Scholartistry bridges arts and sciences, connecting them through aesthetics, which we take as the intimate relations in the experience of thinking, sensing, feeling.
- *Flexible, context-sensitive pragmatics.* Scholartistry works in and through specific scenarios and circumstances, whether culturally, socially, or historically mediated, and is oriented toward communicating and making.

We hope it is clear that scholartistry is not something new. We introduce the concept to draw attention to a specific configuration of learning and knowing, a pragmatics that addresses the particular challenges of complexity.

Interjection in the Form of a Scenario

"A scenario? What do you mean, really? I mean—sorry to say—but this sounds so airy-fairy to me!"

The setting is an imagined inspirational meeting, one in a number of workshops at LARC, a make-believe liberal arts college, scholartistically invented for this chapter with inspiration from design methods, such as scenario and persona development.

The personae are Jean Deanison, the dean of LARC, who is in charge of redesigning the college profile and curriculum for the future. Deanison has convened a number of inspirational workshops, where LARC faculty, students, and administrators are presented with visions for the future of liberal arts education. The workshops are dialogical, seeking to relate future-forward innovations to the challenges of higher ed institutions. For today's session focusing on scholartistry, the dean has invited a small team of participants: Fac DeYoung, an assistant professor of history at LARC; and two student representatives, Dewie Johnson and Harriet Chipman.

The dean smiles but also repeats her somewhat brusque comment: "What do you mean? This sounds so airy-fairy to me!" She elaborates: "As you know, I love the reframing of the liberal arts that you are offering, but frankly the idea of scholartistry is difficult for me to grasp! I mean, how does it relate to the goals of liberal arts education—to offer students learning that will help prepare them to deal with diversity, change, and complexity?"

Complexity and Change

We are faced with complexity, we live in changing environments, business realities are in flux, and everyday lives rest on shaky foundations. We regularly confront unpredictable and high-risk phenomena, such as illness, inequality, political instability, and climate change.

Complex phenomena unveil limitations in ways of thinking about the world that are modeled on knowability—on the assumption that it is possible to fully describe the world and to make predictions about the course of events.[6] To deal with complexity is to deal with processes of change that have emergent and dynamic features. What happens in complexity is unpredictable, irreducible, and nonlinear.[7] If something is complex, there will always be limitations in our understanding of it. It is not possible to generate complete, absolute, or final knowledge about complex phenomena. As a response, we have to develop competencies and tactics for acting on the basis of insecurity and incomplete information. We must develop capacities for navigating amid complex processes of change.

Scholartistry builds on the idea that creativity, the capacity to integrate, and flexibility in action help us navigate these complex processes of change.

Creativity for Complexity Navigation

We emphasize creative competencies in our concept of scholartistry. Creativity is an effective response to change. Creativity may be defined as "the development of original ideas that are useful or influential."[8] For individuals and collectives, creativity is tied to flexibility, and this flexibility is fundamental for the capacity to cope with change, whether it comes in the form of advances and opportunities or disruptions and breakdowns. Creativity is the capacity to produce new ideas, approaches, and models of thinking and doing. This capacity potentially is played out in all spheres of life and across the whole life span. Creativity, hence, is not just about the arts; it is also a key concern of organizations and businesses because of its role in entrepreneurship and innovation. Creativity is about moving beyond conventional modes of thought and practice, regardless of where you are.

It is significant that Tom Kelley and David Kelley of the design consultancy IDEO, a long-standing partner with the Stanford School of Engineering, called their book about design thinking *Creative Confidence*. They emphasize the creative competencies that we are associating with scholartistry.[9] Richard Florida has presented much research regarding the emergence of a "creative class."[10] Daniel Pink caused quite a stir when he proposed that the new master of business administration needed to be a master of fine arts (!) precisely because of its foundations in creative competencies.[11]

Creativity is something you can learn, involving flexible thinking as made manifest in combinatory and associative techniques, open-ended exploration, divergent thinking, lateral thinking, problem finding, and problem solving. Creativity is crucial both in reactive, problem-solving activities and in proactive, inventive processes. Creativity is a driving force in cultural evolution, which is seen in the rapid adaptations taking place from one generation to the next.

The complex issues and heterogeneous and interlocking systems we deal with in our contemporary lives require qualitatively new approaches. Our present-day problems can't be solved by doing more of the same. We need new approaches, and these approaches cannot be developed through practice alone nor through curriculum-based teaching alone. They have to be informed by multiple disciplines and integrated theory and practice in order to foster the skills and sensibilities that make it possible to address complex challenges.

Interjection

The college dean looks around at the others in the preparatory meeting. She has chosen the students and the young faculty member as the participants today in order to allow skeptical voices to surface.

One of the students, Harriet Chipman, a bit hesitantly asks: "Is it like design thinking? I mean, you mention design thinking, and we have heard about design thinking in one of the previous inspirational workshops. Is scholartistry like design thinking?"

Scholartistry, Integrative Capacity, and the Design Connection

A field that has come to stress the creative and integrative capacities we promote with scholartistry is design and, more particularly, design thinking. Let us unpack the connections through some insights offered by Richard Buchanan.

Buchanan's seminal article "Wicked Problems in Design Thinking" emphasizes that designers often engage in conceiving and planning "what does not yet exist, and this occurs in the context of indeterminacy of wicked problems."[12] "Wicked problems" are complex and ambiguous problems to which there is no simple solution. Buchanan calls design thinking the "new liberal art of technological culture" and points toward its potential in integrating the knowledge of the natural, social, and humanistic sciences into adequate solutions to wicked problems.[13] Buchanan also asserts: "Without integrative disciplines of understanding, communication, and action, there is little hope of sensibly extending knowledge beyond the library or laboratory in order to serve the purpose of enriching human life."[14]

In another article, Buchanan connects design practice with rhetoric because design, as creative conception, planning, and implementation, is grounded in implicit or explicit argumentation.[15] Design works in and through communication and dialogue around values, and makes cases for innovation and change for a better life.

Rhetoric here is understood as the art and science of argument and persuasion, of exploring the possibilities of engaging with audiences so as to effect desired outcomes. Rhetoric is the poetics of building and performing statements, arguments, demonstrations, fantasies, hopes, fears. Rhetoric is the erotics of mobilizing desires, connecting with others so as to achieve desired ends. While rhetoric is typically associated with verbal and written communication,[16] Buchanan is right to take a much broader view of rhetoric as material discourse, as creative process, as the production of case or argument: intentional, directed, engaging maker with audience, and including the material conditions necessary for such creative work. The point is, of course, that rhetoric was long a key component of the liberal arts. Rhetoric is part of the liberal arts *and* a field of design that deals with a complex world of ambiguities, uncertainties, and challenges.

Rhetoric and design integrate, answer challenges, make cases, and address audiences, communities, clients, constituencies. They deal in dynamic flows of experience and communication in the complexity of everyday life, which orthodox academic disciplines and fields of specialized expertise often fail to capture.

The connection between design and the liberal arts has been suggested from another standpoint. After a class shared between Bard Graduate Center and Stanford University in the fall of 2014, which explored the research practices and creative outlooks of eighteenth-century antiquarians, our colleague Peter Miller wrote an article in the *Chronicle of Higher Education* suggesting that design thinking was a recent manifestation or transformation of the liberal arts.[17] The predisciplinary and worldly praxis of antiquarians, those pioneers of empirical and field research, roamed freely by means of broad competencies. While Miller's proposition was intended as a provocation in debates around STEM (science, technology, engineering, math) curricular programs, with calls for a crucial creative component (STEAM adds arts to STEM),[18] we reassert the deep historical roots of design thinking in traditions that also cover the liberal arts.

Interjection

Fac DeYoung decides to try to pursue the same line as the dean: how will this be actionable? It sounds fine, wanting to address the goal of educating students to deal with change and complexity, but it also sounds a bit esoteric, a bit oblique.

"OK, let's agree that we need to bring in creative skills. How might we do this? What might scholartistry look like in action?"

Scholartistry at Stanford

An example of scholartistry in action in a liberal arts curriculum is our Design of Cities class at Stanford. It is a studio-based class capped at thirty-two participants. Students are guided through a process of exploring urban dwelling through ethnography, qualitative fieldwork, and arts-based research. Students work with cultural mapping, creative writing, storytelling, and media production. The class is an open-ended studio wherein students are guided in exploring urban dwelling as processes, such as flowing, enclosing, mobilizing, calculating, place making.

Throughout the class, students are asked not only to observe and interact but also to creatively work with images and other media. The objective is to creatively reconceptualize and even reframe how we can handle human experience under the premise that any effective planning or design must be grounded in an understanding of such experience. The orthodoxy is to understand urban dwelling through distinct analytic and administrative categories, such as housing, transport, infrastructure, employment, and recreation, even when it is acknowledged that the experience of urban dwelling cuts right through such categories. So the class addresses directly how we might get a handle on complex human experience. Throughout the studio-based project work, students are confronted with historical case studies that complement the reconceptualization invited by the field explorations and creative encounters with contemporary urban experience. This class in urban dwelling is a class in archaeology and historical anthropology.

Human-Centered Design

Since the late 1960s and 1970s, Stanford has developed design programs, mainly located in the School of Engineering, that have amounted to a platform or paradigm of "human-centered design," an alternative label to "design thinking."[19] There has been considerable cross-fertilization with the IT industry in Silicon Valley, including in and around cognitive science, ethnography, and psychology in relation to the shift of emphasis since the 1960s from industrial to a variety of design approaches. These include service design, interaction design, user-centered and experience design, and a current focus on the design and engineering of complex systems, social innovation, involvement of artificial and augmented intelligence, machine learning, and the mediation of relationships among people, artifacts, and environments.[20]

We are keen to emphasize this broader grounding of design in human experience, including creativity and agency. Between 2001 and 2009 the Stanford Humanities Lab ran experiments in project-based hybrid learning, following the precept that the humanities and arts are a platform for collaborative bridge building across disciplines and through the cultural archive and for addressing matters of contemporary concern.[21] Our purpose was to focus on the cultural and historical breadth of human experience in human-centered design.

These are efforts to deal with the relation of learning in the academy to worlds beyond, which are not organized in disciplinary ways. Human experience doesn't take place in neat disciplinary categories. Involved are shifts from formal instruction to participant-driven learning—making education experience-driven!

While not explicitly associated with a liberal arts agenda, which has been more a feature of educational institutions in the United States, particularly, of course, liberal arts colleges, Roskilde University has half a century of experience with participant-driven education. The university was established by the Danish state in 1972 to promote and deliver radically student-centered, project-based experiential learning. With the Roskilde model, the university continues to cultivate project- and problem-oriented approaches to knowledge creation and to use transdisciplinarity as a key principle in the way study programs are organized.[22] The university's home page, for example, states that "no major problems are ever resolved on the basis of any single academic discipline alone."[23] The creation of value and knowledge in present-day societies increasingly takes place in collaboration across businesses, organizations, government agencies, teams, and individuals worldwide.

Interjection

"Excuse me." Dewie Johnson finally feels he has a point he can make. "Excuse me, but I don't really think your institutional contexts—at Stanford and a Danish state university—offer an approach that we at our small liberal arts college can achieve in any way. I mean, it is inspiring to hear about, but I just can't see it really fly as a concept here at LARC."

Flexibility and Context-Sensitive Pragmatics

Scholartistry develops capacities for navigating through complex processes of change by engaging with ways of thinking and doing that aren't modeled on predictability, linearity, and reductionism. Scholartistry is a way of developing competencies for acting despite insecurity and incomplete information. This implies, among other things, that scholartistry in educational processes and in research tones down the importance of rationalist formulations of goals, aims, and objectives. Instead, scholartistry is about engaging with processes that are dynamic and emergent. This scholartistry tactic is informed by the educational philosophies of Dewey and Eisner. Eisner writes:

> In Western models of rational decision making the formulation of aims, goals, objectives, or standards is a critical act; virtually all else that follows depends upon the belief that one must have clearly defined ends. Once ends are conceptualized, means are formulated then implemented, and the outcomes are evaluated. If there is a discrepancy between aspiration and accomplishment, new means are formulated. The cycle continues until ends and outcomes are isomorphic. Ends are held constant and are always believed to precede means.[24]

He continues: "But is this true? In the arts it certainly is not. In the arts ends may follow means. One may act and the act may itself suggest ends, ends that did not precede the act, but follow it."[25]

Drawing on Dewey's concept of flexible purposing,[26] Eisner tells of processes where ends shift and where the work yields clues that one pursues. They emerge. Unpredictably. In self-organizing ways: "In a sense, one surrenders to what the work in process suggests."[27] Aims shift while the work is being carried out:

> Flexible purposing is opportunistic; it capitalizes on the emergent features appearing within a field of relationships. It is not rigidly attached to predefined aims when the possibility of better ones emerges. The kind of thinking that flexible purposing requires thrives best in an environment in which the rigid adherence to a plan is not a necessity. As experienced teachers well know, the surest road to hell in a classroom is to stick to the lesson plan no matter what.[28]

Flexible purposing is a key aspect of the situated and context-sensitive pragmatics of scholartistry. These pragmatics imply that the act of planning is reframed: "plans are seen no longer as set procedures simply to be acted out but as guidelines that can be altered in accordance with the situation at hand."[29] And sometimes, there is no plan.

Situated and action-oriented flexibility is an important feature of scholartistry. Scholartistry gives priority to open-ended, creative, and imaginative experiments; these features are a key component of design thinking but may lose ground in favor of a more analytic focus on problem orientation and the engineering of solutions. An engineering mindset has proved to be very effective in delivering solutions to clearly defined problems. Scholartistry emphasizes a complementary mindset that foregrounds the creative imagination, holding off from defining a problem in favor of open-ended experimentation and exploration. Open-ended experimentation and explorative flexibility tie in directly with seeing complexity as a premise in knowledge creation. The mindset of scholartistry acknowledges the inherent ambiguity of complexity; problems may resist definition. In accordance with complexity thinking, scholartistry does not operate from a problem-solution paradigm. Instead scholartistry works with ambiguity and the irreducibility of the wicked problem.

An example: working with various stakeholders in ethnically diverse communities, a strict orientation on narrowing in and defining and solving a problem may close down collaboration, because the involved parties are too far from each other in opinion and vantage point to be able to agree on any such problem definition. Here, it is much more relevant to think of "infrastructuring" conversation through open-ended exploration—to build trust, rather than define problems.[30] This demonstrates the creative flexibility that scholartistry promotes.

Feezell sums up the features of open-ended exploration and play that are at the core of scholartistry: freedom, (serious) nonseriousness, illusion, unreality, purposelessness, make-believe, superfluousness, suspension of the ordinary, internal or intrinsic meaning, diminished consciousness of self, absorption, responsive openness, contingency, spontaneity, improvisation, fun![31]

Scholartistry

Interjection

"Make-believe?"

"Fun?!"

Jean the dean has followed the flow of the conversation and the presentation of scholartistry as a way of developing creative agency amid complexity through integrative capabilities and flexible and pragmatic context-sensitivity—all of which are scalable. Further, their realization perhaps is more about mindset and ingenuity than about institutional size or financial strength.

In a softer tone of voice than her initial barking, Jean says: "In a world of pressing challenges and with limited resources available for education and research, it may seem that we cannot afford play and open-ended exploration. It may seem that play is frivolous—and education must focus on fixable problems. I can certainly hear my board saying something like that."

Value and Creative Skills

The implementation of scholartistry in any institution, like any organizational change, requires the acceptance of the institution and leadership to take risks. The economic value of creative skills has been recognized again and again; this is not a new thing. There are several historical examples. The foundation of European schools of art and design from the mid-nineteenth century onward was mainly to improve the creative potential of industrial design. The Victoria and Albert Museum in London and Cooper Hewitt in Manhattan were also founded to improve design skills. An indication of this in the twenty-first century is the massive investments by the Chinese government in the creation of more than a thousand new design study programs because of the realization that engineering skills are not enough on their own to build capacity for innovation.[32] An important point here is that these are not investments just in humanistic skills but in creative skills.

While the pursuit of open-ended play may be difficult to justify in tightly managed and resourced professional projects, shifting frames of understanding is a key component of innovation,[33] and radical innovation, rather than incremental change, depends on open-ended experimentation. Morozov has made a powerful case that problem-oriented design can easily miss the point; it is easy to assume that a problem is well defined.[34] It is vital to make space for open exploration, to consider alternative perspectives, to consider other frames of reference, and to hold problems and associated solutions in abeyance, deferring any definitive statement, diagnosis, or prognosis. We need such lateral thinking more than ever.

Scholartistry can be applied with a problem-solving attitude, where artistry is harnessed for creativity, aesthetic sensibility, and imagination, but it is crucial to highlight that scholartistry exceeds a problem-solving, we-can-fix-it approach, and this is its autotelic feature. The value of artistry is intrinsic. This implies that scholartistry makes a stand for the legitimacy of seemingly purposeless, exploratory activity, for creative impulse and trying things without justification, following hunches and gut feelings.[35]

The academy has long conceived itself as a protected space for open-ended research and experiment. Student-centered liberal arts education has always encouraged self-directed activities. What is the experimental method without open exploration rooted in the creative imagination? How do we think beyond the here and now? So, yes: play!

Notes

1. Benjamin Schmidt, "The Humanities Are in Crisis," *Atlantic*, August 23, 2018.

2. For a fascinating exploration of early science, art, and craft, see Pamela H. Smith, *The Body of the Artisan: Art and Experience in the Scientific Revolution* (Chicago, IL: University of Chicago Press, 2004).

3. Michael Shanks and Connie Svabo, "Scholartistry: Incorporating Scholarship and Art," *Journal of Problem Based Learning in Higher Education* 6, no. 2 (2018): 15-38.

4. John Dewey, *Art as Experience* (New York: Capricorn, 1958), 333.

5. Elliot W. Eisner, "Artistry in Education," *Scandinavian Journal of Educational Research* 47, no. 3 (2013): 373-384, 374.

6. Andrew Pickering, *The Cybernetic Brain: Sketches of Another Future* (Chicago, IL: University of Chicago Press, 2010).

7. John Urry, "The Complexity Turn," *Theory, Culture and Society* 22, no. 5 (2005): 1-14, 8.

8. Mark A. Runco, "Creativity," *Annual Review of Psychology* 55 (2004): 657-687, 658.

9. Tom Kelley and David Kelley, *Creative Confidence: Unleashing the Creative Potential within Us All* (New York: Crown, 2013).

10. Richard Florida, *The Rise of the Creative Class: Revisited* (New York: Basic, 2014).

11. Daniel Pink, *A Whole New Mind: Why Right-Brainers Will Rule the Future* (London: Penguin, 2006).

12. Richard Buchanan, "Wicked Problems in Design Thinking," *Design Issues* 8, no. 2 (1992): 5-21, 17.

13. Buchanan, "Wicked Problems," 3.

14. Buchanan, "Wicked Problems," 6.

15. Richard Buchanan, "Declaration by Design: Rhetoric, Argument and Demonstration in Design Practice," in *Design Discourse: History, Theory, Criticism*, ed. V. Margolin (Chicago, IL: University of Chicago Press, 1989).

16. George A. Kennedy, *Classical Rhetoric and Its Christian and Secular Tradition from Ancient to Modern Times* (Chapel Hill: University of North Carolina Press, 1999).

17. Peter Miller, "Is 'Design Thinking' the New Liberal Arts?," *Chronicle of Higher Education*, March 26, 2015, https://www.chronicle.com/article/Is-Design-Thinking-the-New/228779.

18. John Maeda, "STEM+Art=STEAM," *STEAM Journal* 1, no. 1 (2013): article 34.

19. Tim Brown, "Design Thinking," *Harvard Business Review* 86, no. 6 (June 2008): 1-10.

20. Michael Lewrick, Patrick Link, and Larry Leifer, *The Design Thinking Playbook: Mindful Digital Transformation of Teams, Products, Services, Businesses and Ecosystems* (Hoboken, NJ: Wiley, 2018).

21. Jeffrey T. Schnapp and Michael Shanks, "Artereality (Rethinking Craft in a Knowledge Economy)," in *Art School: Propositions for the Twenty-First Century*, ed. S. H. Madoff (Cambridge, MA: MIT Press, 2009), 141-158. See also Michael Shanks and Lynn Hershman, "The Scientist and the Artist," in *Science Is Culture: Conversations from the Seed Salon*, ed. Adam Bly (New York: HarperCollins, 2010), 177-192.

22. Anders Siig Andersen and Simon Heilesen, *The Roskilde Model: Problem-Oriented Learning and Project Work* (Heidelberg, Germany: Springer, 2015).

23. Roskilde University, https://ruc.dk/ruc_en, accessed July 31, 2019.

24. Eisner, "Artistry in Education," 378.
25. Eisner, "Artistry in Education," 378.
26. John Dewey, *Experience and Education* (1938; repr., New York: Simon and Schuster, 1997).
27. Eisner, "Artistry in Education," 378.
28. Eisner, "Artistry in Education," 378.
29. Jesper Simonsen et al., eds., *Situated Design Methods* (Cambridge, MA: MIT Press, 2014), 5, referring to Lucy A. Suchman, *Plans and Situated Action: The Problem of Human-Machine Interaction* (Cambridge: Cambridge University Press, 1987), viii.
30. Erling Bjögvinsson, Pelle Ehn, and Per-Anders Hillgren, "Design Things and Design Thinking: Contemporary Participatory Design Challenges," *Design Issues* 28, no. 3 (2012): 101-116, 108.
31. R. Feezell, "A Pluralist Conception of Play," in *The Philosophy of Play*, ed. E. Ryall (New York: Routledge, 2013), 23.
32. Wai Michael Siu and Giovanni Contreras, *Design Education for Fostering Creativity and Innovation in China* (Hershey, PA: IGI Global, 2017).
33. Kees Dorst, *Frame Innovation: Create New Thinking by Design* (Cambridge, MA: MIT Press, 2015).
34. Evgeny Morozov, *To Save Everything, Click Here: The Folly of Technological Solutionism* (New York: Public Affairs, 2013).
35. Connie Svabo, "Performative Schizoid Method: Performance as Research," *PARtake: The Journal of Performance as Research* 1, no. 1 (2016): article 7. See also Shanks and Svabo, "Scholartistry."

Afterword
The Age of Connectedness

Leo Lambert
President Emeritus, Elon University

I read this important volume from the perspective of one who has been privileged to serve more than forty years in higher education at diverse institutions, including a nineteen-year tenure as president of Elon University. The great conviction of my life is that higher education remains the most important force in our nation to promote economic mobility, advance a democratic society, fuel innovation and creativity, and uplift the human spirit. Consequently, the quality of undergraduate education in our nation should matter a great deal to every citizen. This book makes a powerful case for why liberal learning—long the bedrock for higher education in the United States—is more essential than ever, and it offers inspiring examples of how faculty are leading its reinvention and thereby allowing it to flourish.

The Case for Coherence

The overarching vision of this book is the creation of new models of liberal education that are integrated and connected, rejecting the old practices of general education checklists and transactional advising experiences that sign off on a schedule of classes for the next term with little, if any, meaningful conversation about how those classes are related to students' goals for life. Instead, this book contains rich illustrations of how to create coherent pathways through the curriculum and help students create genuine synergy between the curriculum and the cocurriculum, between the liberal arts and the professions, and between learning on campus and learning in the broader world. But it is also about employing integrative pedagogies, integrating student voices and lives into the teaching and learning process in meaningful ways, and integrating students—especially vulnerable students—into our institutions by demystifying the academy's codes and committing to building cultures for student success. At a time when the liberal arts and particularly the humanities and social sciences are facing enormous pressures on our campuses, this is a hopeful book that points the way to remaking the case that the liberal arts are not only relevant but indispensable for our times.

This Is for Everyone

What I admire most about this book is the great overall challenge it suggests: that this integrated and powerful vision of the liberal arts is scalable for every student, including and especially, I would argue, students in community and technical colleges. The qualities the liberal arts impart and for which employers are clearly searching—critical thinking, creativity, multifaceted communications skills, quantitative reasoning—are critical for advancement in the twenty-first century for *everyone*. While the institutions in this volume represent the Ivy League, liberal arts colleges and universities, and public comprehensive and research universities, President Gail Mellow of LaGuardia Community College reminds us that nearly 40 percent of the 18 million college students in the United States attend community colleges, in contrast to the 0.4 percent who attend Ivy League campuses. Community colleges educate the majority of low-income, first-generation students, and 25 percent of community college students are trying to both hold down a full-time job and pursue a full academic schedule.[1]

That's why I so deeply admire institutions like LaGuardia Community College and Stella and Charles Guttman Community College (part of the City University of New York) for their leadership in advancing the liberal arts in the two-year college context, ensuring that their students are not only prepared for careers, but also will gain the knowledge and

Afterword

foundational preparation to adapt in a fast-changing world and the opportunity to ask the great questions of their lives, such as "What gifts do I have to offer my community?" LaGuardia's comprehensive approach, for example, includes an emphasis on an integrative pedagogy and curriculum to help students find connectedness; a multifaceted and comprehensive peer-mentoring program; a transformed first-year seminar and system of advisement; and an e-portfolio for students organized around big questions like "Who am I and who am I becoming?"

The Classroom and the First Year Matter a Great Deal

This volume also recenters our thinking on what a critical place the classroom remains in helping students find challenge, direction, and inspiration. Two colleagues and I did a poll in 2018 of 4,000 college graduates nationally and asked them to reflect on the number of important mentors they had in college—be they faculty members, staff members, or influential peers. The poll found that "graduates who had seven to ten significant relationships with faculty and staff were three times more likely to report their college experience as 'very rewarding' than those with no such relationships. Similar effects were found for peer relationships in college."[2] But most relevant to this volume is that 79 percent of graduates reported meeting their "most influential peer" and 60 percent reported meeting their "most influential faculty member" during the first year of college, and the classroom was most frequently cited as the place graduates met these important influencers. That the first-year experience is a defining part of many innovations profiled in this volume—including those at the University of Wisconsin-Green Bay, Smith, Rollins, and Connecticut College—leads me to expect that students will experience a double benefit through these curricular reforms: the understanding of the need to create coherent pathways through their undergraduate experience *and* mentoring by strong and committed faculty.

The Liberal Arts and the Professions Must Collaborate

Both the George Mason case and the Elon German studies case in this book provide compelling examples of how professional school colleagues can be powerful partners in the advancement of liberal education. The old model is the us-against-them mentality of competing for majors and enrollments. In this old model, liberal arts faculty are inevitably on the defensive, given the practical appeal of professional schools to many career-minded students and parents. The Elon German studies faculty offer a pathways approach; their case describes four distinct pathways through the program's curriculum, some of which include courses taught by faculty from the Schools of Business and Communications. This approach underscores the liberal arts perspective that many professional school faculty bring to their teaching and scholarship. It also makes the German studies program more appealing to prospective students by allowing them to align their chosen pathway with their goals for career or graduate school.

The George Mason approach is quite different. Its innovators have created a seven-course, liberal-arts-based Foundations sequence within the School of Business, taught by faculty from a variety of liberal arts fields who teach side by side with business school faculty.

Both approaches argue for low walls (better yet, no walls) between the liberal arts and the professions, focusing instead on collaboration and delivering meaningful, cutting-edge curricula that serve their students' needs and interests.

Integrative Pedagogy Matters

The vice provost for education at Georgetown, Randy Bass, makes a profoundly important point about the state of undergraduate education nationally:

> The general pattern of students is that they have a relatively homogeneous, relatively unsatisfying set of academic engagements until, at best, they get into upper division and major courses. I think we need a far greater variety of learning contexts in the first two years [that are] intentionally designed for the heterogeneity of engagements that . . . would give us faculty and students a much greater variety of interactions.[3]

Another crucial theme that resonates throughout *Redesigning Liberal Education* is the hand-in-glove integration of creative pedagogy with innovative curriculum design. Encountering "messy problems" at Lasell, employing design thinking strategies at Smith, and taking a campus-wide approach at Georgetown to promote experiential, problem-based, integrative learning—all of these point to how creative and engaged pedagogies can help renew liberal learning.

Leadership for the Work

Each chapter in this volume underscores the personal and intellectual leadership that is required to develop a new vision for the liberal arts. As has been noted, curriculum making is hard work—and general education reform is perhaps the most complicated task that can be undertaken on campus. I came away from reading this book with a renewed appreciation for the leadership that makes this innovative work possible, leadership that is boundary spanning, patient, consultative, experimental, and willing to risk failure and learn from mistakes.

When I think of such leaders from my own experience at Elon, they include deans who walked the talk, such as the former business dean, John Burbridge, who was an active and ardent champion of the institution's quest to shelter a chapter of Phi Beta Kappa and make significant investments in the liberal arts. I also think of the former School of Communications dean, Paul Parsons, and his faculty, who created incentives for students to pursue a double major in an arts and a sciences discipline. I hold in high regard the essential leadership of chairs and faculty who champion the liberal arts by celebrating the accomplishments of liberal arts alumni, actively recruiting majors, advocating for creative pedagogy, staffing first-year classes with dynamic faculty members, advancing the message at every opportunity—including on social media—and serving as bridge builders across campus. This committed and often unheralded leadership reenergizes liberal education in our institutions.

A Word about Advising

Professor Richard Light of Harvard has noted that "good advising maybe the single most underestimated characteristic of a successful college experience."[4] Great academic advising is not the transactional variety: it is about encouraging students to seek many mentors, think about the big questions of what they have to offer the world, and develop plans for their education so that it will lead to meaningful careers and lives. All of the valiant efforts described in this volume to create coherence for students need to be connected to many other dimensions of university life, including the entirety of the curriculum, opportunities to pursue high-impact practices, and leadership in clubs and organizations. Helping students seek integration and find connections among all of these dimensions of the undergraduate experience is an unfolding process. Mentors and advisors should be at the hub of helping students make these connections and can be strong allies in communicating the value of a liberal education. We must not overlook the importance of these partnerships.

Revaluing the Civic Purposes of Higher Education

One of the most distressing and dangerous trends of our time is that higher education is increasingly regarded merely as a private commodity for personal advancement, disconnected from—to quote the authors of the College of the Holy Cross case—"a sense of responsibility for the good of society, not just the individual." This volume promises the revitalizing of these civic purposes by integrating community-based learning into our vision for liberal education. Having our students grapple with authentic, real-life, messy, complicated twenty-first-century problems—local, global, or both—is the surest way to help them appreciate deeply that bold interdisciplinary thinking will be essential to confronting the problems requiring their generation's leadership. The practice of applying that thinking in conjunction with community partners in the field is an invaluable experience that will serve them throughout their lifetime.

Reclaiming the Narrative for Higher Education

As was noted in the introduction to this volume, the general public narrative about higher education in the United States might be described as skeptical, at best. As I write this afterword, a major scandal about wealthy families employing unethical means to gain admission to elite universities for their children is dominating the media. Concerns run deep about the cost of college, student loan indebtedness, and campus climates. Our campuses are places that value a robust exchange of views and academic freedom, but they are often regarded by the public as a staging ground for the culture wars. The liberal arts have come to be confused with liberal politics, and holders of liberal arts degrees have been falsely trivialized in popular media and by politicians as unemployable. It is my view that leaders in higher education have done a poor job of communicating an alternative narrative to the broader public that speaks to the life-transforming learning that takes place on our campuses every day and emphasizes that liberal education is at the heart of it. Our collective failure in this regard is worrisome.

As I read the innovative work described in this volume, I remarked to myself time and again, "This is a great story. More people need to know about this innovation." And so my final thought and challenge to readers is that we need to carry this new case for the liberal arts to our neighbors outside the academy. We urgently need to tell the story of what it will take for our graduates to truly be prepared for twenty-first-century work in plain terms, avoiding the jargon of which we academics are so fond. We need to communicate the power and practicality of a new vision for the liberal arts, one that anticipates students succeeding in a high-tech world, integrates high-impact practices like internships and undergraduate research, and employs teaching strategies that link our students with the broader community to confront and solve real-world problems. We have a hopeful, exciting, optimistic, and forward-looking message to convey, so let us seize this opportunity and make a new case for liberal learning.

Notes

1. Gail O. Mellow, "The Biggest Misconception about Today's College Students," *New York Times*, August 28, 2017, https://www.nytimes.com/2017/08/28/opinion/community-college-misconception.html.

2. Leo M. Lambert, Jason Husser, and Peter Felten, "Mentors Play Critical Role in Quality of College Experience, New Poll Suggests," *The Conversation*, August 22, 2018, https://theconversation.com/mentors-play-critical-role-in-quality-of-college-experience-new-poll-suggests-101861.

3. Personal communication, November 12, 2018.

4. Richard J. Light, *Making the Most of College: Students Speak Their Mind* (Cambridge, MA: Harvard University Press, 2004), 81.

Appendix 1

This guide offers information about the focus of each chapter's instructional level, the university or college's size and scope (according to the Carnegie classification system), private or public control, and themes. See appendix 2 for the contents of this book organized by theme and by instructional level.

Chapter Number	First Author	Chapter Title	Instructional Level
1	Bartell	Problem-Focused Liberal Education in a First-Year Learning Community at the University of Wisconsin–Green Bay	first year
2	Artze-Vega	Attending to Local Context, Culture, and Language at Florida International University	first year
3	Gallagher	The Experiential Liberal Arts: An Integrative Model for Twenty-First-Century Education at Northeastern University	core curriculum
4	Reder	Creating Connections: An Intentional, Integrated Liberal Education at Connecticut College	core curriculum
5	Russell	Building a Developmental, Interdisciplinary General Education Curriculum for the Future: Rollins Foundations in the Liberal Arts	core curriculum
6	Britt-Smith	Exploring the Borderlands: Using Interdisciplinarity to Build Civic Literacy at the College of the Holy Cross	first year
7	Daley	Redesigning Learning through Multidisciplinary Teaching: Voices from a Sophomore Core Experience at Lasell University	sophomore
8	Wright	Intergenerational Partnerships to Support Liberal Learning Goals at Brown University	cocurricular
9	Mikic	The Design Thinking Initiative at Smith College	cocurricular
10	Pope-Ruark	Immersive Learning in the Studio for Social Innovation at Elon University	upper class
11	Debelius	Failing Forward: Writing, Design, and Organic Curricular Change at Georgetown University	cocurricular
12	Gring-Pemble	Educating Business Leaders for a Better World at George Mason University	core curriculum, major/minor
13	Windham	Educating for Global Civic Participation and a Career: German Studies in the Twenty-First Century at Elon University	major/minor
14	Bodinger de Uriarte	Pursuing Major Passions: Innovative Minors That Blend Professional Skills and Liberal Education Values for Civic Pursuits at Susquehanna University	major/minor

Theme	Instructional Level	Size and Scope	Control
civic engagement	first year	R1	public
curriculum design	sophomore	DOC	private (not-for-profit)
design thinking	upper class	M	
diversity, equity, and inclusion	cocurricular	BC	
multidisciplinary learning	core curriculum		
problem-based learning	major/minor		
professional programs			

Size and Scope		Control	Theme 1	Theme 2	Theme 3
M	master's colleges and universities: medium programs	public	diversity, equity, and inclusion	problem-based learning	civic engagement
R1	doctoral universities: very high research activity	public	diversity, equity, and inclusion	civic engagement	
R1	doctoral universities: very high research activity	private	curriculum design		
BC	baccalaureate colleges: arts and science focus	private	curriculum design		
M	master's colleges and universities: larger programs	private	curriculum design	multidisciplinary	
BC	baccalaureate colleges: arts and science focus	private	civic engagement		
M	master's colleges and universities: medium programs	private	curriculum design	multidisciplinary	
R1	doctoral universities: very high research activity	private	problem-based learning	multidisciplinary	
BC	baccalaureate colleges: arts and science focus	private	design thinking	multidisciplinary	
DOC	doctoral/professional universities	private	design thinking	multidisciplinary	civic engagement
R1	doctoral universities: very high research activity	private	design thinking	multidisciplinary	
R1	doctoral universities: very high research activity	public	professional programs	civic engagement	
DOC	doctoral/professional universities	private	professional programs	civic engagement	
BC	baccalaureate colleges: arts and science focus	private	civic engagement		

Appendix 2

This is a guide to some of the major themes in the case study chapters and the instructional level(s) that each chapter addresses. Readers are encouraged to focus on the chapters relevant to their interests.

Theme

Civic engagement	Chapters 1, 2, 6, 10, 12, 13, 14
Curriculum design	Chapters 3, 4, 5, 7
Design thinking	Chapters 9, 10, 11
Diversity, equity, and inclusion	Chapters 1, 2
Multidisciplinary learning	Chapters 5, 7, 8, 9, 10, 11
Problem-based learning	Chapters 1, 8
Professional programs	Chapters 12, 13

Instructional Level

First year	Chapters 1, 2, 6
Sophomore	Chapter 7
Upper class	Chapter 10
Cocurricular	Chapters 8, 9, 11
Core curriculum	Chapters 3, 4, 5, 12
Major- or minor-specific	Chapters 12, 13, 14

Contributors

Isis Artze-Vega is the vice president for academic affairs at Valencia College, providing strategic leadership in the areas of curriculum, assessment, faculty development, distance learning, career and workforce education, and educational partnerships for equity. Her work is fueled by a commitment to equity and justice, and implemented through love and service.

Denise S. Bartell is the associate vice provost for student success at the University of Toledo and was the founding director of the Gateways to Phoenix Success program. She regularly leads workshops at state and national levels on developing assets-focused learning experiences for underserved students and on infusing equity-minded professional development opportunities into student success programs.

Randy Bass is the vice provost for education and a professor of English at Georgetown University, where he also leads the Designing the Futures initiative and the Red House incubator for transformative learning initiatives. He focuses on the role of innovation strategies in transforming higher education to better serve the whole person, the common good, and a human future.

John Bodinger de Uriarte is an associate professor of anthropology and the chair of the Sociology and Anthropology Department at Susquehanna University, where he directs the museum studies and diversity studies programs. His research interests include pedagogy, study abroad programs, Native American sovereignty, and contemporary museum, casino, touristic, and photographic representational practices.

Laurie Ann Britt-Smith received her PhD from Saint Louis University, served as an associate English professor and writing program administrator at the University of Detroit Mercy, and is currently the director of the Center for Writing at the College of the Holy Cross, which combines WAC/WID duties, teaching, and oversight of the Writer's Workshop.

Jacquelyn Dively Brown is the chair of Business Foundations in the School of Business at George Mason University, where she teaches professional skills courses. She has received several teaching awards and is working on a PhD in writing and rhetoric, focusing on professional writing, emotional intelligence, and classroom management.

Phillip M. Carter is an associate professor of linguistics and English at Florida International University in Miami, where he is also the director of the Center for Humanities in an Urban Environment. He is a coauthor of *Languages in the World: How History, Culture, and Politics Shape Language*.

Nancy L. Chick is the director of the Endeavor Foundation Center for Faculty Development at Rollins College. She is the editor of *SoTL in Action*, coeditor of two *Exploring Signature Pedagogies* books, and founding coeditor of *Teaching and Learning Inquiry*, the journal of the International Society for the Scholarship of Teaching and Learning.

Michael J. Daley is an assistant professor in the Warner School of Education at the University of Rochester. Prior to this position, Daley was the coordinator of the sophomore multidisciplinary program at Lasell University. In addition to traditional science courses, he teaches multidisciplinary courses and courses on science education.

Maggie Debelius is the director of faculty initiatives at the Center for New Designs in Learning and Scholarship and a teaching professor in both English and learning, design, and technology at Georgetown. Her research areas include graduate education, pedagogy, and faculty development. She is the coauthor of *So What Are You Going to Do with That? Finding Careers Outside Academia*.

Janelle Papay Decato works in Elon University's Global Education Center as the assistant director of study abroad. She manages operations for faculty-led programs and advises students about global engagement opportunities. Decato came to Elon in 2013 after finishing her EdM in college student affairs and completing a Fulbright in Germany.

Peter Felten is a professor of history, the assistant provost for teaching and learning, and the executive director of the Center for Engaged Learning at Elon University. His books include *The Undergraduate Experience*, *Transforming Students*, and the forthcoming *Relationship-Rich Education: How Human Connections Drive Success in College* with Leo M. Lambert. He is one of four coeditors of the *International Journal for Academic Development* and a fellow of the Gardner Institute.

Ashley Finley is the senior advisor to the president and vice president for strategic planning and partnerships at the Association of American Colleges and Universities. She was previously the associate vice president for academic affairs and founding dean of the Dominican Experience at Dominican University of California and a national evaluator for Bringing Theory to Practice.

Dennis A. Frey Jr. is an associate professor of history and the associate dean of curricular integration at Lasell University. In the latter role, he facilitates the ongoing integration of Lasell's core curriculum throughout the university and also directs the RoseMary B. Fuss Teaching and Learning Center. Regularly teaching history, Frey specializes in the social and cultural history of early modern Germany.

Chris W. Gallagher is the vice chancellor for global learning opportunities and a professor of English at Northeastern University. His work has appeared in a wide range of writing studies and education journals, and he is the author or coauthor of five books, including *College Made Whole: Integrative Learning for a Divided World*.

Evan A. Gatti is an associate professor of art history at Elon University. In addition to teaching art history courses on premodern art, historiography, and museums, Gatti served as the associate director of the Elon core curriculum from 2014 to 2019. Gatti's research focuses on medieval art from northern Italy.

Lisa Gring-Pemble is the director of Global Impact and Engagement and an associate professor in Foundations at the School of Business, George Mason University. She is a Mason Teaching Excellence Award recipient and an OSCAR Mentoring Excellence Award recipient, and was named the George Mason University Alumni Association Faculty Member of the Year. She leads and supports university-wide programs in social innovation, including the Honey Bee Initiative, which she cofounded.

Kristína Moss Gudrún Gunnarsdóttir is completing an EdM at the Harvard Graduate School of Education with a concentration in organizational change management and innovation. She is the recipient of a Fulbright-García Robles fellowship and has presented on the topic of innovation in undergraduate admission policy at a number of national conferences, including SXSW EDU and the Ashoka U Exchange. Prior to graduate school, she served as the interim dean of admissions and financial aid at Hampshire College, her alma mater.

Anthony Hatcher is a professor of journalism and a former journalist with a PhD in mass communication research. He also teaches and conducts research in religion and media. Since joining Elon in 2002, he has led study abroad students to Germany, Poland, England, France, the Czech Republic, and South Africa.

Toni Strollo Holbrook is the assistant provost for institutional effectiveness in the Office of the Vice President for Academic Affairs and Provost at Rollins College in Winter Park, Florida. Her responsibilities include assessment of student learning, administrative effectiveness, college accreditation, and strategic planning for all programs of the college.

Derek Lackaff is an associate professor of communication design at Elon University and the associate director of the university's Center for the Advancement of Teaching and Learning. He mentors the next generation of interactive media professionals in the interactive media master's program and is interested in digital opportunities for indigenous and minoritized languages.

Leo Lambert is a professor of education and a president emeritus of Elon University, where he served as president for nineteen years. He is the coauthor of *The Undergraduate Experience: Focusing Institutions on What Matters Most* and the forthcoming *Relationship-Rich Education: How Human Connections Drive Success in College* with Peter Felten. In 2009, he received the inaugural William M. Burke Presidential Award for Excellence in Experiential Education from the National Society for Experiential Education.

Kristin Lange is an assistant professor of German at Elon University. She graduated from the interdisciplinary doctoral program in second language acquisition and teaching at the University of Arizona. Her research is in second language teaching with a focus on multiliteracies, curriculum development, and the use of authentic second language material.

Sherry Lee Linkon is a professor of English and the director of the Writing Program at Georgetown University. Trained in American studies, her research and teaching cover a wide range of fields, including American literature and culture, interdisciplinary teaching and learning, working-class studies, and writing studies.

Anne M. Magro is the senior associate dean for strategy and impact at the School of Business at George Mason University. She has served in various leadership roles within Mason Business, including leading the undergraduate curriculum revision and serving as the first chair of the Business Foundations group. She also serves on the advisory council of the UN Principles for Responsible Management Education initiative.

Maud S. Mandel is the president of Williams College, a professor of history, and a member of the program in Jewish studies. She is the author of *In the Aftermath of Genocide: Armenians and Jews in Twentieth-Century France* and *Muslims and Jews in France: History of a Conflict*.

Jessica Metzler is a senior associate director at the Sheridan Center for Teaching and Learning at Brown University. She holds PhD and MA degrees in English from Cornell University and has taught writing and literature courses at Cornell, Florida State, and the University of Nebraska, Lincoln.

Borjana Mikic is the R. B. Hewlett '40 Professor of Engineering at Smith College. She helped to spearhead the creation of the Design Thinking Initiative at Smith, serving as its inaugural faculty director. Currently, she serves as the associate dean of integrative learning.

William Moner is an assistant professor of communication design at Elon University. He teaches professional writing, visual design, and interactive design in the communication design BA, the interactive media MA, and the media analytics BA programs. His work draws from his experience in media studies and professional web design and development to explore innovation and design-driven approaches in the classroom and beyond.

Phillip Motley is an associate professor in the School of Communications at Elon University, where he teaches visual communication and interactive media courses to undergraduate and graduate students. His research interests include pedagogies of design and experiential learning, especially service learning and social innovation. He is currently serving a two-year term as Elon's Center for Engaged Learning scholar, which allows him to research and explore immersive learning strategies in higher education.

Matthew Pavesich is a teaching professor of English at Georgetown University. His research emerges from the intersections of rhetorical ecologies, postpedagogy, design, and the public humanities, and it has appeared in *enculturation*, the *Journal of Basic Writing*, *Technoculture*, and the *WAC Journal*, as well as in the DC/Adapters project (dcadapters.org).

Uta G. Poiger is a professor of history and the dean of the College of Social Sciences and Humanities at Northeastern University, where she led the introduction of the university's new general education curriculum, NUpath. Among her publications are *Jazz, Rock, and Rebels: Cold War Politics and American Culture in a Divided Germany* and *The Modern Girl Around the World: Consumption, Modernity, and Globalization*.

Rebecca Pope-Ruark is a faculty teaching and learning specialist in the Center for Teaching and Learning at the Georgia Institute of Technology. Previously, she taught professional writing and rhetoric at Elon University through a mix of project-based learning, service learning, and design thinking approaches. She is the author of *Agile Faculty: Practical Strategies for Managing Research, Service, and Teaching*. Her next book project focuses on aspects of faculty burnout.

Michael Reder directs the Joy Shechtman Mankoff Faculty Center for Teaching & Learning at Connecticut College. He works regularly with a variety of institutions to help them provide effective support for their faculty, create holistic and integrated curricula, and use assessment evidence—all focused on improving students' learning and experiences. His work on educational development has appeared in *Peer Review*, *To Improve the Academy*, and the *Journal on Centers for Teaching and Learning*.

Michael S. Roth has been the president of Wesleyan University since 2007, where he also teaches interdisciplinary humanities courses. An intellectual historian, he is the author of several books, including *Beyond the University: Why Liberal Education Matters* and *Safe Enough Spaces: A Pragmatist's Approach to Inclusion, Free Speech and Political Correctness on College Campuses*.

Emily Russell is an associate professor of English and serves as the associate dean of academics at Rollins College, where she is responsible for the administration of general education programs. She is the author of *Transplant Fictions: A Cultural Study of Organ Exchange* and *Reading Embodied Citizenship: Disability, Narrative, and the Body Politic*.

Heather Russell is a professor of English and a senior associate dean in the College of Arts, Sciences and Education at Florida International University. She is the former chair of the English Department. Her academic work resides at the intersections of literary and cultural studies, Caribbean and African diaspora studies, the humanities, and the social sciences.

Ann Schenk is the assistant director of student support at Connecticut College and a first-year seminar staff advisor. Previously, she served as the academic assistant to the Joy Shechtman Mankoff Faculty Center for Teaching and Learning, where she supported the Connections curriculum by helping to develop events for faculty and staff. She also has taught courses in dance at Connecticut College and other institutions.

Michael Shanks is a professor of classics at Stanford University. Shanks's research interests include design history and research, archaeological

Contributors

theory, heritage studies and archaeologies of the contemporary past, the archaeology of Greco-Roman urbanism, and the regional archaeology of the English-Scottish borders.

Susan Rundell Singer serves as the vice president for academic affairs and provost at Rollins College. Previously, she directed the Division of Undergraduate Education at the National Science Foundation and was the Gould Professor of Biology at Carleton College. She pursues a career integrating science and education, which is aimed at improving undergraduate education at scale.

Andrea A. Sinn is the O'Briant Developing Professor and an assistant professor of history at Elon University, where she coordinates the Jewish studies program. She teaches modern German and Jewish history and has published widely on German-Jewish experiences during the Nazi dictatorship and the rebuilding of Jewish life in Germany after 1945.

Christina Smith is an assistant director for undergraduate instructional development at the Sheridan Center for Teaching and Learning at Brown University. She holds a doctoral degree from Oregon State University and a bachelor's degree from the University of Utah, both in chemical engineering.

Alison K. Staudinger is an associate professor of democracy and justice studies at the University of Wisconsin–Green Bay. Her coedited volume *Gender in the Political Science Classroom* argues for inclusive education in the discipline. She thinks teaching in Gateways to Phoenix Success is super fun.

William M. Sullivan is a senior scholar at the New American Colleges and Universities. He was formerly a senior scholar at the Carnegie Foundation for the Advancement of Teaching. He is the author or coauthor of many volumes, including *Habits of the Heart* and *Liberal Learning as a Quest for Purpose*.

Connie Svabo is an associate professor of performance design at Roskilde University, a Danish university that challenges academic conventions and develops new ways of creating knowledge. Svabo promotes the integration of creative competencies in academic research and teaching through the concept of scholartistry, developed in collaboration with Stanford professor and archaeologist Michael Shanks.

Meredith Twombly is the vice president for admissions and financial aid at Clark University. She has held leadership positions in college admissions, retention, institutional research, and assessment over the last fifteen years. Her current work focuses on designing a more constructive and evidence-driven admission process that better aligns with unique institutional missions and values.

Betsy Verhoeven is an associate professor of English and an associate dean of the School of Arts and Sciences at Susquehanna University. She also serves as the director of the professional and civic writing minor. She is currently at work on a multidisciplinary National Endowment for the Humanities project about encouraging civil rhetoric in polarized times.

David J. Voelker is a professor of humanities and history at the University of Wisconsin–Green Bay. He coedited *Big Picture Pedagogy: Finding Interdisciplinary Solutions to Common Learning Problems* and the *Debating American History* series. He taught in the Gateways to Phoenix Success program for two years.

Scott Windham has a PhD in comparative literature from the University of North Carolina, Chapel Hill, and joined the Elon University faculty in 2002. He founded the German studies board and minor. His teaching and scholarship are focused on helping students develop the linguistic and cognitive tools to analyze German literature, film, and other cultural products.

Mary C. Wright is the director of the Sheridan Center for Teaching and Learning and a professor of practice in the Department of Sociology at Brown University. She is a former president (2016–2019) of the US Professional and Organizational Development Network in Higher Education.

Catherine Zeek recently retired from her role as dean of curricular and faculty innovation at Lasell University and currently holds the title of professor emeritus. Her research focuses on integrating high-impact teaching practices and effective supports for faculty, as well as providing leadership and support for the development and assessment of Lasell's core curriculum.

Index

Academy for Innovative Higher Education Leadership, 272
accreditation, 34, 86, 94
ACT, 268
Addams, Jane, xiii-xv
admissions: certificate programs, 62; conditional admission, 27; preadmission requirements, 167; process, 62-63, 248, 268-69, 271-79; scandal, 305
agency: agents of change, 19-20, 29, 126; emergence and, 235; individual, 23, 125, 134, 228, 282-85, 291; student, 9-10, 89-91, 111, 214
agile project management, 139-43; Scrum and, 144, 149
American Association of Collegiate Registrars and College Admissions Officers, 271
American Association of University Professors (AAUP), 6
American College Health Association, 209
Andrew W. Mellon Foundation, 35, 47, 73, 79, 190
Aoun, Joseph, 41, 47, 54, 154; cognitive capacities, 230-31. *See also* humanics
Aristotle, 143, 194
artificial intelligence (AI), 7, 41, 223, 226, 230-31, 291; era of, 44; master's program, 53
Arum, Richard, 241-42
Ashoka, 267
Ashoka U, 173, 272

assessment (institutional): admissions requirements and, 278; culture of, 82, 252; of curriculum (re)design, 41, 55, 73-74, 181; methods of, 207; of minors, 200; multivariate program, 116, 118-21, 146, 181; multi-year, 88; program impact and, 100, 112; of programs, 27, 55, 80, 83, 94; of promising pedagogies, 252, 262
assessment (of students): career, 35, 81; institutional, 255-56; learning, 36, 56-57, 76, 79-81, 92, 133, 161, 177; performance-based (K-12), 270; personal/social development skills, 213, 215; self-, 117, 161; "soft" skills, 207; transactional approach and, 256-57
assets-based approaches, 19-29, 33-36, 40, 144
Association of American Colleges and Universities (AAC&U): defining liberal education, xi, 4-6, 127, 206; designing liberal education, 8; essential learning outcomes of, 2-3, 232-33; General Education Maps and Markers, 214; inclusive excellence, 224; "Liberal Arts Imperative in the Digital Age," 54; Liberal Education and America's Promise (LEAP), 63, 73, 76, 78, 258; on preparedness of students, 270; Valid Assessment of Learning in Undergraduate Education (VALUE), 81, 82-83, 215. *See also* high-impact practices
automation, 7, 44, 54, 223, 226

Bass, Randy, 8, 13, 221, 302
Biesta, Gert, 221, 225, 236
Brown, John Seely, 230, 235
Brown University, 111-21
Buchanan, Richard, 238, 288-89
Butterfield, Victor, xiv, xv

capacity (of learners), 1, 63, 226, 228, 240; to act, 283; civic, 8; cognitive, 230-31; creative, 284, 287-88; design thinking and, 124-28, 134, 144; effective practice and, 276; enhancement of, xiii; high-impact practices and, 209-10; information retention and, 267; for innovation, 295; liberal arts and, 49, 52-54, 194; liberal education and, 2, 9, 44-45, 225, 221; meritocracy and, 21-22; problem-focused, 25-26, 62, 103, 105, 163; reading and, 258-59, 261-62; reflection and, 255; scholartistry and, 292; twenty-first-century skills and, 7, 206, 227, 258; for workplace success, 5-6, 222-23
capacity (of programs), 68, 230, 233; advising, 186
Castano, Emanuele, 258-60
change leadership (Kotter's model), 173-74
changemakers, 164, 171, 267
citizenship, 4-5, 8, 14, 45-46; citizen-subjects, 194, 199; civic literacy and, 85-86; educational quality and, 299; engaged, 85, 125, 165; global, 44, 58, 73, 82, 125; liberal arts and, 68, 283; social problems and, 23-24, 26
civic(s): community engagement and, 29, 99, 212-15; engagement, 24-26, 87, 164, 169, 200; ideals, 252; knowledge, 3; learning, 181, 226; liberal education and, 91, 177-78, 180-81, 184, 304; life, 2, 152, 154-58, 179-80, 200; literacy, 85-87, 92-94, 96; navigating unpredictability related to, 55; participation, 181, 187; responsibility, 54, 168-70, 183; skills, 214-15; writing, 190-93, 195, 197-99
Clark University, 276-78
cocurriculum, 114, 171-73, 209-10
College of the Holy Cross (MA), 85-97, 304
community college, xiv, 34-35, 205, 215, 300
Connecticut College, 58-71, 301
"Copernican moment," 112, 226

Creative Confidence (Kelley and Kelley), 145, 287
curriculum: business, 164-66, 169, 171; change and, 126-27, 131, 161, 267; community engagement and, 212-13, 216; core, xi, 98-102, 142, 151, 178, 283, 303; dispositional learning and, 226-34; diversity and, 32, 34-37, 39, 41; experiential learning and, 7, 45-57; futures, 153, 288; general education, 72-83, 88-89, 100, 107; German studies, 180-89; hidden, 19-20, 22-24; humanities, 284; K-12, 270-71; minors, 191, 193-94; open, 112-14, 120; outcomes, 276-77; pathways, 177-78, 181, 299-302, 304; project-based, 145-46, 149, 231; redesign, 10-12, 86, 173-75; skills, 3; specialization, xii, xiv-xv; speed of, 256-58, 262-63. *See also* writing across the curriculum

Davidson, Cathy, xii, 6-8, 154
Deep Work (Newport), 255
democracy: aspirations for, 240, 252; education and, 108, 112, 232; institutions promoting, 8; participation, 213; practice, 190; society and, 2, 4, 248, 299
Democracy and Education (Dewey), 100
demographics: in higher education, 1, 33, 186, 208; in society, 248, 267
design thinking, 125-28, 132-35, 139-40, 291, 294; curriculum, 145, 270; methods, 129-32, 149, 153; pedagogy, 124, 143, 155, 288-90; process, 144; strategies, 152, 303; tools, 276
Design Thinking (Cross), 245
Dewey, John, xiii-xv, 7, 74, 100, 285, 293
dispositional learning, 222, 226-30, 233
dispositions, 283-85
diversity: competency, 105, 170, 205; contexts, 23-24, 163, 285-86; design thinking and, 127; disciplines, 46, 53-54, 56, 66; faculty and staff, 65, 107, 188, 211; inclusion and, 81, 131, 224; institutional, 165, 224, 234, 299; learning experiences and, 98, 170, 224, 294; liberal education and, xi, xv, 3-5; program design and, 73, 178-79, 185; in STEM, 117; of students, 20, 32-36, 41-42, 130-31, 207-10, 215, 225; study of, 167, 193; teamwork and, 26, 99,

206, 216, 227; twenty-first-century
economy and, 207
Du Bois, W. E. B., xiii-xv, 32

economics (higher education): challenges, 21-22, 25, 29, 103, 207; changes, xii–xiv, 2, 14, 41; educational system and, 266-69, 282-83; inequity, 19, 240-48; students and, 34, 99, 295; uncertainty and, 25
Eisner, Elliot, 285, 293
Eliot, Charles, xi-xii
Elon University, 299; Design Thinking Studio in Social Innovation, 138-50; German studies, 177-89, 301-2; School of Communications, 303
enrollment: competition, 302; decline in humanities, 283-84; in liberal arts, xiv, 46, 52-53, 190-91; limits, 133-34, 148; new curriculum and, 69, 80, 165, 173, 175; of underserved students, 21, 27, 33-35, 40, 115, 208
equality. *See* inequality
equity, 19, 21, 29, 32, 130-31, 216; inclusive excellence, 223-26
ethics: attention and, 254, 258; behavior and, 3, 5, 7, 9, 100; capacity, 1; competency, 26, 63, 85-88, 91-92, 170; development of, 178, 200; liberal arts and, 282-83; questions, 91; reasoning, 44-46, 48-50, 54-55, 78, 128, 181-83, 215; reflection on, 87; skills, 105-6, 107, 109, 167-72, 273
Excellent Sheep (Deresiewicz), 241
Eynon, Bret, 8

Florida, 72, 76; South Florida, 33-34, 36-37, 39
Florida International University, 32-43
frameworks: agile, 141; design thinking, 143; essential learning outcomes, 2-4, 232-33; experiential liberal arts, 48-52, 56; full participation, 64; general education, 213-14; learning collaborative, 113; learning outcomes and, 181-83; for liberal arts, x; pathways, 66. *See also* writing across the curriculum
Freeland, Richard, 8
Freire, Paolo, 23, 160
Fuzzy and the Techie, The (Hartley), 7

Gage, John, 194
George Mason University, 163-76, 214, 301-2
Georgetown University, 151-62, 206-7, 214, 302-3
German studies, 177-89, 301-2
Gutmann, Amy, 47

Hartley, Scott, 7
Harvard University, xii, 269, 304
Hassan, Zaid, 143, 145
heritage language instruction, 39-42
Higher Education Act, 34
high-impact practices (HIPs), 20-28, 59-63, 69, 142, 167; advising, 305; applied, 231; in cocurriculum, 114; pedagogies, 100, 102; soft skills and, 207-13, 216
high schools, 246-49, 268-76
Hispanic-serving institutions (HSIs), 11, 32-33, 40
hooks, bell, 23
Hoover, Eric, 274-75
human-centered design, 6, 9, 126-27, 132, 291-92
humanics, 7, 45, 54-55, 230

identity (institutional), 25, 89; academic model of, 121; disciplinary, 88; in society, 242
identity (student), 64-65, 126, 131; belonging and, 279; as designer, 124; fostering adult, 85; intersectionality and, 20-22, 29, 39, 103
IDEO, 143, 287
inequality, xii-xiii, 223, 233, 286; socioeconomic, 99, 213, 241-49, 252
innovation: challenges of, 223, 229, 233-35; courses and, 37-41; curricular, 45, 48-52, 73-75, 126-27; entrepreneurship and, 165-73; multidisciplinary sophomore year and, 99, 101-2, 107; paradigm shift and, 266-80; program creation and, 88, 94; social, 139-50, 231; technological, 34; writing and, 153-54, 159
intersectionality, 20-22, 29, 39, 103, 195
Ivy League, 111, 242, 300

Jesuit (Catholic order), 86, 88-89, 151, 214

K-12 education, 268-71, 274-77
Kahneman, Daniel, 234, 257

Kelley, David, 145, 287
Kelley, Tom, 145, 287
Kidd, David, 258-60
Kolb, David, 184

Labaree, David, 232
LaGuardia Community College, 215, 300
land-grant university, 5, 37, 205
language, 32-43, 61-62, 77-78, 179-84, 258-59
Lasell University, 98-110, 303
Latinx populations, 33, 35, 37-40
Latour, Bruno, 192-93, 195
learning goals: animating question and, 59, 64, 66-68, 225-26; personal, 9, 171
liberal arts: in business, 164-74; experiential, 11, 45-56, 272, 277; future, 39, 221-23, 227, 233, 282-87, 299-303; historical origins of, x-xi; lifelong learning and, 6; slow, 254-63
liberal arts colleges, xii-xv, 1, 5, 57, 60, 65, 86-88; faculty, 79, 82, 200
living and learning communities, 20-30, 89-90

machine learning, 223, 291
machines, 3, 7, 54; learning and, 226, 230; liberal education and, 222-23; workforce concerns about, 34
Making Sense of the College Curriculum (Zemsky et al.), 74
Mellon Foundation. *See* Andrew W. Mellon Foundation
mental health (student), 214; anxiety and stress, 209; inequality and, 243-48, 252, 269
mentoring: advising and, 69, 177-78, 182-88; applied learning and, 232; diversity and, 35; faculty, 24, 99; importance of, 301; peer, 20, 23-30, 112, 121; personalization, 61; professional, 87, 171-72; programs, 214-16, 301
Milner, Murray, 247-49
mindsets: academic, 214; creative, 294-95; design thinking, 125-29, 131, 135, 144; entrepreneurial, 105, 117, 158, 215, 226-27; technocratic, 242
Minds on Fire (Carnes), 249-50
Modern Language Association (MLA), 47, 258-59
museum studies, 190, 192-93, 196-98

National Association of Colleges and Employers, 273
National Survey of College Counseling Centers, 209
National Survey of Student Engagement (NSSE), 63, 69
New Education, The (Davidson), 154
Newport, Cal, 255
Northeastern University, 7, 11, 44-57, 230

Olin College, 275, 277-78
Open and Integrative (Bass and Enyon), 8
Ostrow, James, 100-101, 103

participatory action research, 23
pedagogy, xiv-xv; civic literacy and, 86; connected learning and, 98-103; design studio and, 124-26, 136, 142, 155-60; diversity and, 32, 35; experiential, 270-72; faculty development and, 72-74, 79-81, 118-23, 175, 267; heritage language and, 39; imaginative, 240-41; integrative, 300-303; pace of, 256, 262; political economy and, 283-84; postpedagogy, 153-54; redesign and, 41; rhetoric and, 192; signature, 232; simulation, 248-52; Students as Partners (SaP), 113; teamwork, 273; traditions, 88
Pell Grant recipients, 33, 42, 163-64
Pickett, Kate, 244-46
politics: advocacy for change, 266; division and, 240, 248; economics and, 25-26, 29; German studies and, 180-81, 183; identity and, 42; instability, 286; learning and, 49, 258; liberal arts and, 282-83, 131, 193, 305; liberal education and, xv, 5-6, 14, 20-21, 91, 211; policy and, 255-56, 258; political science, 52, 90, 167, 170, 250
pragmatism, 285-86, 292-93; liberal education and, ix-xii, xv, 3; outcomes of, 13; purposes of, 179
precarity in higher education, 19, 21-22, 28-29
problem-based/problem-focused learning, 19-21, 23, 153, 167, 169; curriculum and, 165, 168, 231; inquiry and, 156; twenty-first-century education and, 25
problem-solving: abilities, 62, 163, 273, 296; curriculum, 276, 303; exercises, 104, 288;

experiences, 164; perspective, 126, 296; process, 105, 116-17; skills, xi, 5, 127, 213, 242

Qualley, Donna J., 259

Reacting to the Past (educational method), 249-52
retention: of students, 65, 165, 211-12; of underserved students, 21-22, 27-28, 39
Robot Proof (Aoun), 7, 54, 154, 230, 255
Roksa, Josipa, 241-42
Rollins College, 72-84, 301
Roskilde University, 292

SAT, 268, 278
scholartistry, 282-96
Scobey, David, 112-13, 226
Simon, Herbert, 125
Simon Fraser University, 214
Slow Professor, The, 254
Smith College, 124-37
social innovation, 138-50, 171-73, 231, 272, 291
Social Labs Revolution (Hassan), 143, 145
socioeconomic status. *See* economics
Socrates, xiii-xiv; Socratic method, x
soft skills, 206-16
Spanish (language), 38-39
Stanford University, 257, 284, 290-92; d.school, 143; School of Engineering, 287
STEAM (science, technology, engineering, arts, mathematics), 290
STEM (science, technology, engineering, mathematics), 115, 117; courses, 27, 120; disciplines, 7, 44, 47, 119, 129, 133
strategic planning: common goals and, 135-36; opportunity and, 21, 129, 132, 174; university process and, 40, 48, 57, 60
Susquehanna University, 190-202

theory: choice architecture, 274; cognitive apprenticeship, 101; game design, 170; interpellation, 192, 193, 198; of learning, 87-88, 252; of mind, 258-60; practice and, 222, 232; problem solving, 115; self-authorship, 20, 55; situated cognition, 101; things as, 190, 191, 192, 195, 197

Thinking, Fast and Slow (Kahneman), 234, 257
Thompson, Robert, 7
transfer: far, 230-31; in liberal education and, xi, 5; of skills, 73, 78-79, 104, 127, 163; teaching for, 153-54, 157-59, 161, 192, 261
transfer students, 34-35, 208, 271
twenty-first-century skills: applied, 193-95; business, 163-72; citizenship and, 23-27, 304; competencies and, 58, 65, 85-94, 106-7, 109, 111; creativity and, 278-79, 284-96; design thinking and, 124-27, 134-35, 139-40, 147-48, 154-55, 295; dispositions and, 227-32; diversity and, 32-36, 41; humanics and, 54-57; integrative, 44-47, 80; interdisciplinary, 72, 74-75, 99-100; in liberal education, 2-7, 300; now, 205-9, 216-17; pathways to, 177-83; play and, 261; teaching partnerships and, 112, 114; values and, 267, 270

underrepresented students, 35, 115-16
underserved students, 19-21, 34, 164, 208-12, 215; education of, 29-30; retention of, 27
University of Wisconsin–Green Bay (UWGB), 19-31, 301
U.S. News and World Report, 275-77

vocational instruction, 21, 85, 95, 232, 284; liberal education and, xiii-xiv, 5-6

Wabash National Study of Liberal Arts Education (WNS), 60-61, 63
Wesleyan University, xiv-xv
wicked problems: in context, 169, 213, 223; in course design, 140; in design studio pedagogy and, 160; scholartistry and, 288-89, 294; solving, 228; wicked students and, 26; in writing, 151-52
Wilkinson, Richard, 244-46
writing: applied, 142, 146; civic, 109-99; collaborative, 90, 112-15; program, 151-61; requirements, 92-94, 132; rhetoric and, 36-38; teaching of, 81, 250-51; writing-intensive courses, 64-65. *See also* writing across the curriculum
writing across the curriculum (WAC), 87, 90, 115, 172, 194; seminar in, 117-20